Shakespeare's Dramatic Persons

Shakespeare and the Stage

The Fairleigh Dickinson University Press Series on Shakespeare and the Stage publishes scholarly works on the theatrical dimensions of the plays of Shakespeare and his contemporaries. Both individual studies and collections of previously unpublished essays are welcome.

Series Editors: Peter Kanelos (Valparaiso University, peter.kanelos@valpo.edu) and Matthew Kozusko (Ursinus College, mkozusko@ursinus.edu).

Publications in Shakespeare and the Stage Series

Travis Curtright, *Shakespeare's Dramatic Persons* (2016)
Joseph Candido, *The Text, the Play, and the Globe: Essays on Shakespeare and His World in Honor of Charles R. Forker* (2016)
Catherine Loomis and Sid Ray, *Shaping Shakespeare for Performance: The Bear Stage* (2015)
Cary Mazer, *Double Shakespeares: Emotional-Realist Acting and Contemporary Performance* (2015)
R. S. White, *Avant-Garde Hamlet: Text, Stage, Screen* (2015)
Kathryn M. Moncrief, Kathryn R. McPherson and Sarah Enloe, *Shakespeare Expressed: Page, Stage, and Classroom in Shakespeare and His Contemporaries* (2013)

Related Recent Publications

Kristine Johanson, *Shakespeare Adaptations from the Early Eighteenth Century: Five Plays* (2013)
Laury Magnus and Walter W. Cannon, *Who Hears in Shakespeare?: Shakespeare's Auditory World, Stage and Screen* (2011)
Peter Kanelos and Matt Kozusko, *Thunder at a Playhouse: Essaying Shakespeare and the Early Modern Stage* (2010) (Susquehanna University Press)
James C. Bulman, *Shakespeare Re-Dressed: Cross-Gender Casting in Contemporary Performance* (2008)
Frank Occhiogrosso, *Shakespearean Performance: New Studies* (2008)
Paul Menzer, *Inside Shakespeare: Essays on the Blackfriars Stage* (2006) (Susquehanna University Press)
Nancy Taylor, *Women Direct Shakespeare In America: Productions From The 1990s* (2004)
James E. Hirsh, *Shakespeare And The History Of Soliloquies* (2003)
Hardin L. Aasand, *Stage Directions In Hamlet: New Essays and New Directions* (2002)
Susan Young, *Shakespeare Manipulated: The Use of the Dramatic Works of Shakespeare in Teatro Di Figura in Italy* (1996)

On the Web at http://www.fdu.edu/fdupress

Shakespeare's Dramatic Persons

Travis Curtright

FAIRLEIGH DICKINSON UNIVERSITY PRESS
Madison • Teaneck

Published by Fairleigh Dickinson University Press
Copublished by The Rowman & Littlefield Publishing Group, Inc.
4501 Forbes Boulevard, Suite 200, Lanham, Maryland 20706
www.rowman.com

Unit A, Whitacre Mews, 26-34 Stannary Street, London SE11 4AB

Copyright © 2017 by Travis Curtright

All rights reserved. No part of this book may be reproduced in any form or by any electronic or mechanical means, including information storage and retrieval systems, without written permission from the publisher, except by a reviewer who may quote passages in a review.

British Library Cataloguing in Publication Information Available

Library of Congress Cataloging-in-Publication Data
The hardback edition of this book was previously cataloged by the Library of Congress as follows:

Names: Curtright, Travis, author.
Title: Shakespeare's dramatic persons / Travis Curtright.
Description: Madison : Fairleigh Dickinson University Press ; Lanham, Maryland : Co-published with The Rowman & Littlefield Publishing Group, Inc., [2016] | Series: Shakespeare and the stage | Includes bibliographical references and index.
Identifiers: LCCN 2016038095 (print) | LCCN 2016058874 (ebook) | ISBN 9781611479386 (cloth : alk. paper) | ISBN 9781611479393 (Electronic)
Subjects: LCSH: Shakespeare, William, 1564-1616--Stage history--To 1625. | Shakespeare, William, 1564-1616--Dramatic production. | Theater--England--London--History--16th century. | Theater--England--London--History--17th century. | Shakespearean actors and actresses. | Acting--History--16th century. | Acting--History--17th century.
Classification: LCC PR3095 .C87 2016 (print) | LCC PR3095 (ebook) | DDC 822.3/3--dc23 LC record available at https://lccn.loc.gov/2016038095

ISBN: 978-1-61147-938-6 (cloth : alk. paper)
ISBN: 978-1-61147-940-9 (pbk. : alk. paper)
ISBN: 978-1-61147-939-3 (electronic)

∞™ The paper used in this publication meets the minimum requirements of American National Standard for Information Sciences Permanence of Paper for Printed Library Materials, ANSI/NISO Z39.48-1992.

Printed in the United States of America

To Mary

Contents

Acknowledgments		ix
Introduction: Actors and Orators		1
1	*King Richard III* and Characters as Actors	13
2	Kate's Audacious Speech of Submission	45
3	Much Ado about Personation	75
4	Iago's Acting Style	97
5	Marina as Char*orator*	117
Conclusion: Direct Address as an "Original Practice"		145
Bibliography		159
Index		173
About the Author		185

Acknowledgments

It is a pleasure to acknowledge those who have made this book possible. I wish first to thank the editors at Fairleigh Dickinson University Press: To Peter Kanelos and Matthew Kozusko for their interest in and cultivation of *Shakespeare's Dramatic Persons*; and to Harry Keyishian for his editorial leadership. I am also indebted to Cary M. Mazer, whose review and suggestions were especially helpful.

Shakespeare's Dramatic Persons benefited from the careful reading, honest advice, and critical intelligence of many other colleagues and friends. In particular, I thank Yu Jin Ko for his comments on an earlier version of chapter 4; Scott Crider, for his insights into my introduction and conclusion; and Gerard Wegemer, for his review of this manuscript in its entirety. Sections of several chapters were first presented at the meetings of the Shakespeare Association of America, the Center for Thomas More Studies, and at the Blackfriars conferences of the American Shakespeare Center, and I am indebted to those who offered me advice, objections, and welcome on each of those occasions.

I am grateful to the following presses for permission to use previously published material: An earlier version of chapter 4 appeared as the essay "'Stops in the Name of Love: Playing Typological Iago," in *Shakespeare's Sense of Character: On the Page and From the Stage*, edited by Yu Jin Ko and Michael W. Shurgot (Farnham, UK: Ashgate, 2012), 209–22, which is here revised and expanded. Portions of chapter 5 first appeared in the article, "'Falseness cannot come from thee': Marina as Character and Orator in Shakespeare's Pericles ," Literary Imagination 11: 1 (2009): 99–110.

Finally, I thank family and friends who supported me during the long process of research and writing. I recall with special gratitude the inspiration and friendship of Ralph Alan Cohen. My parents, Robert and Lorraine, along with my children, were full of encouragement. Mary, my wife, reviewed every chapter; she has waited the longest for this book, and it is dedicated to her. Without her intelligence, devotion, and genuine regard for the theater and Shakespeare's plays, this book would not have been completed.

Introduction

Actors and Orators

In an often cited description of Richard Burbage's own acting style, Sir Thomas Overbury's *Characters* (1615) records: "what we see him personate, we think truly done before us." Of note is the fact that the same source testifies to Burbage's skills of oratory: "Whatsoever is commendable in the grave orator is most exquisitely perfect in him."[1] Burbage's description is titled "An Excellent Actor" and its account connects what appears as "truly done" upon the stage with the rhetorical tradition of performance, an alliance of lifelike dramatic action and oratory that continues to invite scrutiny.

To think of actors as orators, after all, need not invoke all the assumptions about "Elizabethan acting" that are at least as old as M. C. Bradbrook's famous assertion from 1938 that gesture was "formalised" and speakers employed "conventional movement and heightened delivery."[2] Though of course the actors who first performed in William Shakespeare's plays would possess a different set of skills from those required for proscenium theaters today, the critical debate over and definitions of "natural" and "formal" acting styles obscure our perception of early modern "personation" and how the Chamberlain's and King's Men might practice it.[3] To refine our understanding of early modern acting styles, *Shakespeare's Dramatic Persons* explores how the classical rhetorical tradition would inform an actor's personation of character in ways that could enhance the illusion of what was "truly done" upon the stage.

Such an understanding of rhetoric's importance for the acting style of personation and in the creation of lifelike stage illusions will renegotiate the longstanding critical dichotomy between formalism and naturalism. Twentieth-century studies of early modern acting styles like those of Bradbrook and, later, Alfred Harbage, historicize the performance of character by contrasting a rhetorical style of acting, or formalism, with distinctively modern practices, or naturalism. As I will show, this line of comparative argumentation, howsoever accurate within a general history of ideas, ultimately misconstrues the theatrical workings of rhetoric. Though early and later proponents of formalism rightly caution against ahistorical naturalism or the imposition of proscenium-based aesthetics upon an early modern thrust stage, they underestimate the potential of the classical rhetorical tradition to fashion lifelike individual characters through personation's art.

The ways in which early proponents of formalism approach or define "individual characters" illustrate how rhetoric's own arts come to be regarded as a backward or indelicate form of stage behavior, a primitive if not an embarrassing episode of theater history. Though it "seems clear" that Shakespeare is "appreciated" by his contemporaries "because of individual characters in the plays," argues Bradbrook, these characters are what Samuel Johnson calls "just representations of nature" or types. As a result of the early modern reliance upon types and the actors' "formalised" modes of delivery, Bradbrook infers that a serious misunderstanding of Shakespeare's characters begins in the nineteenth century when romantics like Samuel Taylor Coleridge turned away from the stage, and "the *dramatis personae* were detached from their play and their background." Characters who are "real, all-round, solid human beings, judged by the standards, including the moral ones, of ordinary life" become critical inventions that vastly differ from early modern performance practices. Though Bradbrook's criticism of Coleridge's treatment of character still seems correct to me, she leaves underdeveloped how type characters, precisely because they are rhetorical constructs, would direct an actor's oratorical performance. I will return to the question of typological character in my first chapter, but here I wish to emphasize how naturalism and formalism, individual character and type, and realistic and rhetorical styles set antithetical parameters of discussion about character and its enactment. Bradbrook, accordingly, contrasts formalism and its type characters with modern approaches to individual persons and the representation of consistent characterological traits and "motivations."[4] Such a mode of comparison between early modern and modern acting styles influences the debate over the "real" or "all-round, solid human beings" quality of Shakespeare's characters in performance for decades to come.

Thus, Harbage subsequently explores and defines "natural acting" as the "logical alternative to formal acting" and contrasts a modern actor's "subjective" and "imaginative" performance with the "objective" and "traditional" rhetorical prescriptions of the Elizabethan stage. For Harbage, the Globe theater itself necessitates the formal style because it suits "the open-air theater of Shakespeare's day, with its un-localized, relatively unadorned, and centrally placed stage." The player must "act with his body" and is "part of a statuary group rather than a picture." So, too, "his attitudes must have been statuesque" because a "considerable portion of his audience" could not see his face. "The whimsical smile, the arched brow, the significant sidelong glance would not do," Harbage imagines. As a result of statuesque performance, Elizabethan acting emerges as not only formal but also crude in comparison to modern techniques, which allow the actor to "lose himself" in the character he plays.[5]

Because of how early formalists depict the influence of rhetoric upon the Elizabethan stage the same dispute over "formalism" and "naturalism" erupts again with the publication of Bertram Joseph's *Elizabethan Acting* (1951). Joseph describes the actor's art in terms of how the classical oratorical tradition guides the performance of "passion," "gesture," "voice," and "countenance";[6] his account amounts to what Marvin Rosenberg calls the culmination of "the orthodox formalist movement."[7] In reply to *Elizabethan Acting*, John Russell Brown attacks Joseph's connection of acting with oratory and Rosenberg for depersonalizing an actor's performance with stock traits and gesticulations; both believe that the personation of Shakespeare's characters imparts more of a lifelike acting style than formalists acknowledge. Though Brown writes "formalism" is never "properly defined," he nevertheless argues thus: "formalism on the stage was fast dying out in Shakespeare's age, and that a new naturalism was a kindling spirit in his theatre."[8] Meanwhile, Rosenberg complains that Joseph's position requires great actors like Burbage to "symbolize" a character rather than become one, turning actors into "mannered mouthpieces who recited the dramatic poetry," offering what Harbage earlier referred to as statuary performance.[9] Joseph, in turn, modifies his original claims but does so for polemical purposes. By the time the second edition of his *Acting Shakespeare* (1969) appears, Joseph maintains a connection between the rhetorical style and an actor's "real inner feeling," yet he lacks the historical sensitivity of his first analyses of oratory and the stage.[10]

As a result of Rosenberg and Brown's assessments, Joseph's *Elizabethan Acting* appears largely discredited until the publication of Joseph R. Roach's *The Player's Passion* (1985). In an important advance, Roach vindicates Joseph by pointing out how "the tiresome debate over the relative formalism or naturalism" of acting styles arises because of the "disinclination of both sides to understand the historic links between acting, rhetoric, and ancient physiological doctrines."[11] Roach successfully demonstrates the connection between classical rhetoric and its effects upon the actor's physical person by using Quintilian's *Institutes* and Galenic theories about how a humoral body and its experience of passion could transform players and their audiences alike.[12] As Roach himself claims, his argument follows up and expands upon Joseph's original insight that the rhetorical principle of *actio* or delivery "merely showed through speech and gesture the state of physiological secretions within the body, as well as what went on in the soul."[13] Yet Roach goes much further. He shows how, according to early modern belief, an artful actor could experience passion in his person and render the same feeling in those who witness his performance.[14] The rhetorical or formal style of acting, it turns out, would be natural according to the scientific paradigms of mind, body, and passion of the time.

The Player's Passion suggests the limitations of defining the rhetorical or formal style of acting in terms of its contrast to Romantic notions of character or other modern attempts at naturalism.[15] Bradbook's treatment of character emerges in argument with Coleridge and A. C. Bradley's literary criticism while Harbage's case that the two acting styles represent "logical alternatives" to the stage hazards tautology; both represent how early proponents of formalism range too broadly across the history of ideas in their treatment of the performance of character. "Elizabethan acting" could aim at an illusion of life or naturalism precisely because such mimesis occurs within the horizon of early modern rhetorical techniques that actors would employ. For the same reason, the claim above about Burbage—"what we see him personate, we think truly done before us"—does not refer to a newly developed or more natural acting style but to the lifelike or mimetic effects that an actor's expert employment of oratorical *technê* may provide.[16] Thus, when Thomas Nashe writes of Shakespeare's early histories in 1592 how it would "have joyed brave Talbot, the terror of the French, to think that after he had lien two hundred years in his tomb he should triumph again on the stage, and have his bones new-embalmed with the tears of ten thousand spectators at least, at several times, who in the tragedian that represents his person imagine they behold him fresh bleeding," he testifies to the mimetic power of the rhetorical style upon Elizabethan audiences.[17] Instead of a transition from types and declamation to a heightened stage realism that occurs during the span of Shakespeare's theatrical career, the rhetorical style of acting already had produced claims of lifelike characters.[18]

Roach's argument remains a landmark, but he leaves largely unimagined how a rhetorical acting style could impart lifelike impressions in Shakespeare's specific characters and plays. So even if we now better understand comments like those of Thomas Nashe, Harbage's original concern about such testimony still challenges our conception of how rhetoric instructs actors in performance. "We are told *what* the actor did (in the estimation of the spectator)," writes Harbage, "but not *how* he did it."[19] In the chapters that follow, I will investigate the *how* of performance in terms of where and in what ways rhetoric informs character and directs its performance. Though it is impossible to retrieve all the original conditions of Shakespeare's Globe or how various actors performed in his plays, we can specify where scripts incorporated the classical oratorical tradition. My aim is to pinpoint specific rhetorical genres, typological characterizations, artistic appeals from *ethos*, figures of speech, and oratorical techniques that could aid an actor in the performance of character as an early modern illusion of real life.

To describe such individual characters as lifelike, I will use the terms "person-effect" or "character-effect" interchangeably. Character or person-effects begin as the result of all those rhetorical techniques that early modern texts employ for the sake of crafting dramatic persons but are actualized for audiences with personation, the performance of all such techniques played upon a stage.[20] A mimetic approach to character should be indicated or qualified by "effects" less because of how character has been deconstructed or shown to be a construct and more because dramatic persons are designed to become present only when they are performed.[21] As Anthony B. Dawson explains, for the Elizabethans, a dramatic person is an "embodied character, a real fiction" because there are "linkages between the living being of the actor and that of the character he represents." Materialist criticism tends to overlook "the way that self, role, and body form a kind of trinity, three in one, inseparable but distinct." Dawson seeks to develop a model of "interiorized personhood based on at least the illusion of depth, and providing a paradigm for what we mean by 'character,' even by 'self.'"[22] Such "illusions of depth," I agree, are ultimately the result of an "embodied character" upon the stage; but such presence first and formally emerges from the linguistic structure of dramatic persons, a rhetorical structure that provides the eluctionary, relational, behavioral, and dialogical purview for actualization of "embodied characters" upon the stage.[23] Character or person-effects, therefore, capture the potentialities of the text or a particular role to provide audiences with mimetic action.

Performance returns us to the question of early modern acting styles. When acting styles are misunderstood, it becomes impossible for critics to imagine accurately what choices were available to actors for the vivification of their roles. In Yu Jin Ko and Michael W. Shurgot's recent collection, *Shakespeare's Sense of Character: On the Page and From the Stage* (2012), Ko points out how the hyperboles of romantic conceptions of character parallel those "in the postmodernist caricature of the supposedly reigning, essentialist view of dramatic character as a pre-social, inviolate, transcendent subjectivity." In a significant turn to his argument, Ko observes how most critiques of character-based approaches rely upon historicized distinctions of acting styles, which in turn employ similar arguments to the one rehearsed above—the divide between early modern rhetorical or formal styles from later forms of naturalism. Behind the opposition of either constructivist or postmodern ideas of personhood with those that posit an autonomous self as the subject of mimesis, there is an older and still unresolved dispute over theatrical practice. The current emphasis upon "non-naturalistic practices proceeds from the position," Ko observes, "that such practices are incompatible with the host of qualities associated with psychologized personhood, like inwardness and lifelike forms of inner disunity." The effects of "non-naturalistic" practices, however, deserve further investigation and may produce surprisingly lifelike depictions of persons. Ko therefore calls for "performance-oriented" approaches that expand "the critical vocabularies that character criticism can work in."[24]

Though Ko's concern is for "character criticism" and mine for how rhetoric would inform the performance of early modern *dramatis personae*, his call for exploration of "non-naturalistic" practices represents shared ground and highlights the potential significance of such work. Instead of a Whiggish history about the ostensible progress of naturalism in early modern acting styles, though, *Dramatic Persons* investigates how the classical rhetorical tradition already anticipated supposedly later techniques of personation, including the illusions of interiority or inwardness. With attention to how "performance" may "infiltrate the very composition of character itself,"[25] I will proceed dialectically, interrogating the formal rhetorical quality of dramatic persons in terms of personation techniques and vice-versa.

My first chapter, "*King Richard III* and Characters as Actors," argues that Richard's typological background provides an "illusion of depth" precisely because of what Shakespeare discovers in Thomas More's *The History of Richard III*.[26] Characters like Richard often speak as if to distinguish themselves from rhetorical constructs, especially types, even as they enact such roles. Thus, Shakespeare's tyrant questions his actions in light of his conscience, leaving the impression that he may choose other than he does. Rather than a result of Cartesian anthropology or "bourgeois" notions of "subjectivity,"[27] the character-effect of Richard's "interiorized personhood" derives from Shakespeare and More's own immersion in classical humanism's exploration of and techniques for contrasting invisible, secret purposes with outward, public displays. By tracing Richard's genealogy from Shakespeare back to More's own sources—those of history and comedy, Tacitus's *Annals* and Terence's *The Woman of Andros*—I demonstrate the intersection of typology and theatricality and suggest how characterization and personation constitute different points on the matrix of one dramatic person.

Chapter 2, "Kate's Audacious Speech of Submission," examines the relationship between character as a rhetorical construct and the actor who embodies his or her part by analyzing Kate's final lecture about wifely obedience from *The Taming of the Shrew*. To do so, I call upon Henry Peacham's idea of "mimesis" as a function of how an "orator counterfeits" speech and action, which is "always well performed, and naturally represented in an apt and skillful actor."[28] In the Tudor grammar school, Peacham's idea of mimesis allies the offices of orator and actor in order to produce the quality of "audacity" in students, an attribute that I claim the boy actor who played Kate would transfer to her dramatic person. By revisiting Kate's last speech as a schoolroom exercise in declamation, I will validate Juliet Dusinberre's earlier observation about how "the boy actor was a spur to the creation of heroines of allegedly masculine spirit." Though Dusinberre believes "the high spirits and sharp repartee which characterised the Children's companies" are the source behind "the quick wits, audacity and independence of Shakespeare's heroines," I locate Kate's trait of audacity in the context of the Tudor schoolroom.[29] Once we historicize the pedagogical aims of training in declamation and identify Kate's final speech as a paradigm of rhetorical exercise, the possibilities for how the boy actor could augment the character-effect of Kate's audacity emerge. Instead of asking if boys could play female parts well, I show how the rhetorical training of boys suggests that Kate should maintain a spirited presence in her so-called speech of submission.

Chapter 3, "Much Ado about Personation," focuses upon acting styles and the controversy over whether a new or recently developed form of individualized character portrayal exists at the end of the sixteenth century and in *Much Ado About Nothing*. After a critical analysis of the word "personation," I argue that Shakespeare's play does not present enhanced acting techniques distinct from those found in rhetorical delivery. Instead, the representations of theatricality arranged by Don Pedro or Borachio—the internal dramas of *Much Ado*, what Jean E. Howard calls its "playlets"—employ explicit language about the rhetorical modes of personation.[30] Even so, characters that call attention to or disavow theatrical representation create the impression that they speak outside of its boundaries. These characters are "personated" by actors according to the same rhetorical techniques that the play trumpets as artifice, but the exposure of theatricality paradoxically creates the potential to magnify an audience's sense of character realism.

"Iago's Acting Style," chapter 4, further questions the current critical conception of the rhetorical style of acting. Theorists deconstruct not only Shakespeare as a poet of nature but also show how modern actors, like character critics, anachronistically understand the performance of character as manifestations of a private self. Modern naturalistic acting, after all, seeks an "illusion of reality" by imitating "the behavior of an actual human being" placed in a character's "imaginary circumstances,"[31] but typological character presents and advertises traits that correspond with oratorical techniques of delivery. Yet even with the historical differences of each approach to human psychology and the experience of language, Iago's typological structure and use of figural language embed dramatic actions not unlike those found in more recent productions of the same play. By first examining Iago in light of Plutarch's description of a flatterer, and then reviewing how rhetorical figures would aid a performance of act 3, scene 3, I show how rhetorical and natural acting styles occasionally overlap in their recommendation of characterological traits.

The significance of rhetoric for the performance of character continues in my examination of Marina's speeches from *Pericles*, which shows Shakespeare's use of forensic discourse and the significance of appeals from *ethos*. In chapter 5, "Marina as Char*orator*," I challenge the romance tradition's elevation of narrative structure over character, which dissociates language from the dramatic person who speaks it. In contrast to historical allegory, autobiographical disclosure, or analysis of Jacobean monarchical politics, I demonstrate how Marina's appeals from *ethos* produce the person-effect of self-knowledge. Classically, *ethos* means an envisioning of the self through speech, an artistic appeal that works in tandem with *logos* and *pathos*. To make such an appeal in *Pericles*, Shakespeare deploys forensic rhetoric, fashioning Marina's self-apologetics in a way that creates the character-effects of memory about past events and speculation about future ones. Because she defends her future by reference to her past, forensic discourse fabricates the impression of continuous self-consciousness in Marina. Coherent or unified selfhood, what materialist critics attack as old-fashioned character criticism, emerges as the logical concomitant to appeals from *ethos*. Instead of a "late style" or a new language for indoor theater, Marina's appeals from *ethos* illustrate Shakespeare's ongoing use of classical rhetoric to fashion dramatic persons in lifelike ways.

I conclude *Dramatic Persons* with an examination of how actors today perform character in productions based upon Shakespeare's ostensible "original practices."[32] Though "original practices" are often described in terms of architectural reconstructions of the Globe or the Blackfriars' theatrical spaces, they emphasize the importance of characters and do so in modern ways. In particular, I explore the convention of direct address to audience members by actors who speak in character from the stage. Though the mode of direct address may be early modern, how do actors trained in post-Stanislavski methods practice it? In a comparison of three recent performances of *Hamlet*, I show how contemporary actors approach and make theatrical choices about how to talk to audiences. At the end, I envision how Burbage himself might have performed the same lines. Thus, my investigation of Shakespeare's dramatic persons concludes with a contrast between how today's actors perform and what we might imagine as "truly done" by "an excellent actor" who was a "grave orator" as well.

NOTES

1. "An Excellent Actor" is cited from Blakemore G. Evans, ed., *Elizabethan Jacobean Drama: The Theatre in Its Time*, (New York: New Amsterdam Books, 1990), 99. The author of the description is probably the dramatist John Webster. The passage's allusion to painting is the reason why scholars posit that Burbage is the model. See E. K. Chambers, *The Elizabethan Stage*, Vol. IV (Oxford: Clarendon Press, 1923), 257. For a summary of early modern testimony about the lifelike quality of Burbage's personations, see Bart van Es, *Shakespeare in Company* (Oxford: Oxford University Press, 2013), 232–48.

2. M. C. Bradbrook, *Elizabethan Stage Conditions: A Study of Their Place in the Interpretation of Shakespeare's Plays* (Cambridge, UK: Cambridge University Press, 1932), 109.

3. For development of the term "personation" in light of performances at the Globe theater, see Jacalyn Royce, "Early Modern Naturalistic Acting: The Role of the

Globe in the Development of Personation," in *The Oxford Handbook of Early Modern Theatre*, ed. Richard Dutton (Oxford: Oxford University Press, 2009), 477–95. I cite the terms "formal" and "natural" from Alfred Harbage, "Elizabethan Acting," *PMLA* 54, no. 3 (September, 1939): 687. See my chapter 3 for critical review of personation and debate over what it means in terms of early modern theatrical practices. My argument focuses on personation as a manifestation of the rhetorical acting style.

4. Bradbrook, *Elizabethan Stage Conditions*, 78–79, 84. For Bradbrook, characters lack "consistency" or adequate "motivation" to be understood as natural, but the sense of naturalism that she disputes in this case is derived from A. C. Bradley, *Shakespearean Tragedy: Lectures on Hamlet, Othello, King Lear, Macbeth* (New York: Penguin Books, 1991).

5. Harbage, "Elizabethan Acting," 687, 704, 708. Harbarge claims that naturalism occurs when the actor either "sinks his personality in his part or shapes the part to his personality" (687) and that formal acting "seems bad when it represents, as it must needs in modern times, the resort of a third-rate actor or teacher of acting, or a disharmonious intrusion upon an established contemporary ideal" (705).

6. B. L. Joseph, *Elizabethan Acting* (London: Oxford University Press, 1952), 3, follows Thomas Wright's *The Passions of the Mind* (1604), which summarizes the oratorical tradition's teaching on effective delivery as *vox* or voice; *vultus* or countenance; and *vita*, life or animation of the speaker. See also Thomas Wright, *The Passions of the Mind in General: A Reprint Based on the 1604 Edition* (Chicago: University of Illinois Press, 1971), 176, who adds: "Action then universally is a natural or artificial moderation, qualification, modification, or composition of the voice, countenance, and gesture of the body proceeding from some passion, and apt to stir up the like." I have modernized the prose of Wright.

7. Martin Rosenberg, "Elizabethan Actors: Men or Marionettes?" *PMLA* 69, no. 4 (September, 1954): 916.

8. John Russell Brown, *Studying Shakespeare in Performance* (Basingstoke, UK: Palgrave Macmillan, 2011), 65–66, but originally published as "On the Acting of Shakespeare's Plays," *Quarterly Journal of Speech* 39, no. 4 (December 1953): 477–84.

9. The quote cited above is from Rosenberg, "Men or Marionettes" at 915 but perhaps the best summation of his attack is at 916–17: "The formalists ask us to believe that things were different in Elizabethan times, that men like Edward Alleyn and Richard Burbage, recognized as artists by their contemporaries, were willing, in an age of individuals, to extinguish their vanity and conform their great talents to stock acting patterns; that they were, in fact, a different breed of man and artist from the great English actors who followed them."

10. Here is the complete quotation is from Bertram Joseph, *Acting Shakespeare*, second edition (New York: Theatre Arts Books, 1969), 84: "But fortunately for us in our problem of fusing the realistic with the unrealistic, the art of the orator in the renaissance was anything but formal and stereotyped; on the contrary, it was a lively and truthful art designed to portray real emotion truthfully, and was based on a deep conviction that 'action' should spring always from *real inner feeling*, not from any conventional system of external clichés" (my emphasis).

11. Joseph Roach, *The Player's Passion: Studies in the Science of Acting* (Ann Arbor: University of Michigan Press, 1993), 30. First published by Associated University Presses, Inc. in 1985.

12. Roach refers to "the association of spirits with psychic phenomena" as *pneumatism*, which empowers the actor to transform himself and "the bodies of the spectators who shared that space with him" (Ibid., 27). For further discussion, see Anthony B. Dawson, "Performance and Participation: Desdemona, Foucault, and the Actor's Body," in *Shakespeare, Theory, and Performance*, ed. J. C. Bulman (London: Routledge, 1996).

13. Joseph, *Elizabethan Acting*, 100 and cited by Roach, *Player's Passion*, at 30.

14. See Allison P. Hobgood, *Passionate Playgoing in Early Modern England* (Cambridge, UK: Cambridge University Press, 2014), 28–30, who elaborates upon Roach's

argument by showing how both "aurally driven 'playgoers'" and "visually motivated 'spectators'" participate in a "Renaissance cultural imagination steeped in Galenic humoralism." Even though "humoral bodies have their own affective specificity," Hobgood rightly challenges us to recognize how those same bodies provide grounds for "acknowledging probable emotional collectivity in the audience."

15. Roach, *Player's Passion*, 228n11, calls Joseph's evolution of thought a "needless concession" to Brown and Rosenberg because "absorption in one's part had everything to do with oratory."

16. The lines on "personation" from "An Excellent Actor" (1615) are cited from Brown, *Studying Shakespeare*, 69, who takes them as evidence of naturalism; but the same passage begins with the sentence cited by Harbage, "Elizabethan Acting," 702, which reads: "Whatsoever is commendable in the Grave Orator, is most exquisitely perfect in him." Those in favor of naturalism cite the sentence on "personation" while formalists use the earlier comparison to oratory.

17. From *Pierce Pennilesss his Supplication to the Devil* (1592) in *Thomas Nashe: Selected Writings*, ed. Stanley Wells (London: Edward Arnold, 1964), 65.

18. See Paul Menzer, "That Old Saw: Early Modern Acting and the Infinite Regress," *Shakespeare Bulletin* 22 (2004): 32–33, who shows how critics of early modern acting styles employ an "evolutionary myth" that allows them "to script fictions of progress" not only in terms of theatrical practices and developing dramaturgy but also in discussions of personation.

19. Harbage, "Elizabethan Acting," 692.

20. Cf. J. Leeds Barrol, *Artificial Persons: The Formation of Character in the Tragedies of Shakespeare* (Columbia, SC: University of South Carolina Press, 1974), 101: "We suppose the dramatist attempted to solve the problem of characterization not by presenting 'very human' actions and reactions at random but by arranging an ordered series of behavioral phenomena related to some kind of sequence (or process) so as to convey to an audience that important fiction, the illusion of a 'person.'"

21. Theory alleges that character studies posit the transhistoricity of a unified self in analysis of Shakespeare's plays, what may be called "essentialism," or the belief in a shared human nature independent of how power circulates within given historical periods [Jonathan Dollimore, *Radical Tragedy: Religion, Ideology and Power in the Drama of Shakespeare and his Contemporaries*, third edition (Durham, NC: Duke University Press, 2004), 155]. Instead, "man is a construct, not an essence," a product of external forces, not a unified self. [Jean Howard, "The New Historicism in Renaissance Studies," *ELR* 16 (1986): 23]. As a result, theorists hold that character considered as a unified self derives from the Enlightenment, which proposes the human person in terms of rational self-conscious agency and poetry's corresponding representation of inwardness or interiority. For early and influential arguments that "subjectivity" or selfhood is historically constructed, see Francis Barker, *The Tremulous Private Body: Essays on Subjection* (New York: Methuen, 1984) and Catherine Belsey, *The Subject of Tragedy: Identity and Difference in Renaissance Drama* (New York: Methuen, 1985).

22. Anthony B. Dawson and Paul Yachnin, *The Culture of Playgoing in Shakespeare's England: A Collaborative Debate* (Cambridge, UK: Cambridge University Press, 2001), 15, 20.

23. Terms like "character-effect" and "person-effect" are most often used because, as Harry Berger explains, "speakers are the effects rather than the causes of their language and our interpretation: in the unperformed Shakespeare text there are no characters . . . there are only dramatis personae, the masks through which the text speaks" [Harry Berger, Jr., *Making Trifles of Terrors: Redistributing Complicities in Shakespeare*, ed. Peter Erickson (Stanford, CA: Stanford University Press, 1997), 220]. See also William Dodd, "Character as Dynamic Identity: From Fictional Interaction Script to Performance," in *Shakespeare and Character: Theory, History, Performance, and Theatrical Persons*, ed. Paul Yachnin and Jessica Slights, 62–79 (New York: Palgrave Macmillan, 2009), 62.

24. Yu Jin Ko, "Introduction," in *Shakespeare's Sense of Character: On the Page and From the Stage*, ed. Yu Jin Ko and Michael W. Shurgot (Burlington, VT: Ashgate Publishing Company, 2012), 5, 11.

25. Robert Weimann and Douglas Bruster, *Shakespeare and the Power of Performance* (Cambridge, UK: Cambridge University Press, 2010), 44.

26. In an early reception history, Shakespeare's *Richard III* appears as his most popular play by reason of its number of reprints. By 1594, play quartos were purchased to be read and *Richard III*, with six reprints, surpasses plays like *Hamlet*, which was reprinted three times. Thus, the degree to which Shakespeare builds his reputation upon More's own powers of characterization indicates the tremendous influence that a "source text" may provide. On *Richard III* and *Hamlet*'s quarto prints, see Andrew Gurr, *The Shakespeare Company, 1594–1642* (Cambridge, UK: Cambridge University Press, 2006), 126.

27. On pre-bourgeois (pre-1660) forms of subjectivity versus Enlightenment forms of subjectivity, see Barker, *The Tremulous Private Body*, 31, 52.

28. On "mimesis," see Henry Peacham, *The Garden of Eloquence* (London: Historical Collection from the British Library, 1593), 138–39. I have modernized the English and cite from a digital reprint from the Historical Collection of the British Library. For an overview of Shakespeare's knowledge of classical authors, see Colin Burrow, *Shakespeare and Classical Antiquity* (Oxford: Oxford University Press, 2013). On the reception of classical rhetoric in early modern England, I can only provide a partial bibliography here: See Quentin Skinner, *Reason and Rhetoric in the Philosophy of Hobbes* (Cambridge, UK: Cambridge University Press, 1996), 19–211. On classical rhetoric and education, see Peter Mack, "Rhetoric in the Grammar School" in *Elizabethan Rhetoric: Theory and Practice* (Cambridge, UK: Cambridge University Press, 2002). For earlier important treatments of Shakespeare's use of classical rhetoric, see Miriam Joseph, *Shakespeare's Use of the Arts of Language* (New York: Hafner Publishing Company, 1966) and T. W. Baldwin, *Shakspere's Small Latine and Lesse Greeke* (Urbana: University of Illinois Press, 1944).

29. Juliet Dusinberre, *Shakespeare and the Nature of Women*, third edition (New York: Palgrave MacMillan, 2003), 251. The first edition was published in 1975.

30. Jean E. Howard, "Renaissance Antitheatricality and the Politics of Gender and Rank in *Much Ado About Nothing*," in *Shakespeare Reproduced: The Text in History and Ideology*, ed. Jean E. Howard and Marion F. O'Connor, 163–87 (New York: Methuen, 1987), 163.

31. Harbage, "Elizabethan Acting," 687.

32. Discussions of "original practice" or "OP" are too numerous to mention more than a selection here. For introductions: On all aspects of OP productions, see Christie Carson and Farah Karim-Cooper, eds., *Shakespeare's Globe: A Theatrical Experiment* (Cambridge, UK: Cambridge University Press, 2008); on acting, see Patrick Tucker, *Secrets of Acting Shakespeare: The Original Approach* (New York and London: Routledge, 2002); on characterization through performance, see Jacquelyn Bessell, "The Performance Research Group's *Antony and Cleopatra* (2010)," in *Shakespeare on the University Stage*, ed. Andrew James Hartley (Cambridge, UK: Cambridge University Press, 2015), 185–200.

ONE

King Richard III and Characters as Actors

Long recognized as an actor-tyrant and a superb role to perform, *Richard III* marks William Shakespeare's discovery of the possibilities of personation. In an early assessment, E. K. Chambers describes Richard as unique, writing how Shakespeare's "presentation of character offers *no parallel* to the vivid analysis of the many-sided Richard, with his grim humor of introspection, his audacities and levities of speech, his irony and mock humility, his plausibility and adroitness, his histrionics and sense of dramatic effect."[1] More recently, Robert Weimann and Douglas Bruster explain that Richard's "histrionics" demand a "kind of interplay between speech and performance," because "the arts of dramatic discourse and the arts of performance interact," but, most importantly, "performance begins to infiltrate the very composition of character itself" in the creation of Richard. Thus, the dramatic person of Richard emerges as a significant moment of artistic development because Shakespeare assimilates "the full thrust and surplus of performance to the semi-tragic shape of a Renaissance protagonist."[2]

Shakespeare's ostensible development of Richard, however, derives from Thomas More's original history of the same tyrant, which raises the question of whether performance "infiltrates" character first and foremost in Shakespeare's source or not. Chambers's early sense of histrionics and subsequent analyses of how Richard's character inscribes performance, I will argue, unintentionally though accurately describe the classical character type of the tyrant, who More in his *History of Richard III* captures for Shakespeare's subsequent development. In fact, More's Richard suggests how the actor of Shakespeare's play could oscillate between dramatic language and an actor's personation of a role or between what Weimann calls the "author's pen and actor's voice."[3] To show why this may be so, I will investigate how typology and personation constitute different points on the matrix of one dramatic person, combining elements of the stage and page and working independently of distinctions of genre, which would disassociate historiography from history plays. For in the case of Richard III, his dramatic person originates in More's *History*.

Before turning to the evidence, it would be best to state in advance the rhetorical technique that I think binds More and Shakespeare's art together. Shakespeare learns from More's depiction of character how the rhetorical exemplum recommended by classical historiography should be displayed through the use of *enargeia*, a practice of particularly vivid description of words or events.[4] Shakespeare's subsequent mode of composing dramatic persons may be viewed as a form of theatrical *enargeia*, an extension of More's art that Shakespeare reconfigures with an explicit performative function.[5] Such artistic technique constitutes an important and early form of inscribing character-effects in Shakespeare's canon because, as Lorna Hutson has recently argued, *enargeia* enacts vivid, realistic portrayals of persons and events by design and definition,[6] encompassing, as we shall see, both historical and dramatic presentations. Shakespeare's depiction of Richard, therefore, emerges less from his appropriation of or competition with rival playwrights and more by way of emulative imitation of both the model and technique that More provides him.

PARODY, IMITATION, AND *ENARGEIA*

To analyze Richard's typological genealogy entails a search for the very models of emulation that Shakespeare might have found useful. Too often, critics ignore More's influence in favor of Marlovian forms of overreaching character types. Thus, Nicholas Brooke, like James Shapiro who follows him, identifies Shakespeare's early Machiavels as an imitation of his rival in characters such as Aaron from *Titus Andronicus* and Richard's depiction in Shakespeare's first tetralogy.

The similarity of Brooke and Shapiro's approach to Richard illustrates why More's influence is often put aside. In a representative example, Brooke cites how Aaron calls Tamora's political ascent and security "out of fortune's shot," beyond "thunder's crack" and "envy's threat'ning reach," which indicates how Aaron associates "empery in terms of the human apotheosis." "It seems to me impossible to hear this," Brooke writes of Aaron's soliloquy, "and not think of Marlowe."[7] Next, Brooke easily finds a parallel in Richard's words: "How sweet a thing it is to wear a crown / Within whose circuit is Elsyium."[8] Shapiro's understanding of Richard, however, finds Shakespeare's Marlovian type overthrown by "the inevitability" of "providential scheme," thereby making Shakespeare's contribution to the same typological character primarily that of narrative structure.[9] In both cases, though, Shakespeare's Richard best compares and contrasts with Christopher Marlowe's heroes.

In Brooke and Shapiro's mode of comparison, Shakespeare "freely imitates" his contemporary's work, as Bart van Es writes, borrowing from and participating in "a kind of house style." Such a style shows Shakespeare's contact with common and easily recognized forms of speech rather than his acquaintance with More's characterization of Richard. Shakespeare becomes a "literary dramatist" in his early career, van Es summarizes, and Richard emerges because of Shakespeare's ability for appropriation and development of vernacular drama.[10]

The argument for "house style," howsoever valuable for understanding context, risks homogenizing character or turning character into a derelict category of poetics, even if the emphasis upon emulation seems correct. Perhaps for this reason, Shapiro prefers the term "parody" to "imitation." By parody, Shapiro means a "self-conscious and critical act of recollection" that establishes distance, formal or historical, between works of art.[11] Shakespeare's plays may be termed a song, or *odos*, that is *para*, or "beside" or "against" another song or play, just as Richard might be compared *alongside* Thomas Kyd's Lorenzo or Marlowe's Tamburlaine.

With the term "parody," Shapiro moves Shakespeare away from Harold Bloom's anxiety of influence by minimizing the psychological drive behind an author's appropriation of another author's work. Yet both avenues of inquiry are complementary and create an impetus whereby critics like van Es understand Shakespeare's "characterization" to move horizontally and with less sophistication during his "early" period of composing plays, a conventional assessment of Shakespeare's early plays. Even so, Shapiro's idea of "parody" opens the door to a more historically extensive genealogical analysis of Richard. To see why, we must reflect upon how both More and Shakespeare would have understood the term *imitatio*, and how their conception of imitation could function like Shapiro's sense of appropriation.[12]

More himself practices a special mimetic art form in the creation of his own actor-tyrant because there is no contemporary person of Richard to observe as a basis of representation. Instead, More visualizes Richard through *enargeia*, what George Puttenham refers to as "Hypotyposis, or the counterfeit representation."[13] Puttenham explains how some "matter and occasion leadeth us many times to describe and set forth many things in such sort as it should appear they were truly before our eyes though they were not present, which to do it requireth cunning, for nothing can be kindly counterfeit or represented in his absence, but by great discretion in the doer."[14] Puttenham's "kindly counterfeiting" means fashioning through rhetoric's art a lifelike or natural representation: this counterfeiting in historiography and in literary art involves imitation of traits like the visage, speech, or countenance of a person absent or dead. Puttenham believes Homer excels in this art because his *Iliad* provides truthful and diverse "personages" from history, such as Achilles and Thersites.

More himself calls upon the ancient Greek painter, Apelles, because he thinks that variegated and lifelike imitations of a single emotion in painting are paradigmatic for understanding typological characters like Richard.[15] Indeed, Apelles spans the century as an exemplar for rhetorical composition of characters, reappearing in Thomas Browne's 1570 translation of Johannes Sturm's *Nobilitas Literata* (1549), what Browne called *A Rich Storehouse or Treasure for Nobility and Gentlemen*, but which I call attention to because of its ongoing emphasis upon *imitatio* as the preferred form of emulating other artists. Sturm writes:

> Neither is it to be doubted but the picture of Venus, which Apelles painted as rising out of the sea, appeared to be sprinkled with some foam of the sea, but yet in such sort as the same did make the form and beauty of the goddess more amiable and lovely. Wherefore *as Apelles left some part of that picture rude and untrimmed, so likewise ought a writer and imitator to do.* . . . Therefore they give good advice, which will us to follow Minerva in Homer, who often *changeth Ulysses into sundry forms*, and sometimes maketh him wrinkled, little ill-favored fellow . . . *even thus must the orator do*, that he come not always forth in a silken and precious garment, but oftentimes also in a worn coat, and common attire, and such as serveth for every day.[16]

Note that Apelles's original picture remains "untrimmed." Sturm's immediate point is that poetic imitation ought to be like pictorial representation because both should leave something to the imagination of the reader or the spectator. More importantly, Sturm indicates that because Apelles left his picture in such an unfinished state other artists may envision his original painting differently. Thus, a model, which is partial because it remains "untrimmed," *should be imagined differently* by later orators, if they are to practice imitation properly.

In the linguistic arts, orators and poets would imitate an original by reimagining it as part of their creative process, what rhetoricians refer to as *inventio*, from the Latin *invenire* or "to find," as in the discovery of the right subject matter, arguments, and style for each occasion and task. So Sturm recommends that orators discover how to revise Ulysses into "sundry forms." Invention means reimagining Ulysses into variegated manifestations of character while following an original, particular, even singular model. In Shapiro's terms, such imitation constitutes parody. For Browne's "imitation" shows how poets may formally distance their work from those whom they follow.

Such inventive or parodic imitation is precisely the art that More employs in developing his own Richard from Tacitus's depiction of tyranny in the *Annals* and, as I will argue in the sections below, the same practice that Shakespeare later uses in imitation of More's own portrayal of Richard. Developed in this way, both authors may be said to practice imitation after the manner Puttenham describes and in order to "counterfeit kindly" the character of Richard.

Indeed, More's model of Richard is the Emperor Tiberius of Tacitus's depiction from the *Annals*, and Tiberius is already more than a historical figure—he is also a fictive character in his own right.[17] Quintilian, Tacitus's contemporary, writes that historiography has a "certain affinity to poetry and may be regarded as a kind of prose poem."[18] So, too, the close relationship between rhetoric, poetry, and history is proclaimed by Aristides, who places historians "between orators and poets," implying an interrelationship of the three arts in a formulation that More himself later echoes.[19]

Enargeia constitutes a common virtue for all three arts and illustrates Aristides's point.[20] Quintilian glosses the Greek term or, "as some prefer to call it, representation," as "something more than mere clearness, since the latter merely lets itself be seen, whereas the former thrusts itself upon our notice."[21] For Quintilian, these effects are the "highest of all oratorical gifts" and come from fixing "your eyes on nature" and following it.[22] Likewise, Erasmus could define the term for More:

> We employ this [*evidentia*] whenever, for the sake of amplifying or decorating our passage, or giving pleasure to our readers, instead of setting out the subject in bare simplicity, we fill in the colours and set it up like a picture to look at, so that we seem to have painted the scene rather than described it, and the reader seems to have seen rather than read.[23]

As in Quintilian's suggestion of a scene that is "thrust" upon one, Erasmus writes of the more effortless action of seeing rather than the labor of attentive reading. The former occurs with "word painting" and, thus, Erasmus calls the practice poetic: "All the poets excel in this skill, but Homer above all."[24] Erasmus combines poetry and oratory, and, in More's use of *enargeia*, what Quintilian and Erasmus refer to in Latin as *evidentia*, both poetry and oratory become part of historiography, following, perhaps especially, Lucian of Samosata's early advice about how to write history.[25]

Lucian, an author More greatly admired and imitated, emphasizes such imaginative shaping to historians because they should "give a fine arrangement to events and illuminate them as vividly [*enargestata*] as possible." For "when a man who has heard him thinks thereafter that *he is actually seeing* what is being described and then praises him—then it is that the work of our Phidias of history is perfect and has received its proper praise."[26] Lucian compares historiography to the plastic art of Phidias in order to emphasize the importance of *enargeia* for sculpting or shaping history into vivid narrative forms. As Andrew D. Walker rightly observes, "Lucian's advice to the historian—and the rich rhetoric tradition on which it depends—shows that *enargeia* is also applicable to descriptions of every sort and to the narratives of history, oratory, and ancient fiction."[27] *Enargeia* also reveals how historical personages become literary characters.

The goal of humanist historians such as More, to borrow the later language of Thomas Hobbes, is to describe events "so evidently" that readers feel as if they were present "in the actions." Hobbes's own treatment of Thucydides is the most succinct statement of humanist reasoning as to why historians should fictionalize so: "For his style, I refer it to the judgment of diverse ancient and competent judges. Plutarch in his book, *De gloria Atheniensium*, saith of him thus: 'Thucydides aimeth always at this; to make his auditor a spectator, and to cast his reader into the same passions that they were in that were beholders.'"[28] Such a stylistic imperative, what Quintilian and Aristides readily acknowledge, blurs the boundaries of the actual and fictive, especially in cases where ancient historians imagine past events, which they know of imperfectly through reports or oral tradition or suspect memories.[29] History appears "untrimmed" like the painting of Apelles and creates an impetus for imaginative fashioning of what remains unknown.

Enargeia, thus, becomes a means of variegated and creative imitation because each author differentiates his or her depiction of persons or events by highly specific details of imagined description.[30] The origins of "lifelike" character-effects emerge in cases such as these as a function of rhetorical craft. The historian, like a poet, places readers in the roles of spectators, auditors, or beholders, allowing them to see bygone events; such an objective already suggests how stage productions may depict history as a form of *enargeia*. To place playgoers in the position of "beholders" of past events actually but also rhetorically qualifies what a playwright hopes to accomplish in crafting history plays for performance.

More himself writes history within this rhetorical tradition, which licenses the following: fabricating speeches, inferring motivations, accentuating events or adjusting their timing to sharpen *pathos*, even the invention of details. All of these practices sharpen the presentation of past events and persons.[31] The detail of persons is especially important. Here I mean more than the critical commonplaces that Tacitus introduces personality into history or that More follows Tacitus in this regard. Both historians allow us to see how the tyrant acts as a deceiver, oscillating between an interiority of political schemes while managing public shows of civic-mindedness. More uses *enargeia* especially well to describe such turns, which correspondingly endows his Richard with the character-effect of an "inner self," a Richard in possession of an internal reservoir of secrets and hidden stratagems. Considering Thomas More's *History* as a contribution to English literature, Leonard F. Dean writes: "It is suggestive to think of *Richard III* as an intermediate stage in the history of the use of the biographical or historical example. That history is part of the movement from allegory to realism."[32] If we consider how both More and Shakespeare use *enargeia* to recreate models—in this case, characters derived from history—the interaction between fiction, history, and Dean's "realism" may not be as erroneously conceived as critics who believe "individuality" or "inwardness" is an invention of the Enlightenment would surmise.[33]

TYRANTS AS ACTORS

Let us turn to More's own classical models for Richard. As in Shakespeare's later depiction, character begins as a type. The Theophrastan tradition defines character as a "description, delineation, or detailed report of person's qualities" (number 14 from *Oxford English Dictionary* [*OED*]), which is based upon a single, well-defined moral attribute. That same general approach belongs to Tacitus's *Annals*, More's own source in composing his history of Richard, because Tacitus's "view of character depends primarily on his ethical convictions, and character is regarded as generally fixed and self-consistent."[34] So Tacitus employs a variety of such characters—including "the opportunist" or "informer," the "victim," the "collaborator," and "intransigents"—but above all the type of tyrant, whose fundamental trait is deception or dissimulation.[35] Tiberius's character, we are told, includes a nature both "secretive and guileful in its fabrication of virtues,"[36] which provides a thumbnail portrait similar to the depiction of Theophrastus's dissembler:

> Dissembling, to put it in outline, would seem to be a false denigration of one's actions and words. The dissembler is the sort who goes up to his enemies and is willing to chat with them. He praises to their faces those whom he has attacked in secret, and commiserates with people he is suing if they lose their case.[37]

In these classical descriptions of deceptive character types there are coincidental resonances with Chambers's account of Shakespeare's Richard. Chambers's sense of Richard's "mock humility," "irony," and the "plausibility and adroitness" of "histrionics" parallel Tacitean "guile" and what Theophrastus later refers to as "the dodges and contradictions it is characteristic of dissemblers to invent."[38]

The same classical depiction of deceptive character types are incorporated by More into his description of Richard III. More writes that Richard was

> close and secret, a deep dissembler: lowly of countenance, arrogant of heart; outwardly friendly where he inwardly

hated; not refraining to kiss whom he thought to kill; pitiless and cruel, not for evil will always but more often for ambition, and either for the safeguard or increase of his position.[39]

Like Tacitus's overall depiction of Tiberius, but unlike that of Theophrastus's dissimulator, Richard's insincerity must be a function of his concern to acquire or maintain power. The evil "Machiavel," so often discussed in terms of the English Renaissance stage, originates with Machiavelli's own iteration of or reflection upon the deceptive rhetoric originating in Tacitus's world of tyrants.[40] So, too, with Richard's pretense of good will in arguing for the princes to be under his protectorate, in his feigned indignation when accusing Edward's Queen and Jane Shore of witchcraft, and even in his initial rejection of the crown that Buckingham offers him, Richard successfully dissembles for the sake of acquiring power.

In order to glimpse how More employs imitation, it is instructive to note how More's English version of the *History* compares with the same episode in his Latin version. As Richard Sylvester points out, "the Latin and English texts indicate that More did not 'translate' his Richard"; instead, More practices "simultaneous composition of both narratives, with neither Latin nor English commanding an absolute priority." For Sylvester, More provides a composite "History-Historia," a "unique narrative," which is "almost without parallel elsewhere in literature."[41] Most importantly, this unique approach to writing history reveals More's attempt at various imitations, or sundry forms, of the same character type.

In More's Latin version of Richard's ascent—*Historia Richardi Tertii*—he adds an important though often ignored detail. More writes that Richard "could adopt any role [*personam quamlibet induere*], then play it out to perfection, whether cheerful or stern, whether sober or relaxed, just as expediency urged him to sustain or abandon it."[42] More thereby re-describes Richard's dissembling traits, elaborating upon his English *History*, with reference to how well Richard *performs* acts of dissimulation. Of Richard, thus, "there was modesty in his countenance when in his heart there was arrogance, uncontrollable, boundless, and monstrous. He would speak flatteringly to those whom he inwardly loathed [*verbis adblandiens his quos intus impense oderat*] and would not hesitate to embrace those whom he had decided to kill."[43] The English "outwardly friendly where he inwardly hated" mirrors the ability for sycophantic speech More mentions in the Latin account; similarly, the English "not refraining to kiss" parallels the Latin account of embracing those whom Richard will later kill, what Shakespeare later depicts in Richard's treatment of Clarence. In these traits, More composes Richard's speech and action for performance as a character type.[44] Tacitus combines the classical version of a dissembler with unlimited political aspirations in his emperor Tiberius and More provides a king who speaks falsely for ambition's sake.

More's Richard, however, is identified as something else beside: a consummate and eager actor.[45]

The transition of the tyrant's type from Tacitus to Shakespeare through More may be especially noted through the use of *effictio*, a figure that operates by "representing and depicting in words clearly enough for recognition the bodily form of some person," another manifestation of *enargeia*.[46] Tacitus typifies the tyrant's figure by linking moral character to physical deformity. He describes Tiberius's features: "a spindly and stooping loftiness, a summit denuded of hair, and an ulcerous face, generally patched with cosmetic medications."[47] More's Richard is "little of stature, ill-featured of limbs, crook-backed, his left shoulder much higher than his right, hard-favored of visage."[48] More portrays and even *invents* Richard as a hunchback in these lines, providing a detail absent from Polydore Vergil and a famous, if not factual, flourish of *enargeia*.[49] Shakespeare's Richard, finally, calls himself "rudely stamp'd," "curtail'd of this fair proportion," and "deform'd, unfinish'd."

Yet Shakespeare's Richard claims his deformation is caused by a "dissembling nature."[50] The fact that Richard was born feet first into the world, had teeth from the womb, and is hunchbacked, all of these are signs of an evil nature; Richard understands his physical deformities as manifestations of his immoral disposition. Any sign of comeliness is absent in each depiction of the tyrant because the body mirrors the tyrant's moral identity. Because Shakespeare's Richard is "cheated of feature by dissembling nature," and since he cannot "prove a lover," he is determined "to prove a villain" (1.1.19–30).[51] Alongside ambition, Shakespeare adds resentment as motivation for usurping the crown.

If the same basic type remains, Shakespeare, like the expert orator described by Sturm, produces variation by rearranging and re-imagining some details in the creation of Richard's dramatic person. Shakespeare's Richard provides a first person account of what More provides in narrative—the tyrant's type as consisting of false denigration of one's words and actions. Richard echoes More's character, thus:

> Why, I can smile, and murther whiles I smile,
> And cry "Content" to that which grieves my heart,
> And wet my cheeks with artificial tears,
> And frame my face to all occasions.[52]

As in More's depiction, Shakespeare's Richard can "frame a face" or, as More puts it, "adopt any role" in order to gain a crown. Both represent the classical models of tyrants and deceivers but they emphasize character as a function of theatricality or performance.

Shakespeare's own practice of *enargeia* assumes theatricality in composition and in presentation upon the stage, what I have referred to in terms of character-effects and dramatic persons. Richard speaks the lines above in soliloquy and, thus, by presenting one version of Richard's motivations to audiences in soliloquy and contrasting motives through dialogue with other characters in the play, the playwright dramatizes More's narrative mode of depicting tyrants. Despite the difference in genre, Shakespeare's depiction follows More's suggestion that Richard is a role-playing actor.

Both Richards, too, stem from their authors' shared assumption about the close relationship between classical oratory and historiography and the importance of *enargeia*. Shakespeare's Richard spells out his identity as a dissembling type in terms of *actio*, or delivery, the art of an orator. He defines this practice: "I'll play the orator as well as Nestor, / Deceive more slyly than Ulysses could."[53] More's Richard is an actor and Shakespeare's an orator, but the terms indicate the same office. As More and Shakespeare fashion what Sturm might call "sundry Richards," *enargeia* still constitutes a bringing to life of characters for both authors.

On stage, theatrical *enargeia* includes dialogic and relational dramatic action with other characters alongside that of confession to audiences of the deceiver's actual aims. Brian Vickers aptly calls this general practice "dynamic dissimulation" whereby "the pretence of good is not merely a cover for the continuing practice of one's own faults, whether grave or trifling, but is the method by which a person develops new ones, tries to reach some clearly defined goal. It is a pretence or imposture adopted in order to achieve power, or riches, or sensual gratification, all types of the fulfillment of desire."[54] Vickers's description summarizes the purpose and function of Richard's type, but his emphasis upon "dynamism" and Shakespeare's imperative for Richard to "play the orator" iterates the connection between a rhetorical acting style and the composition of dramatic persons.

For "dynamic dissimulation" is a function of what the rhetorical tradition defines as an orator's "action." As Juan Huarte Navarro's *The Examination of Men's Wits* (1594) typifies, "action" — from the Latin, *actio*, or oratorical delivery — is the "most important of all" properties orators should possess. Action imparts "being and life to the things which they speak, and with the same do move the hearers." "Being and life" are performative: they are results of how a speaker delivers his or her words. Navarro's sense of "action" includes motions and gestures, countenance, vocal changes in pitch or speed, and emotional changes which the body incarnates in specific ways.[55] His orator describes the skills of an early modern actor or what More qualifies as the ability to play various roles. Navarro advocates a skillful and complete itinerary of mimicry, what Shakespeare's Richard encapsulates in claiming the ability to "frame his face" to any occasion. Rhetorical *actio*, in sum, indicates how an orator would practice Richard's "dynamic dissimulation."

Thus, the "actions" described in Richard's soliloquy of ill-intent itemize not just a list of attributes to feign but also indicate how person-effects may be actualized by an orator's artificial though expert display of kinesics, voice, and overall mimicry. A paradox about the tyrant's type emerges as a result. If an actor plays type, his "being and life" upon the stage will occur despite the fact that he calls attention to those actions which signify what he is not. Richard is not kindly or open or concerned for others but plays such traits in order to pursue his own advantage. For Richard is not Richard. The paradox of disclosing the tyrant's character by calling attention to the performance of attributes he doesn't possess, but only feigns possession of, heightens the illusion of agency. By directing attention to what is performed as performance, Shakespeare's Richard appears to possess intentionality independent of theatrical or poetic illusion.

MORE'S DRAMATIC *ENARGEIA*

To see further how More's *History* could suggest dramatic forms of *enargeia* to playwrights, we must first examine how he engaged his own Roman sources. More uses *enargeia* to amplify and appropriate his readings in Roman history into poetic anecdotes with polemical purpose. In Suetonius's *Lives of the Caesars*, More read how Tiberius's "stairs of Mourning" were qualified: "Since ancient usage made it impious to strangle virgins, young girls were first violated by the executioner and then strangled."[56] That prosaic statement—a grim, brief aside to the narrative—More would borrow years later in a response recorded by William Roper to the bishops who had invited More to attend Anne Boleyn's coronation. Their invitation causes More to "remember" an emperor who addressed the difficulty of virgins who were accused of committing a "certain offense" that carried the death penalty:

> Now it so happened that the first committer of that offense was indeed a virgin, whereof the Emperor hearing was in no small perplexity, as he that by some example fain would have had that law to have been put in execution. Whereupon when his Council had sat long, solemnly debating this case, suddenly arose there up one of his Council, a good plain man, among them, and said, "Why make you so much ado, my lords, about so small a matter? Let her first be deflowered, and then after may she be devoured."[57]

More turns the recorded "fact" about Tiberius into a story, beginning with the detail of the "first committer." The original only describes the contradiction of committing rape in the name of the law, but More dramatizes the scene with speakers, creating a council that deliberates with protracted and "solemn" argument. Already, such details heighten the irony that accompanies More's practice of *enargeia*. At last, More's "good plain man" speaks, recommending the ultimate and brutal solution. *Enargeia* functions as the master trope behind More's amplification of Suetonius, an episode More brings to conclusion by playing with "de-flower" and "devour" through parallelism and alliteration to provide an epigrammatic close.

For More, the immediate point of his story was that the innocent who attend to the king's new marriage will become "devoured." After a new queen is crowned, the bishops, who were first only to attend the coronation, will have to "preach for the setting forth of it" before writing "books to all the world in defense thereof."[58] Yet as an insight into how More read Roman history—not simply as model to replicate, but as rhetorical scaffolding or scenery for staged conversation and action to be imagined and developed—Roper's anecdote illustrates how More reads and subsequently creates. More enters the narrative, rearranges its parts, and adds or subtracts from them, employing a poet's sense or a polemicist's purpose.[59] More's art is not merely that of duplicating models but of "re-creating nature" through language.[60]

More's dramatic *enargeia* in the *History* may be especially noted in his embellishments to the story of William Lord Hastings, which follows Tacitus's *Annals* more so than Polydore Vergil's account of the same event.[61] When Hastings is killed in the *History*, Richard issues a proclamation to justify the execution, an episode which is full of More's inventions. "Much matter," More writes, was "devised to the slander of the lord chamberlain," including: giving evil counsel and keeping evil company, "sinister procuring, and ungracious example" and "vicious living and inordinate abuse of his body."[62]

Sylvester finds the model for the betrayal of Hastings in book 4 of the *Annals*,[63] but the propaganda More attributes to Richard seems better situated in the context of book 6. There, Tiberius kills his grandson, Drusus, and soon after produces a series of public allegations as justification for doing so, apart from the now commonplace charge of treason. In the *Annals*, "Bodily abuse" [*probra corporis*] combines with "day by day descriptions" [*descripta per dies*] of Drusus's criminal actions and words.[64] Of such a proclamation, Tacitus opines: "That there had stood by, through so many years, persons to catch his [Drusus's] looks, groans, even his secret murmurs, and that his grandfather could have heard . . . these things were scarcely credible."[65] Similar to Tacitus's presentation, More's Richard accuses Hastings of "inordinate abuse of his body," which construes *probra corporis*—literally, "disgraces of the body."[66] More also specifies Tacitus's *descripta per dies* with allegations of "sinister procuring" and "ungracious example."[67] More follows Tacitus by including several general vices without specific instances in order to retain a sense of concocted propaganda.

More's Richard assumes Hastings need not be proven guilty of any one crime if people are convinced Hastings is a generic moral reprobate, but Richard pays little attention to the suspicious timing of the charges he makes. More writes of Richard's proclamation that it was "made within two hours after that he was beheaded, and it was so curiously composed, and so fairly written in parchment in so well a set hand, and therewith of itself so long a process, that every child might well perceive that it was prepared before."[68] What was "scarcely credible" in the *Annals* becomes that which "every child" could perceive as a hoax.

More amplifies the hoax through *enargeia*. In his version, a schoolmaster, reading the proclamation and "comparing the shortness of the time with the length of the matter"—or the timing of Hastings's death with the elaborate trappings of the accusation—rightly infers that the allegations were created beforehand as ideological cover for what amounts to a political assassination. As More's anecdote of capital punishments and virgins includes the words of a "good man," a merchant answers the schoolmaster: the indictment "was written by prophecy."[69]

As a testimony to More's signature craft, other printed accounts of the same events fail to provide the same intense *enargeia*.[70] Rich and vibrant accounts of Richard's call for strawberries or the memorable addition of Jane Shore, the accused "witch" with whom Hastings allegedly conspired, belong to More alone. Even in Polydore Vergil's account, which is second only to More's for detail, we only learn how "the citizens and all other people" eventually perceive that "Richard would spare no man" in order to gain the crown.[71] There is no official promulgation against Hastings that a schoolmaster and merchant address. More's use of *enargeia* appears livelier than a rendition of historical or factual details because of how he describes events with a dramatic or dialogic emphasis between or among speakers.

More's own explicit invocation of theatrical space may be understood in light of a comparison of passages from the *Annals* and the *History*. In the former, during a crisis in the food supply, the theater employs "more license" against Tiberius than usual and so a rebuke follows at Tiberius's instigation. The castigation of plebs, however, is delivered through the senate and the consuls because Tiberius wished to avoid making an unpopular denunciation. The ruse fails because the emperor's public silence "was interpreted not (as he believed) as citizenlike but in terms of haughtiness."[72] Here the narrative structure is manipulated to expose Tiberius, creating what Richard Sylvester calls a "double vision by distinguishing dramatically between the smooth surface of events and the ruinous moral vacuum that lies beneath them."[73] Tacitus's "double vision" simply declares what the populace thinks; he does not provide them, like More will do, with dialogic exchanges that are full of colorful metaphors or ironic quips among several speakers.

More would appear to retain Tacitean "double vision" in depicting events but his use of *enargeia* differentiates him. The most pronounced instance of when Richard shows his desire for popularity occurs when he pretends to reject the crown that Buckingham coaxes the people to offer England's protector. As in Tiberius's ruse, this scheme is designed to show "citizenlike" behavior on the part of Richard, but, instead, the people "talked and marveled of the manner of this dealing" *because* it was performed as if it were not orchestrated in advance. As with the anecdote about virgins and capital punishment, More enacts the scene.[74] So others in the crowd reply that the same sort of theatrics occur with the consecration of a bishop: Thus, the candidate refuses the offer of an office before accepting it and such feigned reluctance seems typical. The argument evolves into a metaphor for the theater: As in a stage play, when a shoemaker plays a sultan, no one should call the player by his real name and break the dramatic illusion. So neither should the people point out Richard's charade. Because More enacts this argument as a conversation among the people, we infer how Richard's attempt at an aloof, statesmanlike pose reduces to a public relations disaster; no one believes his words are authentic but all comment upon his performance. After the back and forth of the commoners' debate, More concludes:

> And so they said that these matters be kings' games, as it were stage plays, and for the more part played upon scaffolds. In which poor men are but the lookers-on. And they that wise be, will meddle no farther. For they that sometimes step up and play with them, when they cannot play their parts, they disorder the play, and do themselves no good.[75]

The significance of More's comment about "kings' games" isn't just that of thematic content upon the travails of politics; it points toward a dynamic, even theatrical mode of presentation. As in the earlier examples of Hastings or a "a plain good man" who speaks in council, More's ability to fictionalize highly specific and individual arguments constitutes a form of *enargeia* that allows readers to "see" and "hear" the commoners through the illusion of spontaneous, brief, and colorful exchange. The commoners, too, concentrate upon Richard's *performance* in refusing the crown, discussing the divide between his outward display and its concealed purpose. More's brilliant pun upon "scaffold"—which means, of course, both a stage for a play and a platform for execution—further suggests the performative nature of Richard's character and his ascent to power.[76]

Sylvester believes More "takes us inside the minds of his characters," showing the same "intense internal drama" Tacitus displays, but More improves upon Tacitus's literary aim in this regard by dramatizing the action.[77] In the "kings' games" episode, the oscillation between Richard's *gestus* and the commoners' reply accentuate a divide between being and doing, intention and action. Where Tacitus often declares arguments, More presents them in dialogic and relational ways between distinct voices or speakers, providing the illusion of agency and thought to characters or even crowds. Such vivid *enargeia* or *evidentia* provides an embryonic model for dramatization upon actual stages. Characterization appears as part of an "intense internal drama" of the dissembler in these cases because of how More writes with an ability to shift the point of view or voice from that of narrator to a variety of characters in seamless fashion.[78] That Shakespeare read More's *History* as a playwright looking for material to stage appears less surprising than the fact that More's narrative had already crafted Richard's story with allusions to and representations of theatricality.

THE INFLUENCE OF TERENCE

Of special note in the case of Hastings, the Louvain, Arundel, and later Paris editions of More's Latin *Historia* eliminate the accusations of bodily abuse and the character of the merchant with his jocular exchange with the schoolmaster.[79] Instead, a plaintive rationale is given. The Paris edition reads: "But allegations were added against Hastings so that the news of his death would be taken more calmly, as if, quite apart from the main offense, it were a penalty for giving evil counsel."[80] The schoolmaster remains, but More, in the voice of his narrator, ironically worries "if the matter were not too atrocious to be a fit subject for witticisms," and so his *magister* quotes Terence on the timing of the proclamation, "You have not spaced these episodes very well, Davus."[81] More's *Historia* thereby alludes to Terence's *The Woman of Andros* by quoting the words of Simo, the father of Pamphilus, who suspects Davus, a clever slave, of orchestrating a plot.

Though often ignored, More's allusion is crucial for understanding his fashioning of Richard in both Latin and English versions of the *History* and for recognizing how More connects *enargeia* with theatrics.[82] In Terence's play, Simo wishes to marry off Pamphilus to a woman he doesn't love, but Davus reassures him (falsely) that Pamphilus will do what he wishes. Meanwhile, Pamphilus's actual lover, Glycerium, is pregnant and about to give birth. In the scene from which More quotes above, Davus and Simo hear Glycerium's offstage cry of labor pain to Juno Lucina, the Roman goddess of childbirth, "help me, save me, I beseech you!" So Simo questions the timing of Davus's lies in the line that More uses before he adds, "have your actors forgotten their cues?" When More references *The Woman of Andros*, then, he contextualizes Richard's promulgation within the horizons of not just dissembling character types but also comic drama, an important insight for how Richard occasionally emerges as comic even within his overall role as villain. In both the English and Latin versions, there are "sundry forms" of Richard, which are complementary revisions of one another. Or, in Shapiro's terms of argument, More parodies himself in simultaneously composing in two languages different versions of the same event.

The allusion to Terence's "spacing episodes" indicates an even larger dramatic design than Richard's bad timing in releasing his proclamation about Hastings. More's own narrative is riddled by such spacing difficulties that constitute or reveal Richard's sometimes clumsy, often comic, attempts at deception. As in Terence, More's episodes become means of vivifying the type of dissembler.

To see why, I return to the scene from Terence to which More alludes. There, Simo actually believes Davus directs a *false performance* of childbirth, replete with feigning offstage screams, in order to trick him into calling off Pamphilius's wedding. Simo, meanwhile, has been conducting his own deception because he plans a wedding between Pamphilius and Chremes's daughter. In addition to the story of lovers, there are rival tricksters at variance because both Davus and Simo attempt to outwit one another. In the same episode from which More quotes, Simo exclaims in an aside from Davus, "this is the first of the tricks he's planning for me," because Simo believes Davus and his allies are only "pretending she's having a baby."[83] The *prima facie* impression of childbirth, of course, represents the truth, thereby introducing confusion and comedy to the practices of deception: Davus, though he wishes to dupe Simo, becomes genuinely flummoxed by Simo's reaction; Davus wants to keep Glycerium's baby a secret, after all. Conversely, Simo understands what is true as Davus's artifice, which he rightly suspects, but his just suspicion causes him to infer erroneously that there is no baby. Davus's actors—his *discipuli*—appear too obviously cued to be sincere and spontaneous, or so Simo reasons. Laughter arises in cases such as these because deceivers appear as buffoons, victims of their own schemes or penchant for deceit, who could not anticipate contingencies such as a mother's labor screams, or whose strange, even perverse cast of mind leads them away from a moment of victory.

In a parallel and equally comic failure at deception, Richard alleges that King Edward was a bastard, an illegitimate heir. To make the case in public, Doctor John Shaa, an unscrupulous preacher, will deliver a sermon on the text, "bastard slips shall never take root" (Wisdom 4:3). The charge against Edward is a lie and further implies that Richard's own mother was an "adulteress,"[84] but Richard's only concern is that he should appear at St. Paul's just at the same moment when Shaa points out Richard as the true heir. The cue lines, from the English version, begin "this is the very noble prince, the special patron of knightly prowess." If Richard enters with the speaking of these words, it will appear to the people "as though the holy ghost had put them in the preacher's mouth," and, thus, the event will move "the people even there, to cry 'King Richard, King Richard.'" In this way, it may be "put out" that Richard "was specially chosen by God and in manner of miracle."[85]

Yet Richard misses his cue, creating a "spacing" problem, which captures the same effect of disillusionment within the context of planned schemes run awry, a specialty of Terence's play. More describes Richard's entrance:

For while the Protector [was] found by the way tarrying, lest he should prevent those words, and the doctor fearing that he [Richard] should come before his sermon could come to those words, [Shaa] hasted his matter to those things: he was come to them and past them and entered into other matters *before* the Protector came. Whom, when he beheld coming, he suddenly left the matter with which he was in hand, and without any deduction thereunto, began to repeat those words again: "this is the very noble price, the special patron of knightly prowess."[86]

Instead of a politically engineered or staged miracle, an elevation of Richard to the crown by way of supposed divine inspiration, Richard's late entrance becomes a moment of bathos. The people "were so far from crying 'King Richard'" that they "stood as [if] they had been turned into stones for wonder of this shameful sermon."[87] In depicting Richard so, More interweaves the Tacitean "double vision" of "the smooth surface of events" and the "ruinous moral vacuum that lies beneath them" with Terence's comic depiction and exposure of deception.

The influence of Terence also accounts for how More considers dissembling characters within a highly theatrical and partially comic design. Dissemblers like Davus are actors, but not altogether successful ones, because Terence uses them to heighten what Colin Burrow, in a different instance, refers to as "the disillusioned perspective of the slave and the illusion-making structures of the play," which ultimately "work together to create a story which is highly self-conscious about its own fictionality."[88] What Burrow thinks of in terms of narrative, though, Terence's own Davus explains in terms of performance: "Do you suppose it doesn't make any difference," he asks Mysis, an *ancilla*, who unwittingly falls into one of his schemes, "whether you are behaving sincerely and naturally or are acting a part?"[89] In the case of Mysis, she acts more "naturally" in deceiving someone if she doesn't know she is doing so. An innocent deceiver is best. Such acting, Davus urges, makes others believe what *he* wishes them to believe. Self-conscious fictionality thus appears to belong as much to the characters' schemes as to the narrative design of the whole.

In Davus's instructions and character, we find another model for how More inscribes histrionics or role-play into his text conception of Richard. As with Davus's advice to Mysis, More's Richard becomes an actor who aspires to display authenticity or sincerity at the moments when he lies or performs in orchestrated deceptions. Richard's aspiration indicates a "natural" though early modern acting style because a failed attempt at credible behavior appears to be More's point. On the one hand, the actor in Richard tries not to be perceived as one by feigning sincerity or surprise with a thespian's expertise; on the other, his performance is exposed as dissimulation by spacing problems or missed cues, even a bad "scene partner," who speaks too soon or too late. In each case, Richard's failed attempt at duping others by feigning honesty manifests his typological design and particular genealogy from both historical and comedic sources.

SHAKESPEARE AND COUNTERFEITING

Shakespeare recreates More's depiction of dissimulation in the exchange between Richard and Buckingham in act 3, scene 5. Richard and Buckingham enter "in rotten armour, marvelous ill-favoured" according to a rare and specific Folio stage direction, which mirrors More's description of Richard and Buckingham in "old ill-faring briganders," pretending as if "some sudden necessity had constrained them."[90] Instead of exposing dissimulation through a dialogue between a schoolmaster and a merchant, though, Shakespeare lets Buckingham and Richard give full voice to the stratagem. Richard asks Buckingham: "Canst thou quake and change thy colour, / Murder thy breath in a middle of a word, / And then again begin, and stop again, / As if thou were distraught and mad with terror?" (3.5.1–4). The embedded stage directions in these lines are transparent, from quaking to appearing mad. So, too, are figures such as *praecisio*, what Thomas Wilson calls "A Stop, or Half Telling of a Tale." It occurs "when we break off our tale before we have told it."[91] We learn from Shakespeare that the actor must "murder" his breath in the "middle of a word" to play a "stop."

Richard, therefore, describes the emotional, vocal, and physical or kinetic attributes of performance. To quake conjoins with changing "colour," a word that generally means "semblance, outward appearance, character," but may specifically refer to a flush of passion.[92] "Change thy colour" anticipates Celia's later observation of Rosalind at the moment when Orlando is revealed as Rosalind's admiring poet in *As You Like It*. "Change you colour?" Celia asks.[93] The word appears in contrast with pallor elsewhere. Buckingham asks Dorset after Richard's announcement of Clarence's death: "Look I so pale . . . as the rest?" To which Dorset replies: "Ay, my good lord, and no man in the presence / But his red colour hath forsook his cheeks" (2.1.84–86). Later, Richard purposefully misreads these physical signs: "This is the fruits of rashness: marked you not / How that the guilty kindred of the Queen / Looked pale when they did hear of Clarence' death?" (2.1.135–37). Richard may lack color or produce it as part of his performance of accusation or indignant innocence because, as with Davus's advice, it is better to play a part in such a way that you seem sincere.

Richard's ability to change colors grants him a measure of acting expertise that others lack. "Give me a cup of sack to make my eyes look red," Falstaff commands just before he assumes the role of Hal's father, so "that it may be thought I have wept, for I must speak in passion, and I will do it in King Cambyses' vein."[94] Facial and eye color signify emotion, Falstaff surmises, but not every actor needs artificial enhancements for feigning passion. In Quintilian's *Institutio*, which critics often use for explicating Hamlet's wonderment at the players, the power of playing passion connects with persuasion's art:

> When we desire to awaken pity, we must actually believe that the ills of which we complain have befallen our own selves, and must persuade our minds that this is really the case. . . . I have often seen actors, both in tragedy and comedy, leave the theatre still drowned in tears after concluding the performance of some moving role. But if the mere delivery of words written by another has the power to set our souls on fire with fictitious emotions, what will the orator do whose duty it is to picture to himself the facts and who has it in his power to feel the same emotion as his client whose interests are at stake?[95]

The orator may be more powerful than the actor *if* he practices *enargeia* because "to picture to himself" the circumstances of a given case will move him. The rhetorical technique for vivid description thereby becomes the actor's means of experiencing emotion. Credible acting or the orator's ability to deliver an appeal from pathos become one art in the speaker who may reimagine persons and events. The actor becomes like the classical historian or the poet, who brings past events to his or her inner-imaginative eye.

Quintilian's emphasis upon tears suggests an explanation for Richard's expertise in role-play. Clarence testifies that Richard could not have ordered his murder: "It cannot be, for he bewept my fortune / And hugged me in his arms, and swore with sobs / That he would labour my delivery" (1.4.243–45). Beforehand, however, Richard steels the murderers' resolve by warning them against pitying Clarence, calling tears the property of "fools' eyes" (1.3.352). So Richard may cry on demand, it appears. Because a successful usurper and an actor or master orator possess the same abilities, each office requires the ability to play passions in speech and body.

Shakespeare emphasizes the point of embodied performance when Buckingham immediately qualifies Richard's question in terms of the stage. He replies: "Tut, I can counterfeit the deep tragedian, / Speak, and look back, and pry on every side, / Tremble and start at wagging of a straw, / Intending deep suspicion" (3.5.5–8).[96] Buckingham's words are not merely a boast but an itinerary of acting techniques. In speaking these lines, the actor could assume a solemn aspect, or become a "tragedian," and enact "starts" and "stops" in speech so as to feign suspicious tones, even to "pry on every side" or look about with anxiety. Buckingham's words prescribe directions for performance or, at least, provide a metatheatrical commentary upon how to play roles. In detailing the action of a "deep tragedian," Shakespeare describes how the person of the actor may "counterfeit" a character.

The word "counterfeit" further illustrates the connection between the rhetorical style of acting and the performance of roles. "Are you not mad indeed, or do you but counterfeit?" Feste asks the imprisoned Malvolio in the much later play, *Twelfth Night*. Just beforehand, Sir Toby praises Feste because he "counterfeits well" the parson, Master Topas. Feste, even though he lacks the right weight and height for the part, assumes the voice, cloak, and fake beard of the parson in his interrogation of Malvolio.[97] In contexts such as these, the word "counterfeit" questions the relationship between verisimilitude and role-playing. Malvolio could be genuinely "mad" or pretending just like Feste pretends to be Master Topas. Even so, "counterfeit" need not denote "falsity" because the word might "simply be used neutrally to mean to make or manufacture," observes John H. Astington of the term in sixteenth-century acting practice, "especially if artistic technique was involved in the making."[98] It is because of Feste's artistic technique, for example, that Malvolio, like Sir Toby and Maria, finds the clown's personation credible, a lifelike counterfeit of Master Topas, even though the design of the scene means that audiences would recognize Feste's impersonation.

Analogous to how Feste plays another character or role within the drama, when Buckingham speaks about counterfeiting a tragedian, an actor would claim on stage and during performance, within the fiction of the play, that he, already an actor, may perform as one. There is an important difference from Feste's case, however. Buckingham and Richard are rehearsing the typological role of dissimulator and, in so doing, describe their own erstwhile and subsequent practices; they are parodies of themselves but not in Shapiro's sense. Dissemblers should appear honest, not advertise how artifice creates the impression of honesty, for that would be too honest a display of deceit. As in More's portrait of Richard's machinations, Shakespeare ironizes his deceivers.

Indeed, when Richard and Buckingham speak so forthrightly of their skills in deception, they call attention to their own capacities for performance and how role-play is an intrinsic part of their schemes. These dramatic persons voice a sense of self-conscious fictionality that originates from and revolves around typological characters who are adept at dissimulation. If and when comedy emerges in these cases, it does so because of the sequence of events, such as More's arrangement of Richard's missed cue, or in light of how characters, like Shakespeare's Richard and Buckingham, comment upon how to dupe audiences while performing before one. Neither comedy nor a moment of irony, however, necessarily implies primitive acting techniques in the performance of type. From Terence's Davus to More's and finally Shakespeare's Richard, dissemblers are condemned or questioned precisely because they are skillful actors.

In elaborating upon the actor within the tyrant, Shakespeare reveals how he reads More's own representation of Richard's devices. "Could it have been More's seductive, insinuating narrator who inspires Shakespeare's novel treatment of his protagonist?" asks James Siemon. "The effect of More's entertaining verbal insinuations," Siemon urges, "constitutes a rough analogue for the effect of Shakespeare's master of ceremonies."[99] Whether More's narrator becomes the voice of Shakespeare's Richard or not, Shakespeare recognized the performative aspects of More's tyrant. The embedded directions for delivery and gesture, or voice and action, in order to "counterfeit" well are not just meta-dramatical moments; they are exegetical assessments, showing how Shakespeare read or assessed characterization in More's *History*.

PERFORMING MORE'S RICHARD IN SHAKESPEARE'S PLAY

"In relation to the other characters," Katharine Maus writes of Richard's tactics, "he exploits the invisibility of his own interior." Maus adds of Richard's courtship that "we see Anne taken in by a false display of inward truth" as Richard dupes her.[100] Invisible interiors and inward truths are other words for subjectivity, thereby making Richard Maus's counterpoint to materialist attempts to locate "the metaphysics of interiority" in a later seventeenth-century—post-Shakespearean—philosophical development. Yet we have seen how "inward truth" or an "invisible interior" remained part of the concealed intentions intrinsic to the Theophrastan type and in Tacitus's own Tiberius or Davus's machinations within Terence's comic plots. In the case of Richard, critical debate over subjectivity too often pays insufficient attention to the fact that classical models already provide a framework in the dissembler character type, and that this type, in turn and by definition, manifests a secret interiority of thoughts and ruses.[101]

More's unique combination of Tacitean seriousness with Terence's levity about deception emerges in the very scene that Maus references as well. After Richard proclaims his intention to marry Warwick's youngest daughter, Anne, he adds, "what though I kill'd her husband and her father?" (1.1.154). Richard further explains himself in terms of dissimulation and boastful glee:

> The readiest way to make the wench amends
> Is to become her husband and her father:
> The which will I, not all so much for love
> As for another secret close intent
> By marrying her which I must reach unto. (1.1.155–59)

Richard's "secret close intent" allows him to speak like More's earlier description of him as "close and secret, a deep dissembler." Yet his statement of "intent" occurs here in soliloquy before he adopts the role of "lover" in dialogue with Anne, and the contrast between Richard's "intent" and his words exemplifies the "dynamic dissimulation" Vickers describes above.[102]

Thus, the courtship of Anne doesn't only suggest Richard's typology; it also stages and tests his ability to personate a lover in a credible manner. Anne returns Richard's greeting by calling him a "devil," who is "inhuman" and "unnatural," implores God to revenge her husband's death, and asks the earth to open and swallow Richard. The dialogue ensues:

> Richard: Lady, you know no rules of charity,
> Which renders good for bad, blessings for curses.
> Anne: Villain, thou know'st nor law of God nor man:
> No beast so fierce but knows some touch of pity.
> Richard: But I know none, and therefore am no beast.
> Anne: O wonderful, when devils tell the truth!
> Richard: More wonderful, when angels are so angry. (1.2.68–74)

Here, Richard and Anne are attempting to win a debate by controlling its topic. At stake is the perceived identity of Richard. Is he a murderer or a lover? The war of perspective culminates in Richard turning Anne's accusation of lying to his hope that he will "lie" in her bedchamber (1.2.113–16). The argument between them, however, dramatizes Richard's ability to act as someone other than himself, iterating again the importance of the actor who plays Richard or the dramatic person of Richard who illustrates the skills of an actor. In Shakespeare's concentration upon performance, the dissembler's distinguishing trait—a false denigration of word or action—unfolds in Richard's own character.

The framework of Richard as a consummate actor provides opportunities for either More or Shakespeare to stage debates among other characters over what Richard actually intends, providing them both with an important means of vivifying the dissembler's type. So the people in More's *History* attempt to understand Richard's motives in contrast to his display of rejecting the crown even as Richard and Anne duel about motive. More and Shakespeare model questions of Richard's character as occasions for speakers to argue in *utramque partem*, on either side of the case, while letting either readers or spectators remain certain of Richard's histrionic essence.[103]

Richard makes a second appeal to Anne, blaming the recent deaths on war's changing fortunes, which have caused him wounds as well.[104] He recounts how Anne's father "told the sad story" of his own father's death and did so full of such tears that he made his listeners weep. Richard claims he cried not even then, but he does so for Anne, coaxing her, "Those eyes of thine from mine have drawn salt tears, / Sham'd their aspects with store of childish drops" (1.2.156–57). In an obvious sense, Richard is attempting to make Anne pity him, hoping that, similar to Othello's wooing of Desdemona, Anne might love him for the dangers he had past, and so he would love her for pitying them. Even so, the appeal from *pathos* here relates to Richard's attempt to refashion Anne's perception of him.

As Richard "frames a face" for Anne's perception, he daringly asks her to kill him, if she will not take him for a lover, for not to possess her sentences him to a "living death." After kneeling before her, baring his chest, and presenting Anne with his sword, he tells her:

> Nay, do not pause: for I did kill King Henry,
> But 'twas thy beauty that provoked me.
> Nay, now dispatch: 'twas I that stabb'd young Edward,
> But 'twas thy heavenly face that set me on. (1.2.182–85)

In these words Richard incorporates Anne's perception of him as a slayer of her king and husband into a new creation, that of a noble lover, whose only motive is to possess Anne's beauty.

Richard combines parallel sentences, repeating his "Nay" and "But" formulations, with *aposiopesis*, which is a figure for "a sudden breaking off" of speech in order to show emotion, an embedded direction for early modern actors.[105] Richard's stipulations about Anne's beauty and heavenly face are located within these *aposiopeses*, indicating where and how an actor should amplify his appeal from *pathos*. In fact, these sudden breaking off points of speech are precisely the traits that Richard recommends earlier to Buckingham, including the vocal art of murdering "thy breath in middle of a word, / And then again begin, and stop again" (3.5.2–3).

In the seduction of Anne, Richard follows his own, earlier directions for performance, yet with a different purpose now. His objective here resembles an overall tactic at work in his approach to Anne: that of employing such stops of speech in an attempt at appearing spontaneous. As authenticity becomes the result of artifice, Richard may appear as emotionally torn. Anne will infer that his display comes from love. In performing so, the two disputed depictions of Richard in the earlier part of the dialogue—murderer or lover?—become reconciled through what could be called rhetorical self-fashioning or, better put, good acting. Richard murdered because Richard was in love.[106] The dissembler's expertise at acting allows him to overleap Anne's reservations with professions of love. At the same time, Richard's success illustrates the sophistication of a rhetorical style of acting.

TYRANTS IN TRANSIT

As a prefiguration of, or design for, Shakespeare's dramatic person of Richard, More's *History* deserves renewed attention. Though early critics comment that "Shakespeare's Richard" is "More's Richard," an observation repeated in recent editions of the play, the question of how or in what ways More influences Shakespeare's characterization is neglected in later twentieth-century criticism because, in large part, materialist theories largely discredit character criticism in general.[107] I have returned to More's influence, however, under the auspices of how typological character could model Richard as a dramatic person who professes and plays a rhetorical style of acting.[108] In the process, I explored how Shakespeare's composition of Richard inscribes performance and showed how an actor-tyrant's type could impart the character-effect of interiority.

To conclude by returning to Richard's courtship of Anne, after she departs, Richard exclaims in soliloquy: "Was ever woman in this humor wooed? / Was ever woman in this humor won?" (1.2.230–31). In his ecstasy, Richard shows something of the glee of Ben Jonson's Mosca, who makes himself giddy by dissembling. Mosca's words—"I could skip out of my skin now like a subtle snake, I am so limber"—capture the elation of Richard's gloating question.[109] Perhaps, too, there remains an echo of Davus in Richard's question, which derives from Terence but which More incorporates into Richard's character. Richard's boast obviously illustrates that he had spoken falsely in courting Anne, but that ability to dissemble, to be "close and secret," reveals him to be a superb performer either for the stage at the Globe theater or for the drama of kings' games, which could be played upon other scaffolds. More gave Shakespeare the idea for both.

NOTES

1. E. K. Chambers, *William Shakespeare: A Study of Facts and Problems*, vol. 1 (Oxford: Clarendon Press, 1930), 303. I refer to both the Duke of Gloucester and King Richard III as Richard throughout.

2. Robert Weimann and Douglas Bruster, *Shakespeare and the Power of Performance* (Cambridge, UK: Cambridge University Press, 2010), 44, 47. Meredith Anne Skura, *Shakespeare the Actor and the Purposes of Playing* (Chicago: University of Chicago Press, 1993), 64, concurs: "It is an ideal acting part; Richard Burbage was known for it in the sixteenth century, and both David Garrick in the nineteenth and Olivier in ours made their reputation playing Richard. In creating his first tragedies Shakespeare thus simultaneously created his *first* histrionic character" (my emphasis).

3. Robert Weimann, *Author's Pen and Actor's Voice: Playing and Writing in Shakespeare's Theatre* (Cambridge, UK: Cambridge University Press, 2000).

4. The term is defined by Richard A. Lanham, *A Handlist of Rhetorical Terms*, second edition (Berkeley: University of California Press, 1991), 64–65. For discussion and qualification of the term as rhetorical in origin and as a means of appropriation, see Stephen Greenblatt, *Shakespearean Negotiations* (Berkeley: University of California Press, 1988), 5–12. In one sense, I reconstruct a "negotiation" of Richard between and among a group of authors. In tracing and developing the impact of *enargeia*, "mimesis" of Richard accompanies a cultural "exchange" but between poets. Even so, the major artistic development, as I argue below, occurs with More's treatment of classical sources.

5. On *enargeia*, its humanist reception, and Shakespeare's use of it, see Heinrich F. Plett, *Enargeia in Classical Antiquity and the Early Modern Age* (Boston: Brill, 2012), 7–36, 65–68, 89–117, 125–82.

6. Lorna Hutson, *The Invention of Suspicion: Law and Mimesis in Shakespeare and Renaissance Drama* (Oxford: Oxford University Press, 2011), 114, criticizes Greenblatt for defining mimesis exclusively in terms of "the fungibility and availability of objects or subjects of cultural representation" and expands the new historicist treatment of mimesis to include "the temporal and narrative aspects of mimesis." I follow her general observation about *enargeia* and lifelike effect: "We are inclined to forget how much is not actually staged in a Renaissance play because the *enargeia*, or vividness and presence, of various characters' narrations of events that take place elsewhere gives us the impression, especially as readers, of *a reality as immediate as that which we imagine to take place on-stage*" (126, my emphasis).

7. Nicholas Brooke, "Marlowe as Provocative Agent in Shakespeare's Early Plays," *Shakespeare Survey* 14 (1961): 35. For Aaron's lines, see *Titus Andronicus*, 2.1.1–4. With the exception of *King Richard III*, all citations from Shakespeare are internally noted by act, scene, and line numbers and are from William Shakespeare, *The Complete Works*, second edition, ed. Stanley Wells and Gary Taylor (Oxford: Oxford University Press, 2005).

8. The Oxford editors title *3 Henry VI* as *The True Tragedy of Richard Duke of York and the Good King Henry the Sixth*, but henceforth I will abbreviate the play with its shorter title. For the lines cited, see 1.2.29–30. Brooke, 37, writes that "Marlowe's villain is still a felt presence behind Shakespeare's, and such a general relationship has always been recognized." Cf. Janet Adelman, *Suffocating Mothers: Fantasies of Maternal Origin in Shakespeare's Plays* (New York: Routledge, 1992), 1–10. Adelman, contrary to historicized studies and comparisons of Shakespeare to Marlowe, hears "for the first time" in Richard's monologue at 3.2.153–68 from *3 King Henry VI* "the voice of a fully developed subjectivity, the characteristically Shakespearean illusion that a stage person has interior being, including motives that he himself does not fully understand" (1).

9. James Shapiro, *Rival Playwrights: Marlowe, Jonson, Shakespeare* (New York: Columbia University Press, 1991), 96, 182n51.

10. Bart van Es, *Shakespeare in Company* (Oxford University Press, 2013), 56, 72.

11. Shapiro, *Rival Playwrights*, 5–6.

12. On *imitatio*, see D. A. Russell, "De Imitatione," in *Creative Imitation and Latin Literature*, ed. D. West and A. Woodman (Cambridge, UK: Cambridge University Press, 1979), 1–16; G. W. Pigman III, "Versions of Imitation in the Renaissance," *Renaissance Quarterly* 33 (1980): 1–32; Thomas M. Greene, *The Light in Troy: Imitation and Discovery in Renaissance Poetry* (New Haven, CT: Yale University Press, 1982).

13. Cf. Greenblatt, *Shakespearean Negotiations*, 5, who uses Puttenham's definition to redefine enargeia as "social energy" (6).

14. George Puttenham, *The Art of English Poesy: A Critical Edition*, ed. Frank Whigham and Wayne A. Rebhorn (Ithaca, NY: Cornell University Press, 2007), 323–24.

15. More invokes Apelles because of the painter's famous ability at verisimilitude, which More applies to a "pageant" that stars a flatterer. See *The Yale Edition of The Complete Works of St. Thomas More, Vol. 12, A Dialogue of Comfort Against Tribulation*, ed. Louis L. Martz and Frank Manley (New Haven, CT: Yale University Press, 1976), 215/6–216/5.

16. *A Rich Storehouse or Treasure for Nobility and Gentlemen* is cited from Colin Burrow, *Shakespeare and Classical Antiquity*, Oxford Special Topics, eds. Peter Holland and Stanley Wells (Oxford: Oxford University Press, 2013), 26–27.

17. For a discussion of "genesis and models" connecting Roman works to More's *History*, see *The Yale Edition of The Complete Works of St. Thomas More, Vol. 2, The History of King Richard III*, ed. Richard S. Sylvester (New Haven, CT: Yale University Press, 1963), lxxx–civ. Hereafter abbreviated as *CW* 2 and cited internally by page and line numbers. Sylvester writes of More's connection with Tacitus: "how thoroughly he

himself read the *Annals*, especially their first six books, is manifested in the pages of the *Richard*" (xci).

18. Quintilian, *The Institutio Oratoria of Quintilian*, vol. 4, trans. H. E. Butler (Cambridge, MA: Harvard University Press, 1922), 10.1.31; cf. Cicero, *Rhetorica Ad Herennium*, trans. H. Caplan (Cambridge, MA: Harvard University Press, 1954), 1.1.1.

19. Aristides is cited from Cornelius Tacitus, *The Annals*, trans. A. J. Woodman (Indianapolis: Hackett Publishing, 2004), xviii. More's version of the liberal arts stipulates that "judgment" is "much ripened" by the study of orators, laws, histories, and, above all, poets. See *The Yale Edition of the Complete Works of Thomas More, Vol. 6, Part 1: A Dialogue Concerning Heresies* (New Haven, CT: Yale University Press, 1981), 132/3–16.

20. For the special emphasis upon *enargeia* in historiography, see Andrew D. Walker, "Enargeia and the Spectator in Greek History," *Transactions of the American Philological Association (1974–)* 123 (1993): 353–77.

21. Quintilian, *Institutio Oratoria*, vol. 3, 8.3.61–62.

22. Quintilian, *Institutio Oratoria*, vol. 3, 8.3.71.

23. Erasmus, *"Copia": Foundations of the Abundant Style*, trans. Betty I. Knott, in *Collected Works of Erasmus*, ed. Craig R. Thompson (Toronto: University of Toronto Press, 1978), 577.

24. Ibid.

25. On *enargeia* and poetry, see S. K. Heninger, *Sidney and Spenser: The Poet as Maker* (University Park: Pennsylvania State University Press, 1989), 95–100; and compare with Travis Curtright, "Sidney's *Defense of Poetry*: Ethos and the Ideas," *Ben Jonson Journal* 10 (2003): 101–15.

26. Lucian, "How to Write History," in *Lucian*, vol. 6, trans. K. Kilburn (Cambridge, MA: Harvard University Press, 1999), 51, 65, my emphasis. On More's admiration of Lucian see the introduction to *The Yale Edition of the Complete Works of Thomas More, V ol. 3, pt. 1, Translations of Lucian*, ed. Craig R. Thompson (New Haven, CT: Yale University Press, 1974) and Travis Curtright, "Thomas More on Humor," *Logos: A Journal of Catholic Thought and Culture* 17, no. 1 (2014): 20.

27. Walker, "Enargeia," 354.

28. Thomas Hobbes, *The English Works of Thomas Hobbes of Malmesbury*, vol. 8, ed. William Molesworth (London: J. Bohn, 1839–1845), xxii.

29. In a famous instance, Thucydides testifies that he resorted to writing the speeches from past orations: "I have found it difficult to remember the precise words used in the speeches which I listened to myself and my various informants have experienced the same difficulty; so my method has been, while keeping as closely as possible to the general sense of the words that were actually used, *to make the speakers say what, in my opinion, was called for* by each situation" (my emphasis). See Thucydides, *History of the Peloponnesian War*, trans. Rex Warner (New York: Penguin Books, 1954), 47. On Thucydides's use of *enargeia* in narrative scenes, see Walker, "Enargeia," 355–61.

30. Plett takes the analogous case of Lucian's description of a lost painting by Apelles, writing: "From the humanistic point of view, the non-tangible past of Antiquity thus acquires the hidden function of immediate, topic presence. The basis for this is not provided by mimesis, since the ancient model has not been preserved and is therefore inaccessible, but by the imagination alone" (17–18).

31. On rhetorical history and Tacitus, see Woodman's introduction, *Annals*, xi–xix. The most helpful discussion of the literary art involved in rhetorical historiography does not address More but Tacitus. Even so, the techniques described for the *Annals* transfer to the *History* in "The Introduction of Non-Factual Material" in B. Walker, *Annals of Tacitus: A Study in the Writing of History* (Manchester, UK: Manchester University Press, 1952), 33–77. Rhetorical or creative historiography reconfigures modern historians' imperative to discover More's sources. Where no source is found, scholars often declare an unknown "oral source," thereby using the lack of evidence to suggest a factual finding, a method often used to exalt the role of John Morton (e.g. *CW 2*,

lxvi–lxix and see Logan's *History*, xxiv–xxvi). Yet the rhetorical context actually granted More the rights of invention.

So, too, if there is a moral component in Shakespeare's Richard at variance with Marlovian heroes, it may be derived from More's *History*. Rhetorical historiography as practiced by humanists indicates that perennial wisdom about the human condition could be transferred from age to age by classical texts. Thus, Pier Paolo Vergerio's "The Character and Studies Befitting a Free-Born Youth" (ca. 1402–1403) declares of the *litterarum disciplinae* that they are a "great help to those who were born for virtue and wisdom [*vertutem et sapientiam*], and they often provide the means for uncovering stupidity or more destructive kinds of wrongdoing." He then proceeds to discuss Roman emperors. See Vergerio's statement in *Humanist Educational Treatises*, ed. and trans. Craig W. Kallendorf (Cambridge, MA: Harvard University Press, 2002), 36–39. More, at least, could fictionalize elements of the past while believing in the perennial moral truth of his depiction of tyrannical character and its practices.

32. Leonard F. Dean, "Literary Problems in More's Richard III," *PMLA* 58, no. 1 (March 1943): 38.

33. For a critique of materialist approaches on the question of "inwardness" or "subjectivity," see Katharine Eisaman Maus, *Inwardness and Theater in the English Renaissance* (Chicago: University of Chicago Press, 1995), 1–34; in reference to the "inwardness" of Shakespeare's *Richard III*, see 47–54.

34. B. Walker, *Annals of Tacitus*, 47.

35. These types are named and described by Walker in *Annals of Tacitus*, 204–43.

36. Woodman, *Annals,* 194.

37. For the passage cited, see Theophrastus, *Characters*, trans. Jeffrey Rusten (Cambridge, MA: Harvard University Press, 1993), 51. For a general explanation of Theophrastus's influence in classical rhetoric, and especially upon the English Renaissance, see Benjamin Boyce, *The Theophrastan Character in England to 1642* (Cambridge, MA: Harvard University Press, 1947), 11–52.

38. Theophrastus, *Characters*, 53.

39. *CW* 2, 8/7–11. I have modernized all quotations from this text in consultation with the glosses from Thomas More, *The History of Richard the Third: A Reading Edition*, ed. George M. Logan (Indianapolis: Indiana University Press, 2005).

40. Tacitism, at least, became synonymous with Machiavellian thought. Giovanni Botero's *Ragione di Stato* (1589), for example, explicitly links Tacitus to Machiavelli. See Peter Burke, "Tacitism, Skepticism, and Reason of State," in *The Cambridge History of Political Thought 1450–1700*, ed. J. H. Burns (Cambridge, UK: Cambridge University Press, 1991), 479–84; and Victoria Kahn, "Machiavelli's Reputation to the Eighteenth Century," in *The Cambridge Companion to Machiavelli*, ed. John M. Najemy (Cambridge, UK: Cambridge University Press, 2010), 241–44. For a political reading of More's own *History*, see Travis Curtright, *The One Thomas More* (Washington, DC: Catholic University of America Press, 2012), 42–71.

41. Sylvester, *CW* 2, lviii.

42. More's *Historia Richardi Tertii* is cited from *The Yale Edition of the Complete Works of Thomas More, Vol. 15, In Defense of Humanism*, ed. and trans. Daniel Kinney (New Haven, CT: Yale University Press, 1986), 325. Hereafter cited as *CW* 15 followed by page and, when available, line numbers. This edition includes More's original Latin. The above quotation translates: *Personam quamlibet induere gerereque et tueri gnauiter / hylarem / severam / gravem / remissam / prout sumere aut ponere suasit commodum* (324/10–13). Sylvester provides a more literal translation of the first part, writing of Richard: "He could assume whatever mask it pleased him to wear and he played the part he had chosen with the utmost diligence" (*CW* 2, comment on 8/7). *Gnauiter*, an adverb, may be translated as "diligence," or "energetically," or "wholeheartedly." More doesn't appear to comment upon the quality of Richard's acting but rather the tyrant's eagerness to practice it.

43. *In vultu modestia / in animo fastus impotens / ingens / immanis / verbis adblandiens his quos intus impense oderat / nec eorum abstinens complexibus quos destinabat occidere* (CW 15, 324/13–15).

44. Though Emrys Jones's assessment refers to More's English version, the point about Richard as an actor remains the same: "Kyd's Lorenzo is a flatly conceived character. Marlowe's Barabas is closer to Richard . . . but is still not quite what Richard is, one who deliberately assumes different roles in such a way as to remind us pointedly of the arts of the theatre." Jones concludes that More "must be seen as giving Shakespeare his inspiration." See Emrys Jones, *The Origins of Shakespeare* (Oxford: Oxford University Press, 1977), 215.

45. More views the expert actor in terms of observing decorum in *The Yale Edition of the Complete Works of Thomas More, Vol. 4, Utopia*, ed. Edward Surtz and J. H. Hexter (New Haven, CT: Yale University Press, 1979), 98/12–14; and see the commentary on these lines.

46. The author of *Rhetorica Ad Herennium*, trans. H. Caplan (Cambridge, MA: Harvard University Press, 1954), defines *effictio*, which means "portrayal," at 4.49.63.

47. *Annals*, 150–51.

48. *CW* 2, 7/19–21.

49. The 2012 discovery and study of Richard's skeleton reveals that he suffered from scoliosis and spinal curvature but was *not* hunchbacked. For scholarly discussion before this discovery, see commentary in *CW* 2 at 7/20. Logan notes how other accounts—contemporary with More's—do not mention Richard was "humpbacked" (Logan,*The History*, 10n69).

50. All citations from Shakespeare's *King Richard III* are from *The Arden Shakespeare*, Third Series, ed. James R. Siemon (London: Methuen Drama, 2009), 1.1.16–21. Hereafter cited internally.

51. Richard's first soliloquy in the play named for him repeats his motivations all over from *3 Henry VI* as if Shakespeare is reminding the audience where he left off. Compare 3.2.146–95 in *3 Henry VI* with 1.1.14–41 from *King Richard III*.

52. *3 Henry VI*, 3.3.182–85. Though the continuity of Richard's character from 2 and 3 *Henry VI* to *Richard III* remains a question, Siemon, *King Richard III*, writes of the speech quoted above: "Here, for the first time, Richard sounds mostly like Richard" (42).

53. *3 Henry VI*, 3.2.182–89.

54. Brian Vickers, "Shakespeare's Hypocrites," in *Returning to Shakespeare* (London: Routledge, 1989), 90–94.

55. Juan Huarte Navarro, *The Examination of Mens' Wits* (New York: Da Capo Press, 1969), 134–35.

56. Suetonius, *Lives of the Caesars*, trans. J. C. Rolfe (Cambridge, MA: Harvard University Press, 1998), 61.4–5.

57. See William Roper, "Life of More" in *A Thomas More Source Book*, ed. Gerard B. Wegemer and Stephen W. Smith (Washington DC: Catholic University of America Press, 2004), 44.

58. Roper, "Life of More," 44.

59. Some of More's debts to Tacitus seem more obvious: As Sylvester points out in his introduction to *CW* 2, More borrows the structure of the *Annals*, charting Richard's rise and fall after that of Tiberius and transferring the trait of dissimulation from Tiberius to Richard.

60. On More and rhetorical imitation, see Logan, *The History*, xxxi–xxiv. On "re-creating nature," see Brian Vickers's gloss of Puttenham and the following analysis in *In Defense of Rhetoric* (Oxford: Oxford University Press, 2002), 333–35.

61. Another model contributing to this episode may be Suetonius, *Lives of the Caesars*, 24. But see Logan, who writes that "Suetonius's gossipy, scandalous work on the emperors . . . is not an important model for More's history" (Logan, *The History*, xxxin32).

62. *CW* 2, 53/19–25.

63. *CW* 2, xciv–xcv.
64. I insert the Latin from Tacitus, *The Annals: Books IV–VI, XI–XII*, trans. John Jackson (Cambridge, MA: Harvard University Press, 1998), 6.24.
65. Woodman, *Annals*, 178.
66. Jackson, however, uses "unnatural vice" in his translation of *Annals* at 6.24.
67. *CW* 2, 53/24.
68. *CW* 2, 54/4–7.
69. *CW* 2, 54/10–11 and 54/14.
70. For More's version in comparison to other more minor sources, such as those by Mancini, Fabyan, or the author of the *Croyland Chronicle*, see Sylvester's commentary on 46/27–47/1 in *CW* 2, 216. On the *Chronicle*, however, Logan rightly asserts that "it is extremely unlikely that More had seen this work" (*H*, xxvii–xxviii). Polydore Vergil includes Richard making an announcement of Hastings's treason and alleging witchcraft similar to More's but does not include Shore or strawberries.
71. Polydore Vergil, *Three Books of Polydore Vergil's English History*, ed. Henry Ellis, (New York and London: AMS Press, 1968), 181–82. I have modernized the English.
72. Woodman, *Annals*, 172.
73. Slyvester, *CW* 2, xcvii.
74. Cf. Vergil's sparse account of the same event reads: "he was creatyd king at West-mynster the day before the nones of July . . . the people rather not repyning for feare than allowing therof, and was cawlyd Richard iiird" (Vergil, 36: 187).
75. *CW* 2, 81/6–10.
76. On More's "kings' games" passage and Richard, see Jones, *Origins of Shakespeare*, 214, who speculates: "It was perhaps from this episode that Shakespeare's whole conception of the histrionic, role-playing Richard took its rise."
77. *CW* 2, xciv.
78. Even the less vivid technique of character portrayal used by Tacitus is claimed to "adhere most closely" to "the novel" in Stephen G. Daitz, "Tacitus' Technique of Character Portrayal," *American Journal of Philology* 81, no. 1 (January 1960): 52n97.
79. See commentary in *CW* 2, 54/9–13.
80. See *CW* 15, 423 for the lines quoted. For the differences referred to above, compare the English in *CW* 2, 53/3–54/14 with the Arundel ms. in *CW* 2, 131/5–26 and the fair-copy and fuller Paris version in *CW* 15, 423. On the latter's textual history, see *CW* 15, cxxxiii–cliii.
81. *CW* 15, 423.
82. How much More enjoyed this play and, in particular, Davus, may be gauged by Margaret's letter of August, 1534. When Margaret, More's daughter, attempts to persuade her father to take the oath of succession and leave the Tower, More tells a parable about wise men and fools before he confesses: "For as Davus saith in Terence (Non sum Oedipus) I may say you wot [know] well (Non sum Oedipus, sed Morus) which name of mine what it signifieth in Greke, I need not tel you." See Thomas More, *The Correspondence of Sir Thomas More*, ed. Elizabeth Frances Rogers (Princeton, NJ: Princeton University Press, 1947), 519/183–88. The line originally belongs to Davus— *Davos sum, non Oedipus*—who uses it to feign innocence in *Woman from Andros* in *Terence*, vol. 1, ed. and trans. John Barsby (Cambridge, MA: Harvard University Press, 2001), lines 194–95.
83. Terence, lines 467–80.
84. *CW* 2, 59/24–28.
85. *CW* 2, 68/1–6.
86. *CW* 2, 68/8–16, my emphasis.
87. *CW* 2, 68/24–26.
88. Burrow, *Shakespeare and Classical Antiquity*, 153.
89. Terence, lines 794–95.
90. *CW* 2, 52/28.
91. Thomas Wilson, *The Art of Rhetoric* (1560), ed. Peter E. Medine (University Park: Pennsylvania State University Press, 1994), 205.

92. For the general sense of "colour" see David Crystal and Ben Crystal, *Shakespeare's Words: A Glossary and Language Companion* [http://www.shakespeareswords.com/Glossary] and (London: Penguin Books, 2004), noun3.

93. *As You Like It*, 3.2.178.

94. *The History of Henry IV* [Part 1], 2.5.387–90. The editor, John Jowett, refers to Falstaff as "Sir John Oldcastle."

95. Quintilian, *Institutio Oratoria*, vol. 6, 6.2.34–36. For further discussion of the actor's use of *enargeia*, see Bruce Danner, "Speaking Daggers," *Shakespeare Quarterly* 54, no. 1 (Spring, 2003): 53–55.

96. When Shakespeare's scrivener enters, the impact of inserting meta-theatrical explanations of the actor's art produces comedy. More's merchant, who gets the punch-line about how the proclamation over Hastings is written by "prophecy," becomes the scrivener's question, "Who is so gross / That cannot see this palpable device?" (3.6.10–11).

97. *Twelfth Night, Or What You Will*, 4.2.116–17; 4.2.20, my emphasis; and see 4.2.7–11. See also Falstaff, or Sir John, from *The Merry Wives of Windsor*, who celebrates his "admirable dexterity of wit" because he was successful in "counterfeiting" the action of an old woman" (4.5.110–13). For an earlier instance, see Hieronimo's words from Thomas Kyd's *The Spanish Tragedy* in *English Renaissance Drama: A Norton Anthology*, ed. David Bevington (New York: W.W. Norton & Company, 2002): "Haply you think—but bootless are your thoughts— / That this is fabulously *counterfeit*, / And that we do as all tragedians do" (4.4.76–78, my emphasis).

98. John H. Astington, *Actors and Acting in Shakespeare's Time* (Cambridge, UK: Cambridge University Press, 2010), 14.

99. Siemon, *King Richard III*, 59–60.

100. Maus, *Inwardness*, 49, 54.

101. For the term "subjectivity" and the materialist argument that "pre-bourgeois subjection does not properly involve subjectivity at all" but emerges as the result of Cartesian thought, see Francis Barker, *The Tremulous Private Body: Essays on Subjection* (London: Methuen, 1984), 31–32, 52–58. See, too, Jonathon Dollimore, *Radical Tragedy: Religion, Ideology, and Power in the Drama of Shakespeare and his Contemporaries*, third edition (Durham, NC: Duke University Press, 2004), , 155.

102. Richard's exchange with Anne is often wrongly understood as derived from Seneca's *Hercules Furens*, which depicts a similar exchange in Lycus's "wooing" of Megara. See Geoffrey Bullough, ed., *Narrative and Dramatic Sources of Shakespeare* (New York: Columbia University Press, 1960), 313–17; van Es provides the most recent case for Seneca's *Hercules furens* in Bart van Es, *Shakespeare in Company* (Oxford: Oxford University Press, 2013), 68–69. In Seneca's version, there is no offered sword for the beloved to use against her lover, yet Richard offers his chest and sword to Anne. More importantly, Lycus never describes himself as one who killed for love of Megara, though Richard's greatest deception may be convincing Anne that he killed her family members for love of her. Instead, Lycus continually threatens Megara with death, if she does not yield.

103. Of argument *in utramque partem*, see Quintilian, *Institutio Oratoria*, vol. 4, 12.25–28. For discussion of this rhetorical form and Thomas More, see Joel Altman, *The Tudor Play of Mind: Rhetorical Inquiry and the Development of Elizabethan Drama* (Berkeley: University of California Press, 1978), 80.

104. This appeal begins at 1.2.156 and ends with Richard's threat of taking his own life, if Anne will not have him at 181.

105. On *aposiopesis*, see Katie Whales, "An A–Z of Rhetorical Terms," in *Reading Shakespeare's Dramatic Language: A Guide*, ed. Sylvia Adamson, et al. (London: The Arden Shakespeare, 2001), 280–81.

106. Richard's account of his love as motivation heightens the theme of dissimulation and comprises Shakespeare's own addition. As I argue above, his addition builds upon More's influence rather than that of Seneca. In Jasper Heywood's 1561 translation of Seneca's *Hercules Furens*, Lycus tells Megara he killed her father and brethren

because "we all togyther [were] led / With wicked luste" (Bullough, *Narrative and Dramatic Sources*, 316). The word "lust" here pertains to the acquisition of kingdoms, not brides. The context is clear from the original, where Lycus claims "war delights in blood [*bella delectate cruor*]. But he fought for his realm, sayest thou; we impelled by insatiable ambition? [*nos improba cupidine acti*]." See Frank Justus Miller, trans., *Seneca's Tragedies* (Cambridge: Harvard University Press, 1960), lines 405–8. Shakespeare's Richard transforms bloodlust into "love" for Anne, attributing his (true) political agenda for power to (false) personal and private motivations to possess Anne's beauty. The subject of the debate between Richard and Anne revolves around Richard's ability to disguise his intentions, whereas Lycus simply pronounces his.

107. R. W. Chambers, *Thomas More* (Ann Arbor: University of Michigan Press, 1958), 117, is an example of such an early critic; for a recent edition that iterates Chambers, see Anthony Hammond, ed., The Arden Shakespeare: *King Richard III*, Second Series (London: Methuen, 2000), 77. On character as a distinctly "modern" development, see Barker, *The Tremulous Private Body*, 24–25, 31–32, 52, 59, 68; and Belsey, *Subject of Tragedy*, 18, 26–34, 40. Yachnin and Slights, *Shakespeare and Character*, 18n6, dub materialist critique as "the practice of character assignation" and suggest a comeback for character studies.

108. On the point of inscribing performance into character, see Weimann and Bruster, *Power of Performance*, 52, who write of Buckingham's speech on counterfeiting, "the act of performance becomes inseparable from representation itself."

109. For Mosca's quotation, see Ben Jonson's *Volpone* in *English Renaissance Drama* at 3.1.5–7.

TWO

Kate's Audacious Speech of Submission

No understanding of *The Taming of the Shrew* may neglect Katherina Minola's final "speech of submission" to her husband, what Barbara Hodgdon calls "a locus of obsessive attention" for directors, critics, and actors alike.[1] In stage productions, the culmination of Petruchio's "taming school" reveals Kate as genuinely in love, a brainwashed victim, or a cunning and cool ironist (4.2.55). Occasionally, she is a performer, who learns from Petruchio how to dupe others while retaining her inner freedom. Behind these Kates are critical categories like harmless "farce" or an object lesson in patriarchal "subordination" or training in "role-playing."[2] Today's actresses typically struggle against a subordinated character even as critics argue "that Elizabethans viewed *The Taming of the Shrew* as concluding with the husband in control and the wife tamed."[3]

Even so, I will present a triumphant Kate, an audacious speaker, but in the Elizabethan context of the boy actor who played her role and his/her particular charge to speak persuasively at play's conclusion.[4] To put it paradoxically, Kate triumphs in delivering an excellent speech upon her own subordination. "The play stands or falls on the apprentice's performance in the last scene, just as Petruchio's wager stands or falls," writes Juliet Dusinberre of the boy actor who voices Kate's oration, "so masters gather round to see whose apprentice will play the big part" like the characters do at the end of the play, listening to Kate's final words.[5] *Taming*, Dusinberre argues, demands that audiences attend to more than one plot—that of the play and a more "covert drama" which is generated by "the actual structures of relationship present in the company" that performs it.[6]

Dusinberre's insight that there is a "covert drama" afoot at the end of *Taming*, especially among the apprentice boy actors, calls attention to the competition between and among them, a relationship that mirrors the contention among pupils in the Tudor grammar school. "Everything in the school," writes instructor John Brinsley in his *Ludus Literarius* (1612), should be done "by emulation and contention for praise," and the boys should be matched "so they would be placed as adversaries [so] that they may contend in all things, whether of them shall do the better."[7] Of note, the awarding of roles, like the school prizes for oration, hinges upon the boys' rhetorical skills of delivery. "Stage-playing and rhetorical delivery were so alike," B. L. Joseph writes in 1951 in a comment that remains fundamentally accurate, "that whoever knows today exactly what was taught to the renaissance orator cannot be far from knowing at the same time what was done by the actor on the Elizabethan stage."[8]

Given the close relationship of acting and oratory, stage and classroom training, the importance of a "covert drama" that impacts the final scene of *Taming*, as Elizabeth Hutcheon and Lynn Enterline have recently argued, manifests the strictures of the humanist schoolroom, where a *magister* sits in judgment of a *puer* and both are concerned with the art of persuasive public speech.[9] For *Taming*, like its predecessor, *Love's Labour's Lost*, richly alludes not just to humanist rhetorical forms and training but also enacts them. In the humanist classroom, the boy student would perform a declamation, which, if it receives approval of a schoolmaster, avoids punishment and achieves reward. Likewise, as Kate's speech delights Petruchio, the two exit in victory over the other couples on stage—if not in happiness, at least, with a bag full of money. Thus, both shrew and the actor who plays her may provide audiences with a fully realized experience of a victorious Kate at the very moment when she speaks of her submission.

A triumphant Kate bears upon the question of how William Shakespeare fashions character-effects because, if she is victorious, she emerges as such because of how well she declaims, an art that signifies lifelike personation in the sixteenth century.[10] Henry Peacham, for example, defines "mimesis" in his *Garden of Eloquence* (1593) as "an imitation of speech whereby the orator *counterfeits* not only what one said but also his utterance, pronunciation and gesture, imitating everything as it was, which is always well performed, and naturally represented in an apt and skillful actor." Yet Peacham's early modern version of "natural" representation, we shall see, indicates declamation's art, which he doesn't distinguish from skillful acting. Such mimesis constitutes a form of what Peacham understands as a manifestation of rhetoric's art whereby "the singular parts of man's mind are most aptly expressed and the sundry affections of his heart most effectively uttered."[11]

To further demonstrate the lifelike possibilities of the rhetorical style of acting in this chapter, I will argue that Kate's final speech reveals a schoolroom exercise in speaking and Peacham's notion of mimesis. The interplay between a boy actor's presence and his representation of Kate illustrates Peacham's original emphasis upon the orator who mimics the "singular parts" of a character's "mind" and "heart."[12] But also Kate's "singular parts" are attributes derived from the boy actor who transfers qualities from his own person to the role he plays. Accordingly, I will examine Kate by keeping both representation and the boy actor's presence in mind,[13] using Shakespeare's representation of Kate's rhetorical expertise to explain the schoolroom exercises in persuasion's arts and vice versa.[14]

In particular, Kate's last speech calls attention to the all-male grammar school's emphasis upon "audacity" in declamation, even though that art requires a student to remain and speak in female character. "When you meet with an act or scene that is full of affection and action," schoolmaster Charles Hoole advises, "you may cause some of your scholars, after they have learned it to act it, first in private amongst themselves, and afterwards in the open school before their fellows; and therein you must have a main care of their pronunciation and acting every gesture to the very life." Instruction in pronunciation and acting "to the very life," we shall see, manifests "audacity" in the performer, which suggests how the boy actor playing Kate's character would appear bold, not necessarily just as a shrew, but especially when she/he declaims at the play's end. "No day in the week should pass on which some declamation, oration, or theme should not be pronounced," Hoole commands, because "by assiduity in these exercises, the scholars may be *emboldened* to perform them."[15] Schoolmasters like Hoole present "the skills of oratory and performance in robust and masculine terms," observes Ursula Potter, because they believe masterful delivery or performance embodies such traits.[16] Instead of a binary opposition between "character" and "actor," I am interested in how the prized trait of audacity from the grammar schools could become a quality that Kate embodies in performance.[17]

Finally, if an audacious Kate is the result of how the boy actor should personate that role, there are grounds for modern productions of *Taming* that, in Paul Yachnin's words, accentuate Kate's "expression of many-sided resistance."[18] Contemporary actresses who play Kate, even if anachronistically or unintentionally, echo the Elizabethan importance of audacity in expert declamation. Though the frame of reference alters from early modern acting styles to modern naturalism, contemporary Kates on the stage today may speak, in Elizabethan terms, like a man, if they declaim with expertise and passion. Instead of asking whether or not Elizabethan boys might play women well on stage, I wonder if their rhetorical training suggests how contemporary Kates, played by especially powerful actresses, rightly maintain a spirited presence in the famous "speech of submission."

AUDACITY AND PERFORMANCE

To recognize Kate's oratorical bravery, we must first define "audacity" in the arts of rhetoric and personation as both school and theatrical exercise present it. Though classical rhetoric has been widely acknowledged as the curricular foundation for grammar schools at least since the publication of T. W. Baldwin's *Shakespeare's Small Latine and Lesse Greeke* (1944), Lynn Enterline's recent *Shakespeare's Schoolroom: Rhetoric, Discipline, and Emotion* (2012) demonstrates the theatrical aspects of that curriculum, showing how corporal and vocal delivery are intrinsic to the boys' education.[19] In doing so, unlike previous and more historical studies, she pursues the question of how or why "the humanist rhetoric training" strengthens or develops "the stability of masculine identity."[20] In this section, rather than rehearse the entire grammar school program so well documented by others, I will follow Enterline by sketching the early modern program for cultivating boldness through rhetorical study and illustrate its connection to the theater. My aim is to recall the already well-established historical context about grammar school performances for the sake of suggesting how a role, or the personated, could blend with the actor, the personator, even when the theatrical and rhetorical cultivation of audacity required boys to mimic vocal, affective, or physical attributes of women. Though the above inference about the transfer of audacity from actor to character seems clear enough, as we shall see at the end of this chapter, its ramifications are seldom applied to Kate's final speech.

To begin, with an all-male schoolroom like Brinsley's, boys would study the *ars rhetorica* because of the humanist ideal of the *vir civilis*, or the *statesman*.[21] Students should become skilled in invention, the creation of subject matter; disposition or the organization of that material; elocution or style, especially in regards to how figures of speech are deployed; memory, including the orator's ability to memorize his speech or the actors' obligation to memorize lines; and delivery, the use of voice and gesture.[22] Humanists argued that an education in rhetoric would afford an opportunity "for the educated lay man in the conduct of government," and English schoolmasters believed in this objective whether or not their students ever pursued such careers.[23]

The theater's role in the classroom becomes clear if we imagine how declamation, daring, and acting could contribute to what John Bale calls the formation of a student's "tender and childish speaking mouth" into the instrument of a future statesman, who would speak "elegantly and distinctly."[24] In Enterline's review of grammar school curricula and ordinances, oratory and acting remain "virtual synonyms" because "schoolmasters thought both acting and declamation were good training in eloquence and the art of gentlemanly behavior." So there is nothing unusual about grammar school ordinances that state how on "every Thursday" students "shall for exercise *declaim* and *play* one act of a comedy."[25] Or that Sir James Whitelock, a student who enrolled at Merchant Taylors' school in London in 1585, would testify on behalf of his old instructor, Richard Mulcaster: "And yearly he presented some plays to the court, in which his scholars were only actors, and I one among them, and by that means taught them good behavior and *audacity*."[26] For "boldness and audacity," Edel Lamb summarizes of grammar school practices, "were crucial traits of the orator," which were considered "masculine traits."[27] A good actor must expertly convey his lines, but to do so requires daring, an antecedent self-confidence. In the classroom, bravery wed to oratory betokens leadership skills. Boldness, thus, emerges as a concomitant to the ideal of grammar school education, which aspires to form statesmen.

Likewise, the importance of audacity resounds in later defenses of the professional or collegiate stages. In perhaps the most famous testimonial to the importance of "emboldending" scholars, Thomas Heywood's *Apology for Actors* (1612) lists each of the same five canons of rhetoric reviewed above in his defense of the theater, following and quoting from the same *Ad Herennium* that inspires the humanist retrieval of classical rhetoric.[28] As in the grammar school, Heywood emphasizes how rhetorical training cultivates bravery, which acting on stages will augment:

> In the time of my residence in Cambridge, I have seen tragedies, comedies, histories, pastoral and shows publicly acted, in which graduates of good place and reputation have been specially parted: this is held *necessary for the emboldening of their junior scholars, to arm them with audacity*, against [in preparation for] they come to be employed in any public exercise.... *It teacheth audacity* to the bashful grammarian, being newly admitted into the private college and after matriculated and entered as a member of a university, and makes him a bold sophister [debater], to argue pro and contra, to compose his syllogisms . . . to reason and frame a sufficient argument to prove his questions, or to defend any axiom, to distinguish any dilemma, and be able to moderate in any argumentation whatsoever.[29]

Though Heywood distinguishes "junior" scholars from more advanced performers, his *Apology* repeats conventional defenses of the study of rhetoric, which already assumed the benefits of classical learning for speaking and disputing in public. Grammar schools, like universities, train boys in rhetoric under the presumption that it prepares students not simply for the clergy but as future statesmen; and, as Harold Newcomb Hillebrand's foundational study, *The Child Actors*, documents in detail, school theatricals were an essential aspect of this training.[30] Heywood appropriates the aims of humanist pedagogy to defend acting as a profession, but, in doing so, he highlights the comprehensive significance of audacity for the classroom and the stage.

How, though, could the study of eloquence develop this early modern trait of masculinity in students? Before "junior scholars" performed at the university level, Heywood's "training in audacity" would occur especially in the practice of declamation, a coincident and complementary exercise to the writing of themes. Themes were elementary and went by the Greek name of *progymnasmata*. Quintilian refers to them as *dicendi primordia* or the "rudiments" of speaking, illustrating the connection between composition and public speaking.[31] "Theme," explains Donald Lemen Clark, "had the same double meaning it has today. It meant both the subject on which one spoke [*argumentum*] and also the school composition on the subject."[32] Already, the alignment between composition and *argumentum* suggests an eristic or competitive enterprise, a cultivation of traits presumed necessary for pursuing victory as adults in public spheres of debate. So Brinsley, like Heywood, claims that memorizing themes and delivering them "will be a great furtherance to audacity," even as Heywood, like the schoolmasters, praises university stages for teaching young men the "audacity" needed to dispute any public question.[33]

To be trained as a statesman after the humanist model, boys would master the fundamentals of public speaking and composition of arguments, the practices of declamation and themes. Both assignments circulate in London through John Colet's St. Paul's School, which used Erasmus's *De Copia* and *De Ratione Studii* as central texts.[34] Erasmus advises teachers to have students compose themes, following guidelines of Cicero and Quintilian, according to rhetoric's different genres—demonstrative (to praise or blame), deliberative (to persuade or dissuade about future courses of action), and forensic or judicial (to accuse or defend), yet he applies the same method to formal oratory and declamation.[35] In the demonstrative class, for instance, a teacher may direct the boys to denounce Julius Caesar or to praise Socrates.[36] Theme composition within any genre and the skills of pronunciation in declamation were considered complementary and interchangeable exercises and assigned as such, forming an upper-tier though crucial part of grammar school education.[37]

The emphasis upon rhetorical genre and delivery required students to assume and play "characters" from the texts they voiced. Boys would write and speak from the point of view of a fictive or historical person, practicing *ethopoeia*, if the speaker were known but the speech created, or *prosopopoeia*, if both character and occasion were imagined. The most influential and popular handbook of the grammar school in this regard was not by Erasmus but by Aphthonius, a Greek sophist of the fourth century, whose introductory exercises "everyone agreed to be indispensable."[38] The examples from Aphthonius's *Progymnasmata* refer to "what Hecuba might say when Troy was destroyed" and to "what words Niobe might say when her children lie dead."[39] These prompts, like that of Erasmus's charge to denounce Julius Caesar or exalt Socrates, suggest demonstrative rhetoric; in the cases of Hecuba and Niobe, a speech of lamentation, which praises the lost and blames those responsible for it. Yet no matter the genre, the exercises require boys to declaim in the voices and characters of women and to do so in order to transform boys into graceful oratorical performers—gentlemen or future courtiers. Peacham's definition of "mimesis" as a particularly skilled declamation refers to the expert discharge of exercises such as these.

Within genre or by way of the assumption of roles, the quality of audacity emerges in and manifests expert delivery because of how the humanist classroom addresses rhetorical pronunciation.[40] Thus, William Kempe, a student of Eton in the 1570s, argues in his 1588 *The education of children in learning*, that students should not only learn "every trope, every figure, as well of words as of sentences; but also the rhetorical pronunciation and gesture fit for every word, sentence, and affection."[41] Brinsley, too, emphasizes the "continual care of pronunciation," claiming it as an architectonic virtue of the entire educative enterprise. Brinsley advises "that from the first entrance" students should learn "to pronounce everything audibly, leisurely, distinctly, and naturally, sounding out specially the last syllable that each word may be fully understood." For "what a grace sweet pronunciation gives unto all learning, and how the want of it doth altogether mar, or much deform, the most excellent speech."[42]

To practice such excellent speech, we have seen, boys trained as actors, but boy actors could refer to their stagecraft in light of their schooling in rhetoric as well. In an oft-cited example of the connections between the school and the stage, Ben Jonson's *Cynthia's Revels* (c. 1600) opens with children actors disputing over who will speak the prologue. In the ensuing argument, the boys conflate the terms "young grammatical courtier" and the "neophyte-player" upon the stage.[43] The courtier is the expert orator the grammar school expects to produce, but the "young grammatical courtier" still lacks rhetorical expertise. By the same token, the "neophyte-player" needs further training in what humanist educators refer to as "rhetorical pronunciation." So Jonson's play suggests the humanist training of grammar schools, which, in turn, understands performance as propaedeutic in the instruction of future statesmen. Heywood, conversely, appropriates the purposes of humanist education by turning them, ultimately, into a defense of the theater.

On the stage or in class, however, we find the same emphasis upon "audacity." Rather than just read or translate Latin texts, students would "declaim" them, preparing boys, as instructor Charles Hoole claims, to "expel that subrustic bashfulness and unresistible timorousness which some children are naturally possessed withal, and which is apt in riper years to drown many good parts in men of singular endowment."[44] To pronounce orations well would transition timorous boys into manly speakers. That masculine identity—a crucial purpose or sign of instruction in eloquence—emerges in and as the result of public performance rather than by way of the actor assuming the attributes of whatever character he happens to play. Acting instructs boys in "sweet pronunciation" and "excellent speech," but all such performances, no matter the gender of the role or the argument assumed, require and teach audacity, a point Shakespeare captures as well.

AUDACIOUS BOYS AS AMBASSADORS OF LOVE

To investigate how Shakespeare represents boy orators in terms of grammar school instruction in bravery, this section will examine the training and speeches of Moth from *Love's Labour's Lost* and Viola/Cesario from *Twelfth Night, Or What You Will*. Though neither part is designated as a grammar school student or defined as an apprentice actor within the fiction, both could have been played by a boy from either station, and the contexts of several of their speeches allude to formal training in rhetoric. In the texts that I analyze below, we will see how Shakespeare's fiction knits together the qualities of audacity, rhetorical speech, and performance, which I will use later as comparative models of analysis for understanding Kate's final declamation. Kate's performance will appear at least as sophisticated as that of Moth or Cesario/Viola, but for now I want to emphasize how boy orator roles, by the strictures of the humanist curriculum, should channel impetuosity into expert displays of oratory within the fiction itself.

First, Moth's training in humanist declamation becomes transparent when Boyet informs his Lady, the Princess of France, about how his "knavish page" prepared for his embassy to her. As Evelyn B. Tribble has shown, King Ferdinand, Berowne, Longaville, and Dumaine coach Moth in the very task at which the page subsequently fails: audacious rhetorical delivery.[45] In Boyet's account of Moth:

> Their herald is a pretty knavish page
> That well by heart hath conned his embassage.
> Action and accent did they teach him there:
> "Thus must thou speak and thus thy body bear."[46]

"Action" above translates *actio*, the use of gesture in particular and delivery more generally. "Suit the action to the word," Hamlet famously teaches, "the word to the action" (3.2.17–18). "Accent" refers to the speaker's ability to control stress within a metrical line. Stress, thus, impacts tone or voice as well. In the passage above, we learn that Moth "hath conned" his speech, or memorized it, along with appropriate "actions" for performance and, therefore, with direction for how to deliver individual lines.

Moth's training indicates a rhetorical acting style, what Heywood explains in terms of emboldening speakers. *The Apology* first describes the same wedding of accent and action in light of rhetoric's teaching, but it connects delivery to what Heywood finds essential in acting for the stage:

> To come to a rhetoric, it not only emboldens a scholar to speak, but instructs him to speak well, and with judgment; to observe his commas, colons, and full points, his parentheses, his breathing spaces, and distinctions; to keep a decorum in his countenance, neither to frown when he should smile, nor to make unseemly and disguised faces in the delivery of his words; not to stare with his eyes, draw awry with his mouth, confound his voice in the hollow of his throat, or tear his words hastily betwixt his teeth; neither to buffet his desk like a madman, nor stand in his place like a lifeless image, demurely plodding, and without any smooth and formal motion. It instructs him to fit his phrases to his action, and his action to his phrase, and his pronunciation to them both.[47]

In this passage, *The Apology* provides a gloss upon the training Moth receives. Heywood's list of what rhetoric provides includes "accent" — how to play punctuation and observe "breathing spaces" — with "action," what Boyet may mime on stage with the word "thus" from his line to Moth, "thus thy body bear." To "bear a body" well, we learn from Heywood, means keeping decorum in countenance, neither frowning nor smiling, for example, when the occasion does not call for such action. Heywood's last point is to avoid a "lifeless image" by using "smooth and formal" motions. His general recommendations for formal delivery resonate with Peacham's definition of mimesis because both assume how artful delivery guarantees a credible impression or persuasive *ethos*.

Yet again, Heywood explains this training in terms of cultivating "audacity." Rhetoric, Heywood thinks, "emboldens scholars to speak" by imparting "judgment" to its disciples about *how* to deliver or play lines. Thus, boldness functions in tandem with oratorical *technê*, a craft-like knowledge of how to compose or deliver speeches. Lamb thinks of Heywood's argument as one for "skills of performance which include the techniques of 'study' necessary for the creation of character on the early modern stage, and this provides the boys with the ability to explore new identities." Her investigation thereby connects an inquiry into how boys "forge their selfhoods" off the stage with performance within a "carnivalesque space" of on stage exploration. "Audacity," she writes, "stimulates their transition from boyhood to manhood."[48] Yet Heywood's point, like Moth's charge, doesn't present the stage or speaking occasions as license for explorations of the self. Rather, it connects daring with *technê*, suggesting how training, like the kind given to Moth, mutually reinforces both aspects of delivery.

If daring pertains to oratorical *technê*, then the expert discharge of either or both would indicate masterful acting or delivery. So Moth's young coaches not only impart instructions for "action" and "accent" but also worry how the pressure of an audience might negatively impact Moth's performance. Boyet says of Moth's instructors:

> And ever and anon they made a doubt
> Presence majestical would put him out;
> "For", quoth the King, "an angel shalt thou see;
> Yet fear not thou, but speak *audaciously*." (5.2.101–4)

The concern here is that Moth will lose his "audacity" in front of the beauty of the princess, but the boy boasts that he will not lose his nerve. "An angel is not evil," Moth replies, "I should have feared her had she been a devil" (5.2.105–6). Moth's bravado makes him apt for the task not simply by manifesting his enthusiasm for it but because audacity, in the context of humanist training, aids or makes the performance of successful orations.

Moth later fails because his audience, the princess and her ladies, ignore his initial supplications. They turn their backs to him according to the stage direction. "They do not mark me," Moth complains to Berowne, "and that brings me out" (5.2.173). Moth thereupon breaks character in speaking to his erstwhile director, abandoning his prepared speech because his audience doesn't respond as planned. In failing so, Moth's ultimate lack of audacity illustrates why that quality connects to the *technê* of expert performance. Moth forgets his lines because of an oblivious or unreceptive audience. He substitutes his own self-consciousness as a speaker in front of an inattentive audience for the assumed role and discipline he should play as Berowne's ambassador.

In a different context but on the same important point, Moth emerges as Shakespeare's "unperfect actor" from Sonnet 23, a poem that obliquely reflects the grammar school and the professional stage's emphasis upon oratorical *technê*. In the sonnet, Shakespeare tellingly uses performance as an analogy for describing why his speaker cannot address "love's rite":

> As an unperfect actor on the stage
> Who with his fear is put beside his part,
> Or some fierce thing replete with too much rage,
> Whose strength's abundance weakens his heart,
> So I, for fear of trust, forget to say
> The perfect ceremony of love's rite.[49]

The speaker is tongue-tied like an "unperfect actor" who forgets his lines and puts "beside his part." Because he experiences some overwhelming emotion, "some fierce thing," which arises independently from those passions he should discover and voice from his part's language and what expert delivery prescribes, he fails in his own embassy of love. The emotion of the speaker, like that of an individual actor, becomes at variance with what he should say of "love's rite."

Moth's failure pertains as much to technique as to the content of Berowne's own notion of "love's rites." "Despite his braggadocio about his 'audacity,'" writes Tribble of Moth, "he flounders when confronted by the dual tasks of remembering lines and coping with audience inattention."[50] Moth fails at these "dual tasks" because his feelings of frustration overwhelm the requisite pluck a successful delivery of his part mandates. "Some fierce thing"—whether it is love, as in the sonnet, or shame, as is probable in Moth's case—renders these speakers "tongue-tied." Where the quality of audacity should overcome such failings, audacity itself falters, and that failure is described according to flawed execution. In terms of boy-orators like Moth, rather than an offstage "forging of selfhood" into a more masculine identity, audacity emerges more simply as a concomitant of artful delivery.

If Moth doesn't succeed, Shakespeare later shows how a boy actor achieves victory by presenting a strikingly similar challenge in *Twelfth Night*. In disguise as Cesario, Viola plays an ambassador from another forlorn lover, Duke Orsino. Like Berowne and friends, Orsino dispatches his messenger to his beloved, Lady Olivia, who greets Cesario in entourage. Just as the boys who would deliver speeches in the voices of Hecuba or Niobe in grammar school exercises, Shakespeare's young male actor will voice Viola, yet in this instance the boy actor plays a girl who, in turn, dresses as a young man, thereby presenting Cesario's embassy on stage as a parallel scene to Moth's charge. As in *Love's Labour's Lost*, the ladies do not mark the speaker. Instead of turning her back, Olivia puts a veil over her face. Cesario, like Moth with the Princess, struggles for Olivia's attention and defends his prepared speech, which is "well penned," and, besides, he took "great pains to con it."[51] Neither should Cesario speak outside of his supposed instructions. Analogous with Moth's own situation, he received strict instructions from his superior. When Olivia asks him where he comes from, Cesario claims: "I can say little more than I have studied" and Olivia's question is "out of my part." So Olivia asks him, "Are you a comedian?" (1.5.173–77).

What Cesario means by "study," in early modern terms, is "rehearsed," just as "comedian" refers to "one who plays in comedies, a comic actor" (*Oxford English Dictionary*).[52] Shakespeare uses the latter in *Antony and Cleopatra* when Cleopatra complains about "quick comedians" who will stage her and Antony's love and an actor will "boy greatness" or play her role (5.2.216–17). Olivia's terminology therefore evokes the practices of the playhouse, which in this case represent exercises in declamation. Like the training that Erasmus recommends, Shakespeare's embassies feature exercises in demonstrative rhetoric or epideictic oratory. So both Moth and Cesario's speeches are in praise of the beauty of a beloved, but Cesario confesses what must be assumed about Moth's preparation, how he "took great pains to study it, and 'tis poetical" (1.5.189–90). In *Love's Labour's*, Berowne coaches Moth during his performance, interrupting and correcting him, but in *Twelfth Night* it is Olivia, Cesario's actual audience, who does so. Olivia is not simply inattentive but proactively hostile, which forces Cesario to improvise. He asks to see her face so that he will be, unlike Moth, marked, but in doing so, Olivia rightly accuses him, "You are now out of your text" (1.5.225).

Cesario's turn from the "text" to improvisation emerges as a crucial example of the importance of audacity. Though Cesario breaks from his "text," he tellingly does not break from his part, role, or charge in doing so. In this context, as Tribble argues, audacity reveals how Shakespeare's "hallmark of expertise is situational awareness, or the aplomb to cope with the unexpected," a trait that Moth lacks but Viola possesses.[53] Cesario, instead, successfully wrests attention from Olivia by demanding to see her face and insulting her by calling her "proud":

> I see you what you are: you are too proud.
> But, if you were the devil, you are fair.
> My lord and master loves you. Oh, such love
> Could be but recompensed, though you were crowned
> The nonpareil of beauty! (1.5.242–46)

In response, Olivia inquires: "How does he love me?" (1.5.247). At this juncture, Olivia "marks" him and, of course, eventually falls in love with the speech Cesario subsequently delivers and the speaker who gives it. Because Olivia falls in love with Cesario, he fails in his embassy as did Moth but not because he lacks audacity or performs poorly. Olivia replies to Cesario's somewhat clichéd speech about how she should pity her beloved, "You might do much" (1.5.269). Cesario's impassioned and perfect delivery, it would appear, moves her. Yet that expert delivery relies upon and is foreground by audacity.

Cesario's speech highlights the connection between spontaneous delivery or the creation of matter *ex tempore* and the significance of bravery, though this point eludes recent commentators and actors. In modern productions, the actor playing Cesario might woo on behalf of Orsino or speak in a way that channels Viola's own love for Orsino; either could be the case once Cesario is put out of his text. "Inspired speech flows from this easy give-and-take as the actor begins to speak more personally," writes critic Mary Jo Kietzman of Viola's words as Cesario to Olivia, which, "in doing so, delivers the thoughts and feelings of the occluded Viola." Yet an "occluded Viola" is a choice that colors how we understand early modern personation. For Kietzman, Cesario voices Viola in instances of "inspired speech" because Shakespeare presents character as "a fiction created by the actor's willingness to explore and express his identity in relation to an other."[54] The charge of unrequited love remains the same in the cases of Viola for Orsino and Orsino for Olivia, after all, which could allow for the motives of an "occluded Viola" to be voiced on stage by the actor. Today's actresses who play Viola/Cesario, therefore, may choose to imagine their character's addressee as an offstage Orsino, of whom Viola secretly dreams. In doing so, like Kietzman, these actresses present a Cesario who speaks for Viola, what Kietzman explores as the onstage creation of a fictive "identity." In reply to Olivia's question— "Are you a comedian?"—Cesario speaks for Viola's romantic hopes, "No, my profound heart, and yet, by the very fangs of malice, I swear, I am not that I play" (1.5.177–79).

On an early modern stage, however, the explicit claim of a fictive self or character in contrast to a role that same self or character plays could indicate something different from an "occluded Viola." "I am not that I play" directs attention not just to boys who play girls but also to how boy actors would enhance delivery by assuming a variety of roles. The boy who plays Viola, for example, also plays a "eunuch" (1.2.53), a term which better describes the apprenticed actor, who could declaim in the voices of boy or female whenever called upon, illustrating his protean capacity and, if expert, his "audacity." That last quality, even within the fiction, discloses daring as a trait that stage versatility coincidentally augments and demonstrates. The insult of Olivia, Cesario's boldest flourish, Shakespeare presents as a turning point, a rough means of disorienting Olivia's truculence. Correspondingly, Orsino advises Cesario—"Be clamorous, and leap all civil bounds" (1.4.21)—which translates into his page's "saucy" and "mad" behavior at Olivia's gates (1.5.192–94), and in his claim to "stand at [Olivia's] door like a sherriff's post" (1.5.143–44). In these details, Shakespeare incorporates rhetoric's emphasis upon the importance of audacity. If Orsino's instructions to "be clamorous" metatheatrically disclose how an older, more experienced actor like the adult who plays Orsino would prepare his apprentice boy for the part of Viola, the conflation of audacious declamation and theatrical performance emerges within the embassy scene itself.[55]

So, too, the question of "inspired speech" in either theatrical or declamatory contexts reveals Shakespeare's representation of spontaneity. Cesario's extemporaneous speech on his "master's flame," within the fiction of the play, could be understood as a reflection of the one Cesario had "conned" or prepared in advance with Orsino's charge or language in mind. Cesario tells Olivia: "If I did love you in my master's flame," I would "write loyal cantons of contemned love" and bless her name "to the reverberate hills." "Oh you should not rest," he tells her, "between the elements of air and earth / But you should pity *me!*" (1.5.256–68). Olivia takes the word "me," ultimately, as an invitation to love not Orsino but his messenger, yet the hypothetical construction indicates that Cesario speaks in the person of Orsino. Cesario's improvised embassy on behalf of Orsino, thus, represents how the messenger reorganizes Orsino's material, given Olivia's initially poor reply. A master of invention, Cesario makes different choices about what ideas his speech to her should include; or his disposition rearranges Orsino's ideas such that the part of praise for Olivia comes later in his interview, after Cesario receives her attention; throughout, elocution reshapes the whole in the moment of actual delivery. Audacity triggers the new synthesis and its successful delivery. There is no original speech of Orsino to which we may make comparison, of course. We only know an Orsino-authored version exists because of Cesario's claim that he "conned" it.

Even so, the reported discrepancy between original and improvised versions shows Shakespeare fictionalizing the orator's art of refashioning previously memorized material on the spot, an indication of rhetorical excellence and the very model of grammar school exercises in extemporaneous speaking. In advice upon the teaching of themes, Brinsley writes that students should learn how to pronounce, memorize, and speak set speeches written by others on a nightly basis, which "must needs help to furnish them with variety of the best matter and fit phrase."[56] But a well-delivered speech, though praiseworthy, is for lower-tier students. The best ones can speak *ex tempore*, inventing matter, which they freely borrow from other sources and suddenly refashion "to very good purpose." Brinsley's testimony suggests that, rather than an occluded Viola, Cesario's discourse upon his "master's flame" shows the expert orator's spontaneous revision of commonplace material, signifying how Cesario should be supposed to reorganize or articulate anew Orsino's own language of unrequited love. But to improvise after this fashion requires audacity, which indicates further how confidence enables decorous pliability, an intelligent adaptability, which rhetoricians praised as an occasion of "great commendation": for this particular kind of speaker may succeed given any audience or speaking venue.[57]

Shakespeare's fiction of Cesario performing outside of his lines, thus, illustrates what Tribble calls "situational awareness," a mark of superb acting skill. "From the perspective of expertise," Tribble writes of the players that visit Denmark in *Hamlet*, "the most salient characteristic of the First Player's performance is its fluency and unflappability." The First Player undergoes Polonius's interruption and may pick up lines that Hamlet originally misremembers. In an example of the same aptitude, Cesario's performance appears highly skilled, but we can now note how "fluency and unflappability" also include or entail rhetorical skills of a higher, more creative order. Cesario's improvisations illustrate not just the audacity that Moth lacks but also the presence of mind to rework or even create material.

Because Shakespeare stages *ex tempore* speaking, he augments the potential for lifelike dramatic action. In modern productions, Viola plays Cesario within the play, which fictionalizes the tension between herself as character and as an actor who plays as a boy; that tension allows Kietzman to infer interiority or to discover an occluded Viola in *ex tempore* speaking occasions. Alternatively, though, Shakespeare's embassy scene could show how boy orators impart the quality of audacity through their expertise in declamation. In this case, audacity is the result of Shakespeare's representation of the rhetorical techniques of improvised speech. Olivia falls in love at this point because of Viola's capacity to use language in fashioning a voice, that of Cesario.

OF WEAK AND IDLE THEMES

In the context of expert oration, Kate's own speech of obedience, much like any of the exercises from the *Progymnasmata*, may be judged in terms of artful execution, even as a representation of speaking extemporaneously. Dusinberre wonders if the puer/Kate "winked" at his magister/Petruchio, or even to any women watching him in the theater, in celebration of his "momentary supremacy by means of a brilliant performance of a speech proclaiming subjection."[58] Perhaps there was no wink, but audiences today often applaud contemporary Kates in stage productions, even if they disagree with her final words. Dusinberre's "wink," too, suggests something more: the poise involved in an expert performance, in this case, of a boy who plays Kate with the daring of an orator or, like that of Cesario, with brilliant self-assertion.

Let us examine Kate's speech more closely in order to see how clearly it reflects schoolroom exercise. Propaedeutic for more advanced oratory, themes indicate both a subject and the composition of it. Remember that in composing themes, boys were supposed to learn moral content from the *argumentum* along with the particular *ars*, technique or art, for composing such an argument. When Puck summarizes the plot of *A Midsummer Night's Dream* as a "weak and idle theme" (5.1.422), for example, he may mean that the play was no more than an exercise in speaking well, which was composed upon a trivial matter.

To see how Kate's declamation pertains to themes, I return to the same schoolmaster cited above, John Brinsley. His *Ludus Literarius*, writes Colin Burrow, remains "our best guide to Shakespeare's school, since it was explicitly designed to assist provincial schoolmasters" like Shakespeare's own King's Free Grammar school at Stratford, which was just fifty miles from where Brinsley himself later taught.[59] Brinsley's account of themes presents a dialogue between two schoolmasters, Spoudeus, a drudge, and Philoponus, who is wise—the voice of Brinsley himself. Spoudeus's students do not respond well to their assignments in themes, which drive him "into exceeding passions" and "to deal over rigorously with the poor boys." So Philoponus–Brinsley elaborates how to proceed, beginning with the first principles of the exercise:

> We are to consider, what is the end and purpose of their making Themes; and then to bethink ourselves, which way they may the soonest attain unto the same. The principal end of making Themes, I take to be this, to furnish scholars with all store of choicest matter, that they

may learn to understand, speak or write of any ordinary Theme, Moral or Political, such as visually fall into discourse amongst men and in practice of life; and especially concerning virtues and vices. So as to work in themselves a greater love of the virtue and hatred of the vice, and to be able with soundness of reason to draw others to their opinion.[60]

The first rule for dealing with slow or less inclined boys is for the teacher to understand what is at stake in the exercise, which is not simply training in an art of speaking but moral improvement through understanding a speech's content. Such was an essential tenet of humanist thought, originating with Erasmus but trumpeted by John Colet for the boys at the St. Paul's school in London.[61] Curiously, however, Brinsley does not address a question of moral philosophy in writing how to teach themes to students. If any of the suggested topics appear "over-hard for childrens' capacities, in regard of the matter of them," we should "make choice of the most easy and familiar."[62] Art will trump content in Brinsley's presentation because the latter will be obvious. If not, the teacher should provide students with an illustration for them to imitate, making the "general matter of it very plain unto them," explaining any difficult phrases, reading a piece of it to them every night, posing "short questions" with easy answers; all of it, Brinsley repeats, "to make every thing plain unto them." Lastly, with such a difficult group, aim for 12 to 16 lines, no more.[63]

Brinsley gives an example of "most easy and familiar" matter for the composition of themes: The proposition that "Children are to obey their Parents."[64] The importance of obedience was one the boys would know well not only from birch-wielding classroom management but also from the school's ceremonial events. From the ordinances at Shrewsbury School, we learn that, upon election of a new schoolmaster, "one of the best scholars shall welcome him with a congratulatory Latin oration, promising obedience on behalf of the school."[65] So obedience as a subject is perfectly elementary. For "if we think first of the Parents what they have been, and are towards the children; and so what the children have and do receive from them . . . any one of understanding shall be able to find out reasons why the children are to obey their Parents."[66] As a spur to invention, Brinsley's prompt will allow children to discover reasons for why they should obey, which they may rank in terms of strongest to weakest and arrange according to Brinsley's tightly governed sense of progression from exordium, narration, division, and confirmation to the end.[67] Students do not discover, analyze, or critique but learn how to artfully argue for a thesis. "Thus let them take special pains to pronounce Themes or Declamations, striving [to see] who shall do best," Brinsley summarizes, tying together composition, delivery, and competition with what Joseph earlier refers to as "identification," for the boys also speak from a character or role's point of view. "And in all their oppositions to dispute," Brinsley urges, the boys should act "as if *ex animo* in good earnest, with all contention and vehemence."[68]

The theme of obedience belongs to Kate as well, but, less obvious, her arrangement corresponds to how Brinsley recommends unruly or otherwise difficult boys ought to proceed. Though many have recognized Kate's final speech as classical oratory, the sort of exercise she performs eludes commentators. For most, her speech about gender roles constitutes a subject rather than the exemplification of a particular rhetorical exercise. Yet Kate's speech is tightly designed according to Brinsley's instructions and these were explicitly for a second-tier brand of student. Beginners require stricter focus; in effect, they have invention given to them in the prompt, so that they may strive for *dispositio*, or arrangement of ideas, after Cicero's basic guidelines. More complex orders that include additional topics of invention, answering objections, adorning speech with classical allusions will come later. "Brinsley would prefer to call the grammar school exercise declamation rather than oration," writes T. W. Baldwin, "and to regard it as an extension of theme-making."[69] Within "theme-making," too, there are levels of development, which a teacher may address with supplementary materials to texts like Aphthonius's *Progymnasmata* or through the kind of advice Philoponus offers. Given such measures, Kate emerges as a beginner, who composes a theme with success following Brinsley's rules of remediation—and with Petruchio's direction. The fact that Kate surpasses these horizons only adds to the surprise of her speech at the play's conclusion.

KATE'S DIVISION AND PARTITION

So Petruchio, like a schoolmaster, assigns the proposition: "Katharine, I charge thee tell these headstrong women / What duty they do owe their lords and husbands" (5.2.136–37). Yet the widow replies: "Come, come, you're mocking. We will have no telling" (137). Like the inattentive or hostile audiences in *Love's Labour's Lost* or *Twelfth Night*, Kate must earn or win a hearing through audacity. Petruchio helps her by targeting the Widow, ordering Kate: "Come on, I say, and first begin with her" (139). Unlike Moth but similar to Cesario's insult of Olivia, Kate's exordium secures a quiet house by beginning in accusation:

> Fie, fie! Unknit that threatening, unkind brow,
> And dart not scornful glances from those eyes
> To wound thy lord, thy king, thy governor.
> It blots thy beauty as frosts do bite the meads,
> Confounds thy fame as whirlwinds shake fair buds,
> And in no sense is meet or amiable.
> A woman moved is like a fountain troubled,
> Muddy, ill-seeming, thick, bereft of beauty

> And while it is so, none so dry or thirsty
> Will deign to sip or touch one drop of it. (5.2.142–51)

Kate's introduction still grabs every auditors' attention just as an exordium should, but, in attacking the Widow, she enacts Brinsley's instructions: "If the Theme be of any person, in accusation or defense of them after the manner of declamations, then that their Exordium may be fitliest taken from the party himself who is accused or defended; from some description of him to his praise or dispraise."[70] "Fitliest" is a rare adverb, which indicates what is most apt or decorous, given the rhetorical circumstances and situation of the speaker, his addressee, and auditors.[71] Such decisions should be made by the speaker himself, but Kate is directed in how to begin, whom to attack, and upon what grounds. Even so, she responds expertly, attacking the widow in the name of the same decorum that Petruchio desires and, as a result, demonstrates her grasp of the concept. The widow is in "no sense meet or amiable" because she is "moved" or angry, which like a "fountain troubled" is "ill-seeming." The widow's behaves inappropriately, in other words, which the simile echoes in the image of a "muddy fountain." By making decorum the basis of her critique, Kate shows she doesn't require Petruchio's direction any more than Cesario would. By speaking with daring and extemporaneously, she surpasses Moth as well.

The second part of Kate's speech, her narration, corresponds to Brinsley's instructions as well. Brinsley advises that the narration be clear, advancing the speaker's claim so that the "auditors may fully understand the matter" and the orator may "proceed more easily." Within the narration, though, a speaker may employ "some short division" of the subject matter or break the subject into its member or parts.[72] Of importance, Brinsley here alludes to Cicero's *Topica* and its distinction between *divisio* and *partitio*, which speakers use to *define* their subject matter. Cicero explains that "in analysis [*in divisione formae*] we have classes or kinds which the . . . Latin authors . . . call *species*." Yet "in an enumeration [*in partitione*] we have, as it were, parts, as for example a body has a head, shoulders, hands, sides, legs, feet and so forth."[73] Division, then, applies to ideas or forms, species that fall under a genus, whereas partition cuts a hole into its components; the former concerns concepts, the latter existent persons or things or actions. Such forms of definition were so essential that only Erasmus's Lady Folly could dispense with the exercise because, as she asks, "what good would it do to present a shadowy image of myself by means of a definition when you can see me with your own eyes?"[74]

What Folly ignores, however, Shakespeare employs with precision. To recall a famous example from *Much Ado About Nothing*, Dogberry accuses Borachio and Conrade:

> Marry, sir, they have committed false report;

> Moreover, they have spoken untruths; secondarily,
> they are slanders; sixth and lastly, they have belied a
> lady; thirdly, they have verified unjust things; and to
> conclude, they are lying knaves. (5.1.211–15)

False report, spoken untruths, slander, and so forth—all of these are species of the same idea or genus. To find these "classes" or "kinds" constitute a rhetorical expansion, which Dogberry practices along with his idiosyncratic and comic way of counting. When Don Pedro replies, he not only ranges from second to sixth to third but also retains Dogberry's division. So Pedro asks such questions as: "what have they done? what's their offense? what you lay to their charge?" Claudio, then, interjects: "Rightly reasoned, and in his own *division*; and, by my troth, there's one meaning well suited" (5.1.216–21). To merely echo Dogberry's irregular numbering, in other words, would not be sufficient to reason after the same "division." Hence, Claudio quips "there's one meaning well suited," which Samuel Johnson explains: "That is, one meaning is put into many different dresses; the Prince having asked the same question in four modes of speech."[75] Shakespeare's comic portrayal of Dogberry, then, presumes that his audience will know exactly why he misspeaks.

A well-dressed meaning, however, differs from partition. Cicero uses division to treat subjects or ideas and partition for objects and things. Thus, *partitio* itemizes something or someone that physically exists. In *A Midsummer Night's Dream*, Shakespeare's Snout provides a joke about the term:

> In this same interlude it doth befall
> That I, one Snout by name, present a wall;
> And such a wall as I would have you think
> That had in it a crannied hole or chink,
> Through which the lovers, Pyramus and Thisbe,
> Did whisper often, very secretly. (5.1.154–59)

The importance of the part—a chink, a hole, a cranny—to the whole of a wall—a rough-cast, or a stone—plays with the term "partition" as that wall which separates the lovers and as the rhetorical device that enumerates a thing into its parts. Hence, Demetrius sardonically comments upon Snout's performance: "It is the wittiest partition that ever I heard discourse" (5.1.166–67).[76]

So, too, in practice, Shakespeare could have the two devices dovetail one upon the other. Baldwin prizes Holofernes's display of division and partition from *Love's Labour's Lost*, in part, because division shades into partition, which demonstrates expert knowledge of both by the speaker.[77] Just so, itemizing by clowns or pedants shows how well Shakespeare grasps its practice. For both devices, though rudimentary, are important for invention and amplification, and Kate's mastery of them indicates how Shakespeare takes pains to show her development as an orator.

For Brinsley, division may distinguish the "general" into its "specials" whereas partition takes a "whole" and describes "his members or parts," and either may provide an overall order to the oration, joining "each part together with fit transitions, to show their passage from one part to another."[78] An entire speech, in other words, assumes an immanent design from defining terms, which are properly conceived and described through division and partition, a form of *copia*. Indeed, Kate's declamation proceeds from defining husbands and their offices to that of wives, illustrating Brinsley's point.

Contrary to Dogberry's practice, Kate's artful division elaborates rather than simply iterates her idea of a husband: "Thy husband is thy lord, thy life, thy keeper, / Thy head, thy sovereign; one that cares for thee" (5.2.152–53). "Husband" thereby is delineated into separate but related kinds, which connect leadership to care of those under one's charge. Even words like "keeper" connote "care" with "oversight."[79] More to the point of the theme, as the Tudor grammar school emphasized a wedding of classical rhetoric and Pauline Christianity, Kate's Ciceronian division captures both aspects of the precept from Ephesians, "wives, submit yourselves unto your husbands, as unto the Lord," and "husbands, love your wives, even as Christ loved the Church, and gave himself for it."[80] Kate's division, in this way, rightfully provokes the question of irony, for Petruchio is "rough and woos not like a babe," yet, as Germaine Greer famously writes, Kate's final speech "rests upon the role of a husband as protector and friend."[81]

In fact, Kate will dictate a husband's duties to his wife, or what Tita French Baumlin calls "man's proper marital virtues," which means that although Kate may address her words to the Widow or to Bianca on stage, she speaks indirectly to the male characters as well.[82] The subsequent part of her speech, at least, continues by specifying duties for men, providing a *partitio* of his body and what it does or should do:

> And for thy maintenance commits his body
> To painful labor both by sea and land
> To watch the night in storms, the day in cold,
> Whilst thou liest warm at home, secure and safe. (5.2.154–57)

Her partition unfolds in a clever contrast. The antithesis between husband and wife serves the case for obedience, but only if he so commits his body for her sake, a qualification that perhaps may exclude the male suitors, if either they or the audience considers it in terms of what these characters have done in the play. Insofar as "proper marital virtue" constitutes mere commonplace, which the men on stage do not take personally, Kate's words may please them. Actors who play Hortensio, Lucentio, and Petruchio have choices to make in response to these lines, from cheering Kate on to howling at their own wives for their opposition to playing some recognition of rebuke.

In Kate's arrangement, too, the parallel to a body committed to "painful labor" is the female body, which she defines as "soft, and weak, and smooth, / Unapt to toil and trouble in the world." Such bodily contrasts form a substantial part of Kate's *confirmatio*, or central argument, because, as she says to the women, "our soft conditions and our hearts / Should well agree with our external parts" (5.2.171–74). Softer parts should result in "love, fair looks, and true obedience," which is owed to their day-laboring men (5.2.159–60). In speaking so, Kate's theme echoes Brinsley's call for clear and easy declaration of the speech's matter, which, "if it concern persons or facts of persons" should "set down all the circumstances to express the nature and manner of it."[83] Overall circumstances, nature, and manner of the persons allows Kate to conceptualize the offices of both husband and wife, which, in effect, means she speaks and prescribes roles to both genders. By division, the genus of husband emerges in its species of lord and sovereign; by partition, the body of such a one is enumerated into specific duties and travails. Finally, the comparison of men and women, husband and wife, their bodies and duties, makes her case for submission. The perfect enactment of such rhetorical design, scripted as extemporaneous performance, indicates that Kate's audacity, previously manifested only by rebellion, emerges in bold address, a speech that confronts her audience without Moth's loss of nerve or Cesario's departure from his assigned oratorical task. When Shakespeare fictionalizes extemporaneous speaking in *The Taming of the Shrew*, he indicates how Kate's improvisations manage to hold together as a persuasive whole, revealing an audacity only matched by expertise.

Such expertise and performance of audacity would be augmented within the theater and during moments of direct address to audiences as well. Kate's question, for example, about "soft conditions and hearts" is a rhetorical one, the figure of speech known as *erotema*,[84] which provides the actor a cue for addressing individual audience members or a group of audience members.[85] Bianca and the Widow, in other words, need not have been Kate's addressees for every line. Indeed, Kate's final speech, if it charms or pleases, must do so for its spectators in the audience as well as those spectators in the form of other characters on the stage.[86] Like Rosalind, who "charges women" in the audience at the end of *As You Like It*, Kate might speak her question about female bodies directly to women in the audience. Kate could even appear to wait for an answer from the audience before she continues because the rhetorical question, like Brutus's to the plebes he has offended, might inspire retort.[87] If targeted women in the audience indicate disagreement or remain silent or combine either reaction with cheers, Kate's reply is already provided for her in the subsequent line: "Come, come, you forward and unable worms" (5.2.175).

So, too, Brinsley's student or Shakespeare's actor would recognize the attempt to affirm or deny a point in the form of a question constitutes rhetorical flourish, another instance or manifestation of training in audacity. As Enterline comments upon Kate's final speech: "The fact that she is engaged in public argument before an audience of peers and a 'master' would remind any contemporary audience member who had been to grammar school that 's/he' is a performer performing, an orator arguing a case from the body s/he does not have in order to succeed in convincing you that s/he does."[88] Either by way of direct address to audiences or within the framework of school exercise, the meta-theatrical aspects of Kate's delivery could blend with the boy's representation of Kate, revealing a bold master of language in the actor who embodies Kate.

PARTITION AS *COPIA*

Partition, finally, makes Kate's last appeal especially powerful. Following Cicero and providing what amounts to a broader formulation of Brinsley's use of the term, Peacham defines partition as "a form of speech by which the orator divideth the whole into parts" and connects it to amplification: "The use of this form of speech serves to minister plenty and variety of matter, and of many fountains of figures of eloquence: there is not one that may be found more fruitful than this, or more plentiful in the multitude of branches."[89] At the end of her speech, Kate finds these plentiful branches by describing her own qualities as superior to the other women on stage. In an address to the Widow and Bianca, Kate professes:

> My mind hath been as big as one of yours,
> My heart as great, my reason haply more,
> To bandy word for word and frown for frown.
> But now I see our lances are but straws,
> Our strength as weak, our weakness past compare,
> That seeming to be most which we indeed least are. (5.2.176–81)

Kate dissects her own "soft, and weak, and smooth" body into further qualities, which serve for comparison's sake. In regard to womanly revolt against husbands, Kate's own inclination, wish or "mind" seems as "big" as either that of Bianca or the Widow. So, too, Kate's "heart" or courageous spirit remains as "great" or as "full of emotion." Finally, Kate's own reason "haply" — or "perchance" or "by luck," an ironical qualification — emerges as superior.[90] The use of "haply" shows Kate speaking carefully, a clue that she knows this last comparison may be disputed or found to be insulting, perhaps, especially by Bianca. Alternatively, Kate could play her lines as if she were taunting her sister. If Kate employs *platea* discourse before, as I speculated above, she must return to the fiction now, addressing her onetime rival.

More than that, Kate's earlier treatment of woman and wife as defined by embodiment assumes new connotations. The list of traits — capacity of mind, greatness of heart, and overall strength — constitute a category of "seeming to be," which she paradoxically claims and disavows at once, especially because they are characteristically masculine traits, which woman should least possess. In a meta-theatrical context, Kate's "seeming" plays with the fact that a boy enacts her role with audacity; but, within the fiction, Kate's dramatic person, as shrew, is more than just a soft body as well. As "seeming being" suggests divergence from actual being, Kate presents a docile exterior through the content of her words while her delivery suggests an actor animated by spiritedness. Such a contrast comports well with how Anna Kamaralli imagines the final scene, which illustrates how Kate's message could present a "staggering contradiction": She delivers the longest speech of the play, speaks without interruptions, whether she remains in center stage or roams, and everyone else attends to her words. "As an audience," Kamaralli suggests, "we are being told that Katharina is the dominant personality by *everything except the words*."[91] Indeed, but instead of a "staggering contradiction" between the speech's content and the "personality" who delivers it, early modern audiences could note what this "seeming" Kate becomes in light of what the boy actor imparts to her stage representation. Kate's declamatory audacity, in other words, demonstrates how the personator and the personated, ultimately, work toward a single impression because the boy actor conveys a masculine spirit to his role, supplying Kate's "dominant personality" with "audacity" throughout her speech on subordination.

Such blurring of personator and personated illustrates how audacity in speech combines intelligence and spiritedness in a particular way, as we saw in the case of Viola's exercise of Cesario and, in more extreme forms, Kate's previous behavior as a "shrew." Yet audacity now manifests itself in decorous *ex tempore* declamation, giving rise to a Kate who, like Cesario, is a character speaking outside of her text, creating matter to "the purpose." By scripting an *ex tempore* speech, Shakespeare embeds person-effects of daring and intelligence in Kate. At the same time, the "submission speech" intertwines the audacity of the personator with the stage representation of Kate for the sake of augmenting an audience's general amazement at the eloquent disavowal of shrewish behavior by a onetime shrew.

Kate celebrates her own rhetorical prowess by claiming that her heart, mind, and reason perform their functions better in herself than in other women. At the play's end, she emerges as the best speaker among the ladies as well. Thus, Kate's supremacy becomes her proof, paradoxically, about the relatively lower status of woman to man. If the best of women, Kate, recognizes the weakness of women in general, surely inferior females should acknowledge their weakness as well. The patriarchal structure of her argument, however, remains contingent upon Kate's gigantic, audacious self-assertion and delivery, a performance that awards and prioritizes her own person over her competitors.

Once we realize what qualities Kate has invested in her person, which the boy actor must supply in expert delivery, the significance of her final gesture becomes clear. She begins in address to Bianca and the Widow but concludes by speaking to Petruchio:

> Then vail your stomachs, for it is no boot,
> And place your hands below your husband's foot,
> In token of which duty, if he please,
> My hand is ready, may it do him ease. (5.2.182–85)

Were the female gender personified after the model of a body politic, Kate would emerge as governor and lord, who directs or curtails appetites. She exemplifies mind, heart, and reason just as Bianca and the Widow now exemplify stomach. Hence, even as her speech debases her as a woman among men, it promotes her above other women. Because of this promotion, perhaps, contemporary audiences may imagine Kate will no longer be debased among men; she is more like them, after all. Her hand is "ready" to go below her husband's foot, which means she need not on stage actually perform what she describes, unless Petruchio calls for it, which he does not in the text. Instead, he celebrates her and calls for a kiss, a commendation of her words and person. Kate's redescription of herself and her body, and both in comparison to other women, elevates the very hand that she offers to bring low. So Petruchio tells Lucentio, "'Twas I won the wager, though you hit the white" (5.2.192). Lucentio was the ostensible winner, pursuing Bianca until he hit the "white," or won his prize bride, but he does not emerge victorious, for he misjudged the sisters.[92] In becoming a "good wife," Kate rises to a star orator at the same instant, replacing her sister in both marital and intellectual categories as supreme.[93] The competition that Dusinberre finds among apprentice actors resolves in Kate's appearance as the bravest, most eloquent, and intelligent speaker. Boy actors from the start and female actresses of today who play her as such a speaker have warrant for their decision.

NOTES

1. *The Taming of the Shrew: Third Series* (Arden Shakespeare), ed. Barbara Hodgdon (London: Methuen Drama, 2010), 118; hereafter cited internally. For a review of critical and theatrical interpretations of this speech, see Hodgdon, *The Taming of the Shrew*, 118–31; for a "liberated Kate," see Velvet D. Pearson, "In Search of a Liberated Kate in *The Taming of the Shrew*," *Rocky Mountain Review of Language and Literature* 44, no. 4 (1990): 229–42; on productions from 1948–1987, see Penny Gay, *As She Likes It: Shakespeare's Unruly Women* (London: Routledge, 1994), 86–119; on recent productions and the difficulties of playing Kate's character, see Anna Kamaralli, *Shakespeare and the Shrew: Performing the Defiant Female Voice* (New York: Palgrave Macmillan, 2012), 89–110.

2. For Kate as victim, see Emily Detmer, "Civilizing Subordination: Domestic Violence and *The Taming of the Shrew*," *Shakespeare Quarterly* 48, no. 3 (1997): 273–94; for *Taming* as a farce, see Robert Heilman, "The Taming Untamed, or, the Return of the

Shrew," *Modern Language Quarterly* 27 (1966): 147–61; on Kate and playing roles, see Robert S. Miola, "The Influence of New Comedy on *The Comedy of Errors* and *The Taming of the Shrew*," in *Shakespeare's Sweet Thunder: Essays on the Early Comedies*, ed. Michael J. Collins (Newark: Associated University Presses, 1997), 27–33. For an important discussion of character and person instead of theoretical approaches to Kate and her final speech, see Paul Yachnin, "Personations: *The Taming of the Shrew* and the Limits of Theoretical Criticism," *Early Modern Literary Studies* 2, no. 1 (1996): 21–31 at http://extra.shu.ac.uk/emls/02-1/yachshak.html.

3. See interviews of three actresses who played Kate between 1978 and 1987 in Carol Rutter, *Clamorous Voices: Shakespeare's Women Today*, ed. Faith Evans (London: The Women's Press, 1988), 21–25; for *The Taming of the Shrew* as "a play that was of its time," see Laurie Maguire and Emma Smith, *30 Great Myths about Shakespeare* (New York: Wiley-Blackwell, 2013), 42.

4. Fiona Shaw's account, in particular, finds Kate's final speech "about how her spirit has been allowed to soar free" in Rutter, *Clamorous Voices*, 21–22.

5. Juliet Dusinberre, "*The Taming of the Shrew*: Women, Acting, and Power," in *The Taming of the Shrew: Critical Essays*, ed. Dana Aspinall (New York: Routledge, 2002), 180.

6. Dusinberre, "*The Taming of the Shrew*," 169.

7. John Brinsley, *Ludus Literarius (1612): A Scolar Press Facsimile* (Menston, England: The Scolar Press Limited, 1968), 50.

8. B. L. Joseph, *Elizabethan Acting* (London: Oxford University Press, 1952), 1. See, too, Edward Burns, *Character: Acting and Being on the Pre-Modern Stage* (New York: St. Martin's Press, 1990), 10, who concurs that "acting and rhetoric are never seen as distinct entities" on the Elizabethan stage.

9. Elizabeth Hutcheon, "From Shrew to Subject: Petruchio's Humanist Education of Katherine in *The Taming of the Shrew*," *Comparative Drama* 45, no. 4 (2011): 315–37; Lynn Enterline, *Shakespeare's Schoolroom: Rhetoric, Discipline, Emotion* (Philadelphia: University of Pennsylvania Press, 2011), 95–119.

10. On how boy actors were received, see Gerald Eades Bentley, *The Profession of Player in Shakespeare's Time, 1590–1642* (Princeton, NJ: Princeton University Press, 1986), 113–18, who provides evidence that the younger male actors did enthrall audiences as female characters; for a critical overview of boy actors and cross-dressed performance, see Phyllis Rackin, "Boys Will Be Girls," in *Shakespeare and Women* (Oxford: Oxford University Press, 2005), 72–94; and for analysis, see David Mann, *Shakespeare's Women: Performance and Conception* (Cambridge, UK: Cambridge University Press, 2009), especially 1–121. See, too, Catherine Belsey, "Shakespeare's Little Boys: Theatrical Apprenticeship and the Construction of Childhood," in *Rematerializing Shakespeare: Authority and Representation on the Early Modern Stage*, ed. Bryan Reynolds and William N. West (New York: Palgrave Macmillan, 2005), 54, who believes the acting was "good," citing Henry Jackson from 1610. In this oft-cited but important passage, Jackson wrote of the boy playing Desdemona: "although she always put her case very well, after her death moved us still more when, lying in bed, she implored the pity of the spectators with her countenance itself." Belsey's appraisal of "good" Elizabethan acting, however, need not always indicate illusionistic theater, especially in moments of meta-theatricality as Mann, *Shakespeare's Women*, 119–21, demonstrates in his analysis of Rosalind's epilogue from *As You Like It*. For the argument that "the text itself, as originally performed by an all-male cast generated deconstructive power of its own by creating a metatheatrical frame," see Michael Shapiro, "Framing the Taming: Metatheatrical Awareness of Female Impersonation in *The Taming of the Shrew*" in *The Taming of the Shrew: Critical Essays: Critical Essays*, ed. Dana Aspinall (New York: Routledge, 2002), 210–35, and 211 for the quotation cited. On "meta-theatricality," see Mary Bly, "The Boy Companies: 1599–1613," in *The Oxford Handbook of Early Modern Theatre*, ed. Richard Dutton (Oxford: Oxford University Press, 2009), 147–49. Cf. Thomas Heywood, *Apology for Actors* (1612), in *Shakespeare's Theater: A Sourcebook*, ed. Tanya Pollard (Oxford: Blackwell Publishing, 2004), 226: "But to see

our youths attired in the habit of women, who knows not what their intents be? Who cannot distinguish them by their names, assuredly knowing they are but to represent such a lady at such a time appointed?" Though anachronistic, evidence from the New Globe theater confirms Bentley and Belsey's historical claims. See Pauline Kiernan, *Staging Shakespeare at the New Globe* (New York: Palgrave, 1999), 117, who writes: "It perhaps needs to be stressed that most, if not all, of the time, if a male actor plays a female role, the audience will take him to be a woman in any other role." Rather than debate illusionistic theatre and boy actors, I argue that attention to the male actor who played Kate shows how the quality of audacity may be augmented in performance.

11. Henry Peacham, *The Garden of Eloquence* (1593) (London: Historical Collection from the British Library, 1593), 138–39.

12. In *The Taming of the Shrew*, there are obvious instances where the cross-dressed convention appears to be questioned or where the covert drama of the Tudor schoolroom intrudes upon the play's fictionality. See Shapiro's list of such instances in "Framing the Taming," 216–30

13. Kate's last line, for example, questions not just her sincerity within the fiction of the final scene but also directs attention to the boy actor who declaims as the character he is not: "But now I see our lances are but straws, / Our strength as weak, our weakness past compare, / That seeming to be most which we indeed least are" (5.2.179–81).

14. Indeed, "the final scene," writes Lois Potter of Kate, "in which she demonstrates how women should behave, may look like a defeat in a modern production; in the 1590's, it would have been in the original sense of the word, the triumphant conclusion to the boy's training." See Lois Potter, *The Life of Shakespeare: A Critical Biography* (Malden, MA: Wiley-Blackwell, 2012), 148–49.

15. Charles Hoole, *A New Discovery of the Old Art of Teaching School*, ed. Thiselton Mark (Syracuse, NY: C. W. Bardeen, 1912), 180, 284. Hoole's treatise is written in 1660 but advertises the "old art" of previous teaching methods. I have adjusted the capitalization and punctuation or modernized the spelling from Mark's edition without damage to Hoole's original sense. On the schoolboy's schedule, see "The constant Method of Teaching in St. Pauls Schoole London" in Donald Lemen Clark, *John Milton at St. Paul's School: A Student of Ancient Rhetoric in English Renaissance Education* (Hamden, CT: Archon Books, 1964), 110–13; and William Nelson, *A Fifteenth Century School Book* (Oxford: Clarendon Press, 1956), 18, which records the following response to the student's workload: "All that was to me a pleasure when I was a child, from three years old to 10, while I was under my father and mothers' keeping, be turned now to torments and pain. . . . For now at five of the clock by the moonlight I must go to my book and let sleep and sloth alone. And if our master happens to wake us, he brings a rod instead of a candle."

16. Ursula Potter, "Performing Arts in the Tudor Classroom," in *Tudor Drama before Shakespeare 1485–1590*, ed. Lloyd Kermode, Jason Scott-Warren, and Martine Van Elk (New York: Palgrave Macmillan, 2004), 149–50.

17. As Anne Blake argues in "'The Humour of Children': John Marston's Plays in Private Theatres," *Review of English Studies* 38, no. 152 (1987): 481, boy actors could draw "attention to the discrepancy between actor and role" for the sake of "celebrating the triumph of the actor in creating the dramatic illusion in spite of the discrepancy."

18. Yachnin, "Personations," 2.16. Cf.: Idem., 2.26: "To resituate power in the sphere of the person is to foreground power's failure to account for the full range of effects produced by the actor's personation of Katherine."

19. See, too, Potter, "Performing Arts in the Tudor Classroom," 143–65, who provides the best account of why the classroom should be considered a stage space, and, in doing so, she rightly comments how "modern studies of Renaissance rhetoric . . . have marginalized the delivery skills that formed an integral part of rhetorical training" (143). The most comprehensive account of the actor as orator according to techniques found in classical and early modern texts is Heinrich Plett, "Actio Poetica: The

Rhetorical Conceptualization of Acting and Poetry," in *Rhetoric and Renaissance Culture* (Berlin: DeGruyter, 2004), 251–93.

20. Enterline, *Shakespeare's Schoolroom*, 11.

21. See Quentin Skinner, *Reason and Rhetoric in the Philosophy of Hobbes* (Cambridge, UK: Cambridge University Press, 1996), 66–87 on "the ideal of the *vir civilis*." For exploration of Skinner's historical studies in the context of Shakespeare's plays, see David Armitage, Conal Condren, and Andrew Fitzmaurice (eds.), *Shakespeare and Early Modern Political Thought*(Cambridge, UK: Cambridge University Press, 2009).

22. On the grammar schools and rhetoric, in addition to T. W. Baldwin *William Shakspere's Small Latine and Lesse Greeke* (Urbana: University of Illinois Press, 1944), see Peter Mack, *Elizabethan Rhetoric: Theory and Practice*. (Cambridge, UK: Cambridge University Press, 2002), 9–47; and Clark, *John Milton at St. Paul's School*; the five canons of rhetoric derive from Cicero, *Rhetorica Ad Herennium*, trans. H. Caplan (Cambridge, MA: Harvard University Press, 1954), 1.2.3.

23. Skinner, *Reason and Rhetoric*, 73.

24. I cite John Bale from Harold Newcomb Hillebrand, *The Child Actors: A Chapter in Elizabethan Stage History* (New York: Russell & Russell, 1964), 18n39: *tum ad formandum os tenerum & balbutiens, quo clarè, eleganter, & distinctè verba eloqui & effari consuesceret. Plurimus in eius museo vidi ac legi tragoedias & comoedias, epistolas, orationes.*

25. Enterline, *Shakespeare's Schoolroom*, 41, the emphasis belongs to the author, who cites the ordinances of the Shrewsbury School. Hillebrand, *The Child Actors*, 20, gives the same quotation, which he speculates derives from Thomas Ashton, the schoolmaster behind productions at the theatre at Shrewsbury.

26. Sir James Whitelocke, *Liber Famelicus of Sir James Whitelocke*, ed. John Bruce (Westminster: J. B. Nichols and Sons, 1858), 12, my emphasis. On the Merchant Taylors School, see E. K. Chambers, *The Elizabethan Stage, Vol. 2* (Oxford: Clarendon Press, 1923), 76.

27. Edel Lamb, *Performing Childhood in the Early Modern Theatre: The Children's Playing Companies (1599–1613)* (London: Palgrave MacMillan, 2009), 99–100. Joseph, *Elizabethan Acting*, 13–15, makes the same point, surveying the same educational literature.

28. On the importance of the *Rhetorica Ad Herennium* and Roman oratory in England, see Skinner, *Forensic Shakespeare*, 11–47.

29. Heywood, *Apology for Actors*, 226–27. The glosses belong to Pollard's edition.

30. Hillebrand's conclusion states: "Certainly, considering how active children were in the field of drama during the hundred years between 1515 and 1616, we ought not to be surprised to find them exercising a marked influence on plays and players" (*The Child Actors*, 253).

31. Quintillian, *Institutio Oratoria*, trans. H. E. Butler (Cambridge, MA: Harvard University Press, 1922), 1.9.1.

32. Clark, *John Milton at St. Paul's School*, 208.

33. Brinsley, *Ludus Literarius (1612)*, 178.

34. For Erasmus's texts, see the *Collected Works of Erasmus: Literary and Educational Writings, Vol. 2: De Copia / De Ratione Studii*, ed. Craig R. Thompson (Toronto: University of Toronto Press, 1978).

35. For rhetoric's genres, see Cicero, *Rhetorica Ad Herennium*, 1.2.2.

36. On themes, see Erasmus's *De Copia*, trans. Brian McGregor, in *Collected Works of Erasmus*, 680–82 and Clark, *John Milton at St. Paul's School*, 217.

37. On themes and their relationship to declamations, see Brinsley, *Ludus Literarius (1612)*, 172–90; for summary of the practice in grammar schools, see Skinner, *Reason and Rhetoric*, 27.

38. Skinner, *Reason and Rhetoric*, 29.

39. "The Preliminary Exercises of Aphthonius the Sophist," in *Progymnasmata: Greek Textbooks of Prose Composition and Rhetoric*, trans. George A. Kennedy (Atlanta: Society of Biblical Literature, 2003), 115–16.

40. See Joseph R. Roach, *The Player's Passion: Studies in the Science of Acting* (Ann Arbor: University of Michigan Press, 1993), 23–57.

41. Kempe is quoted from Joseph, *Elizabethan Acting*, 10, though I modernized the English.
42. Brinsley, *Ludus Literarius (1612)*, 50–51; my modernization.
43. Ben Jonson, "Cynthia's Revels," in *Ben Jonson, Vol. IV*, ed. C. H. Herford and Percy Simpson (Oxford: Clarendon Press, 1932), 3.1.3–4. Two of Jonson's boy actors for this play were grammar school scholars, Salomon Pavy, who was "about twelve," and Nathan Field, who was "about thirteen or fourteen" at the time they acted in *Cynthia's Revels*, according to David Kathman, "How Old Were Shakespeare's Boy Actors?" in *Shakespeare Survey: Writing About Shakespeare, Vol. 58*, ed. Peter Holland (Cambridge, UK: Cambridge University Press, 2005), 223. Kathman's overall findings range up until the 1600s and, in with this larger frame, he concludes: female roles were played by boys "no younger than twelve and no older than twenty-one or twenty-two, with a median of around sixteen or seventeen" (219–20).
44. Charles Hoole is cited from Foster Watson, *The English Grammar Schools to 1600: Their Curriculum and Practice* (Cambridge, UK: Cambridge University Press, 1908), 316. See Enterline, *Shakespeare's Schoolroom*, 9–62, for exploration of the connections between Latin oratory and dramatic performance.
45. I follow Evelyn B. Tribble, *Cognition in the Globe: Attention and Memory in Shakespeare's Theatre* (New York: Palgrave Macmillan, 2011), 118–22.
46. All of *Love's Labour's Lost* quotations are from Shakespeare's *Love's Labour's Lost: Third Series (Arden Shakespeare)* ed. H. R. Woudhuysen (Walton-on-Thames: Thomas Nelson and Sons, 1988), 5.2.97–100. Hereafter cited internally.
47. Heywood, *Apology for Actors*, 227.
48. Lamb, *Performing Childhood in the Early Modern Theatre*, 113.
49. Unless otherwise noted, all citations of Shakespeare are from *The Complete Works of Shakespeare*, ed. David Bevington, seventh edition (New York: Pearson Longman, 2014). For the passage above, see *Sonnet 23*, 1–6. Henceforth cited internally.
50. Tribble, *Cognition in the Globe*, 122.
51. All citations from Shakespeare's *Twelfth Night* are from *Twelfth Night, or What You Will: Third Series (Arden Shakespeare)*, ed. Keir Elam (London: Cengage Learning, 2008), 1.5.168–69. Hereafter cited internally.
52. On the term "study," see Simon Palfrey and Tiffany Stern, *Shakespeare in Parts* (Oxford: Oxford University Press, 2007), 318–20.
53. Tribble, *Cognition in the* Globe, 126. I follow Tribble's comparison of the failure of Moth to the expertise of the First Player from *Hamlet* as well at Tribble, *Cognition in the* Globe , 120–26.
54. Mary Jo Kietzman, "Will Personified: Viola as Actor-Author in *Twelfth Night*," *Criticism* 54, no. 2 (2012): 267, 261.
55. On the designation of "eunuch" and how Orsino's relationship to Caesario alludes to the relationship between master actor and his apprentice, I follow Kietzman, "Will Personified," 261 and 264.
56. Brinsley, *Ludus Literarius (1612)*, 178. "Besides that," Brinsley emphasizes, "this will be a great furtherance *to audacity*, memory, gesture, pronunciation" (Idem). The *ex tempore* format involves higher praise for each of these.
57. Brinsley, *Ludus Literarius (1612)*, 185.
58. Dusinberre, "Women, Acting, and Power," 182.
59. Colin Burrow, "Shakespeare and Humanistic Culture," in *Shakespeare and the Classics*, ed. Charles Martindale and A. B. Taylor (Cambridge, MA: Cambridge University Press, 2004), 12.
60. Brinsley, *Ludus Literarius (1612)*, 174–75.
61. In addition to studying classical literature and "good authors" of "Roman eloquence," Colet intends for "his school" especially "to increase knowledge and worshipping of God and our Lord Christ Jesus." See "What Shall Be Taught" in the *John Milton Statutes of St. Paul's School* in J. H. Lupton, *A Life of John Colet: Dean of St. Paul's and Founder of St. Paul's School* (Eugene, OR: Wipf & Stock Publishers, 2004), 279. Clark, however, avers: "When we read Colet on chaste Latin and pure eloquence we must

bear in mind that as a humanist he is more concerned with the literary manners than with the morals of great writers. He is insisting that his boys learn classical Latin, not medieval Latin" (*John Milton At St. Paul's School*, 102).

62. Brinsley, *Ludus Literarius (1612)*, 176.
63. Brinsley, *Ludus Literarius (1612)*, 177.
64. Brinsley, *Ludus Literarius (1612)*, 180.
65. Cited from Enterline, *Shakespeare's Schoolrooms*, 21.
66. Brinsley, *Ludus Literarius (1612)*, 181.
67. The "parts of a theme" were identical to the parts of Ciceronian oration. Brinsley lists six—*Exordium, Narratio, Confirmatio, Confutatio, Conclusio* (*Ludus*, 179)—following the *Rhetorica Ad Herennium* at 1.3.4.
68. Brinsley, *Ludus Literarius (1612)*, 214.
69. Baldwin, *Small Latine*, 2:359.
70. Brinsley, *Ludus Literarius (1612)*, 179.
71. The *Oxford English Dictionary* (OED) doesn't provide a definition for "fitliest" but does supply one for "fitly": "In a way that is fit; properly, aptly, becomingly, suitably, appropriately."
72. Brinsley, *Ludus Literarius (1612)*, 180.
73. Cicero, *De Inventione, De Optimo Genere Oratorum, Topica*, trans. Harry Mortimer Hubbell (Cambridge, MA: Harvard University Press, 1949), VI.30, 403–4.
74. Desiderius Erasmus, *The Praise of Folly*, trans. Clarence H. Miller (New Haven, CT: Yale University Press, 1979), 13.
75. Johnson is quoted in the gloss on "suted" for 5.1.232 from William Shakespeare, *A New Variorum Edition of Shakespeare: Much Ado About Nothing*, ed. Horace Howard Furness (New York: Dover Publications, 1964). Bevington's note on line 5.1.220 captures Claudio's point but confuses partition and division by glossing "his own division" as "its own partition in a logical arrangement."
76. I am indebted to Garry Wills, *Rome and Rhetoric: Julius Caesar* (New Haven, CT: Yale University Press, 2011), 49–50, for the explanation of and joke about "the wittiest partition" that Demetrius ever heard.
77. Baldwin, *Small Latine*, 2:112.
78. Brinsley, *Ludus Literarius (1612)*, 180. From this passage, Brinsley may be seen to use the term division after the definition in the *Topics*. For "division" as the device by which "we make clear matters are agreed upon and what are contested," see *Ad Herennium*, 1.3.4.
79. See the *OED* on "keeper" as a noun, 1.a.
80. I modernize the English of Ephesians, 5.22–25 from *The Geneva Bible: A Facsimile of the 1560 Edition* (Peabody, MA: Hendrickson Publishers, 2007). See, too, Colossians 3.18–19.
81. Germaine Greer, *The Female Eunuch* (New York: MacGraw-Hill, 1971), 206.
82. Tita French Baumlin, "Petruchio the Sophist and Language as Creation in *The Taming of the Shrew*," *Studies in English Literature, 1500–1900* 29, no. 2 (1989): 250, writes: "This description of man's proper marital virtues is surely directed specifically toward Hortensio and Lucentio, neither of whom appears to be Petruchio's equal in caring for the growth of his partner."
83. Brinsley, *Ludus Literarius (1612)*, 180.
84. *Erotema* would be known as *interrogatio* in Cicero, *Rhetorica Ad Herennium*, 4.15.22, or as "the questioner" in George Puttenham, *The Art of English Poesy: A Critical Edition*, 296–97. See my conclusion for discussion of this figure and its potential for direct address to audience members.
85. Rhetorical audacity in the form of direct address to audience members provides nuance to the conventional understanding of the *platea* discourse, which is too often distinguished from formal speech. See Robert Weimann, *Author's Pen and Actor's Voice*, 180–215.
86. See Bridget Escomle, *Talking to the Audience: Shakespeare, Performance, Self* (New York: Routledge, 2005), 16: "Whereas in naturalistic theatre it is impossible for any

character to desire or have an interest in anything outside of the fiction, Shakespeare's stage figures have another set of desires and interests, inseparable from those of the actor. They want the audience to listen to them, notice them, approve their performance, ignore others on stage for their sake. The objectives of these figures are bound up with the fact that they know you're there."

87. Though it seems impossible to know how much of Shakespeare's audience consists of women, Stephen Orgel, "Nobody's Perfect: Or Why Did the English Stage Take Boys for Women?" *South Atlantic Quarterly* 88 (1989): 8, summarizing comments by foreign visitors to the English stage, writes that "a large proportion of the audience consisted of women." Cf., Stephen Gosson's *The School of Abuse* in Pollard, ed., *Shakespeare's Theater*, 29–31. As Gosson's and other antitheatrical tracts make clear, women were rebuked for attending the theater primarily because it was considered unseemly for them to do so. As a result, we may imagine how Kate's rebuke to actual female audience members could satirize these complaints by enacting their spirit of moral rebuke even while they assume ongoing attendance by women at the theater.

88. Enterline, *Shakespeare's Schoolroom*, 117.

89. Peacham, *The Garden of Eloquence*, 124–25.

90. My glosses for "heart" and "haply" are from Crystal and Crystal, *Shakespeare's Words*.

91. Kamaralli, *Shakespeare and the Shrew*, 108–9. Italics belong to the author.

92. For discussion of the relationship of Bianca and Kate in light of humanist education, see Patricia Parker, "Construing Gender: Mastering Bianca in *The Taming of the Shrew*," in *The Impact of Feminism in English Renaissance Studies*, ed. Dympna Callaghan (New York: Palgrave Macmillan, 2007), 193–209; and Heather James, "Shakespeare's Learned Heroines in Ovid's Schoolroom," in *Shakespeare and the Classics*, ed. Charles Martindale and A. B. Taylor (Cambridge, UK: Cambridge University Press, 2004), 66–88.

93. In the context of the humanist classroom, the elevation of Kate over Bianca may capture how boys were hierarchically arranged underneath an instructor as well. *Monitores* were appointed by the *magister* and were in charge of policing the speech of the younger or less inclined students, prohibiting speech in English rather than in Latin. From the *Annals of Westminster School*, we learn how boys supervise others in the hall, the school, the fields, the cloister, even the washroom; the last are the *monitores immundori* or monitors of the unclean. "The Captain of the School was over all these and therefore called *Monitor monitorum*," or the monitor of all monitors, creating a leader of all the other students. Complaints or accusations were alleged every Friday morning "when the punishments were often redeemed by exercises or favors showed to boys of extraordinary merit, who had the honor (by the *Monitor monitorum*) many times to beg and prevail for such remissions. And so (at other times) other faults were often punished by scholastic tasks, as repeating whole orations out of Tully, Isocrates, Demosthenes: or speeches out of Virgil, Thucydides, Xenophon, Euripides, etc." See John Sargeaunt, *Annals of Westminster School* (London: Methuen & Co., 1898), 281, for these citations, which I have modernized. If the end of *The Taming of the Shrew* represents a schoolroom declamation, it may reflect the hierarchical arrangement of the classroom as well. A student like Bianca could be praised or blamed according to the judgment of the *monitor monitorum*, just as Kate judges and commands another boy actor on the stage.

THREE
Much Ado about Personation

Thus far, I have presented William Shakespeare as a classically educated poet, who fashions character-effects according to the techniques of rhetoric, following the humanist practice of imitation or training in declamation. *Richard III* and *Taming of the Shrew*, therefore, exemplify Shakespeare's early career, firmly establishing an acting style in terms of what orators refer to as delivery, the arts of action and accent. In this chapter, I will ask whether a new and an especially lifelike manner of personation emerges in the late 1590s by examining *Much Ado About Nothing*, a play Shakespeare composes in the same year that John Florio's publication of *World of Words* defines "personare" as a verb that means "to personate, to act, to imitate any person."[1]

To anticipate my argument, instead of an evolving naturalism or acting style, I find that *Much Ado* situates "personation" within the rhetorical tradition but does so in order to fashion the illusion that characters may speak outside of theatrical boundaries. The representations of theatricality within *Much Ado*—its characters who play dramatists, like Pedro and Borachio, or roles within these internal dramas, like Margaret who impersonates Hero—include those who are charged with the task typically reserved to people who are offstage, the office of beholder. In these instances, Shakespeare invites playgoers to understand characters not just as performers within the fiction of the play but also as representations of themselves, actual audience members, spectators who sit in judgment of fictions. "While the theater audience occupies a privileged position in relation to the action of the play," writes Nova Myhill, "the play presents it with audiences that also believe their position privileged and shows how that assumption leaves them vulnerable to having their readings controlled by the play's internal dramatists Don John, Borachio, and Don Pedro." By demonstrating the similarity between spectators within and outside of the fiction, Myhill's argument purposefully and rightly conflates "spectatorship in/of *Much Ado*" and, in the process, explores discrepancies between knowledge and perception with those of spectacle and observer.[2] We shall see how these discrepancies reflect the antitheatrical tracts of the period, but the identification of characters with early modern theatricality suggests something more.

For when dramatic persons direct attention to the actor's craft, they may appear distinct from theatrical representation, even though they remain a function of it. Traditionally, critics understand these instances as meta-theater or "dramatic illusions," which they define in terms of how Shakespeare's plays are about "dramatic art itself," or how plays call attention to the theatrical practices that underlie representation; such analyses usually repudiate mimesis. Pauline Kiernan, for example, describes how "dramatic illusions" differ from "mimetic illusions" because of how an actor calls attention to the fictitious nature of what is performed on stage, what is personated.[3] In *Much Ado*, however, meta-theater ultimately deepens the very illusion of personation that the play calls attention to as a feigned imitation. The disavowal or invocation of theatricality creates the impression that characters may speak and exist in nonrepresentational modes. Characters appear not as dramatic persons but real ones.

PERSONATION AND INDIVIDUAL CHARACTERIZATION

To analyze the critical controversy around the term "personation," I begin with an illustration of Shakespeare's use of it from Maria's plan "to gull" Malvolio in *Twelfth Night, Or What You Will*. Maria says of her plot: "If I do not gull him into nayword and make him a common recreation, do not think I have wit enough to lie straight in my bed."[4] "To make a gull of" indicates "to dupe, cheat, befool, 'take in,' or deceive," a designation I will use to describe scenes that show how characters trick other characters on stage.[5] Here, to gull into a nayword means to make Malvolio's name a byword with a gull; to be Malvolio will mean becoming a dupe.

Maria's talk of "obscure epistles" suggests something else: "I will drop in his way some obscure epistles of love," she says, "wherein by the color of his beard, the shape of his leg, the manner of his gait, the expressure of his eye, forehead, and complexion, he shall find himself *most feelingly personated*" (2.3.154–58). Maria will gull Malvolio first by her credible personation or representation of him in the letter. The details of her description indicate how the term "personation" corresponds to lifelike linguistic portraiture. Thus, personation contrasts with the exaggerated traits—the smiles and "strange, stout" disposition (2.5.167)—that

Malvolio later performs before Olivia, what Maria calls "the trick of singularity" (2.5.148–49).

To gull audiences with personations seems like an apt metaphor for describing the actor's charge to create a lifelike portrayal of character in performing a role. So, too, Maria's lifelike personation and Malvolio's overacting analogously corresponds with two contrary modes of representation upon the early modern stage. As Andrew Gurr has shown, Ben Jonson's lament on the title page of *The New Inn*—that his play was "never acted, but most negligently play'd, by some, the Kings' servants"—shows how "acting" refers to the orator's directions for *actio* and in counterdistinction to mere "playing." Acting supersedes playing because the latter is what amateurs offer upon common stages.[6]

Shakespeare's Philostrate adds to the picture of "mere playing" when he says of Bottom's "players" that there is not a single part well cast or apt word used by them. These are "hardhanded men that work in Athens here, / Which never labored in their minds till now," which means they have "toiled their unbreathed memories" in attempting performance (*A Midsummer Night's Dream*, 5.1.72–75). The "players" are "rude mechanicals," who lack the aptitude for the intellectual labor of *memoria*, the last canon of classical rhetoric (3.2.9). "Unbreathed memories" are unexercised memories: Bottom's players have "conned with cruel pain" (5.1.80) those speeches or lines that both orator and actor would more easily master. Simple "players" lack the requisite training and aptitude for performing roles well.

As the more academic sense of "acting" trumps untrained playing, there is a growing body of scholarship that now posits how a more rarified art of "personation" supersedes *actio* at some point in the late 1590s.[7] Proponents of this development cite Thomas Heywood's *Apology for Actors* (1612), which appears to distinguish the actor from the orator precisely because of how expert actors demonstrate heightened credibility or the lifelike personation of a role. Heywood calls "oratory" a "speaking picture" and painting "dumb oratory," but "neither can show action, passion, motion, or any other gesture, to move the spirits of the beholder to admiration."[8] Next, he speaks of the art of personation:

> To turn to our domestic histories: what English blood, seeing the person of any bold English man presented and doth not hug his fame, and hunny at his valor, pursuing him in his enterprise with his best wishes, and as begin rapt in contemplation, offers to him in his heart all prosperous performance, *as if the personater were the man personated*, so bewitching a thing is lively and well spirited action, that it hath power to new mold the hearts of the spectators.[9]

For Robert Weimann and Douglas Bruster, "Heywood argues that playing exceeds the art of oratory in its studied qualification of 'everything according to the nature of the person personated.'"[10] Gurr concurs, claiming that the creation of a "new" noun—"personation"—suggests "that a relatively new art of individual characterization had begun to develop," what he calls "an art distinct from the orator's display of passions" or that of the "academic actor's portrayal" of character-types.[11] Personation, thus, becomes subject to Whig historiography in these accounts because Shakespeare ostensibly improves upon Kate's declamatory audacity and Richard's vivification of type. Instead, Shakespeare's dramatic persons provide "a relatively new art of individual characterization."[12]

As a result of this reading of Heywood's *Apology* and its application to Shakespeare's plays, personation now registers a continuum of mimetic effects. "Personation is 'role-playing,'" Weimann and Bruster argue, "and the embodiment of a role and its representation through either dialogue or monologue is to give body and voice to something scripted," but this leads to what the authors call "deep characterization." Such depth includes the actor's greater identification with a role. "The characterizing performer surrenders his own body more consistently to the symbolic process," Weimann and Bruster write, because "the actor tends to identify with the represented person to the degree that his or her histrionic competence becomes completely integral to the task in question."[13]

In the context of progressive identification between actors and characters, the distinction between *actio* and "deep characterization" align with what Jane L. Donawerth refers to as the difference between "lively" and "lifelike" acting styles.[14] The performance of passions with an exaggerated gesture and pronunciation of the Marlovian mighty line make for the "strutting and bellowing" of a *lively* performance by actors like Edward Alleyn. *Lively* performance, however, lacks the refinement of Richard Burbage's more *lifelike* personations.[15]

Though these readings of personation remain influential, I think they mistakenly conflate two passages from Heywood's *Apology* and obscure the terms of debate over what might constitute lifelike dramatic action in the 1590s. Though the rule for actors "to qualify every thing according to the nature of the person personated" occurs after the discussion of "dumb oratory," Heywood describes personation according to expert oratorical delivery. He writes that Cicero's *Ad Herennium* requires "invention, disposition, elocution, memory, and pronunciation," all of which are imperfect without "action":

> For be his *invention* never so fluent and exquisite, his *disposition* and order never so composed and formal, his *eloquence,* and elaborate phrases never so material and pithy, his *memory* never so firm and retentive, his pronunciation never so musical and plosive; yet without a comely and elegant gesture, a gracious and *bewitching kind of action*, a natural and familiar motion of the head, the hand, the body; and a moderate and fit countenance suitable to all the rest, I hold the rest as nothing.[16]

Heywood's "bewitching kind of action" is exactly what he recommends to actors in terms of qualifying "every thing according to the nature of the person personated," yet such action signifies the rhetorical technique of gesture. As the passage above illustrates, Heywood situates personation within the five canons of rhetoric derived from the Ciceronian tradition, but he privileges the last canon, delivery. Under delivery, of course, falls the artful management of voice and gesture.[17] Heywood's elevation of a "bewitching kind of action" above the other skills of traditional rhetoric, it turns out, echoes Cicero's anecdote about Demosthenes, which informs us how delivery (*actio*), both in terms of voice and gesture, is "the first thing in speaking" but also "the second, and also the third."[18] Rather than "a relatively new art of individual characterization," Heywood qualifies personation as part of rhetoric's art.

In the *Apology*, a continuum of mimetic possibilities nevertheless remains. Personation is a rhetorical acting style that Heywood contrasts with "over-acting, tricks, and toiling too much in the antic habit of humors, men of the ripest desert, greatest opinions, and best reputations may break into the most violent absurdities."[19] These "over-acting tricks" are condemned along with underacting, what Heywood refers to as standing around like "a stiff starched man."[20] Personation becomes the golden mean between the two, lying between excess and deficiency in delivery. To appropriate terms from *Twelfth Night*, Heywood's golden mean corresponds to Maria's sense of personation that is lifelike, whereas excess or deficiency — over- or underplaying parts — would appear as an unnatural "trick of singularity."

Because early modern actors could personate characters according to Heywood's notion of naturalism, the antitheatrical authors, Heywood's opponents, worried about the impact of performance upon the players. Plays present moral hazard to actors precisely because actors embody characters after a "lively" or, more accurately, lifelike depiction of personhood. John Rainolds's *Th'Overthrow of Stage-Playes* (1599) makes the point about the dangers of representation most succinctly:

> For the care of making a show to do such feats [as in acting roles in comedies], and to do them as *lively* as the beasts themselves in who the vices reign, worketh in the actors *a marvelous impression of being like the persons whose qualities they express and imitate*: chiefly when earnest and much meditation of sundry days and weeks, by often repetition and representation of the parts, shall as it were engrave the things in their mind with a pen of iron, or with a diamond.[21]

"Lively" here does not indicate a rhetorical delivery at variance from "lifelike" personations but conflates oratory and acting at the point of exterior portrayal or behavior, a point Shakespeare himself iterates.[22] Like other polemicists in the debate over the theater and contrary to Donawerth's position, Rainolds uses *lively* to denote *lifelike* characterization.[23] For this reason, Rainolds believes the "lively" performance of roles not only harms audiences, but also the actors whose "representation" of other selves, characters with whom they identify as actors, will engrave "vice" upon their minds.

In responding to opponents like Rainolds, Heywood articulates personation as the apogee of the rhetorical tradition when and if actors perform well. "Actors should be men picked out *personable*," advises Heywood, "according to the parts they present," which suggests how personation signifies typological character and an early modern practice of "typecasting." The actors' bodies and personalities must match the roles or types they are assigned to play.[24] Heywood mentions "zawnies" or clowns, "pantalones" or old foolish men, and even harlequins or mute players. These and other such types are listed along with specific English actors, such as "Will Kemp," who are well suited to play particular parts because of their individual qualities.[25]

With arguments like these Heywood rebuts the largely Puritan attack upon the theater. If acting involves oratorical *technê* in representing character, stage plays constitute no moral infection of the actor. The practice of rhetorical technique absolves the theater from the charge that it forces its actors to sin. So Heywood summarizes—in contradistinction to Gurr's argument that personation differs from orators or the academic actor—that players "should be rather scholars, that though they cannot speak well, know how to speak." Alternatively, actors should "have that volubility that they can speak well, though they understand not what." In either case, "both imperfections may by instructions be helped and amended." The only problem is "where a good tongue and a good conceit fail," because in that case "there can never be [a] good actor."[26] Personation, as an artistic standard, signifies how well an actor's imagination envelops language, movement, intonation, fluency, and becomes internalized in a "firm and retentive memory" in order to produce "a bewitching kind of action."[27]

Thus, personation as an art form becomes essential to Heywood's overall point against the allegation of moral infection. "But to see our youths attired in the habit of women," writes Heywood in reply to the charge that actors are morally damaged by the performance of their parts, "who knows not what their intents be?" The actors' art of personation cannot be so overpowering as Rainolds suggests because, as Heywood questions of the boy actors, "who cannot distinguish them by their names, assuredly knowing they are but to represent such a lady at such a time appointed?"[28] Heywood thereby relies upon the classical understanding of rhetoric as an art and personation as part of that craft. The artistic intention to embody character upon the stage should not be confused with the moral agency or identity of the person who does so.

Heywood's *Apologia* remains vexed in critical discourse because it suggests distinctions between naturalism and affectation or character and playing a role; but such categories exist within the early modern horizon of rhetorical delivery. Instead of an emerging or progressive aesthetic of naturalism, personation remains the consequence of perfecting the techniques of the rhetorical style of acting. That rhetorical style Heywood doesn't articulate as mechanical but as "natural and familiar." Heywood's understanding of what rhetorical technique imparts to actors, not his definition of personation, emerges as the actual but not new "art of individual characterization."

GULLING AUDIENCES

In the above contexts, the *Apology* presents personation as the golden mean between "over-acting tricks" and underacting like "a stiff starched man," allowing for evaluative distinctions about performance. In this section, I explore those distinctions in terms of how gulling scenes from *Much Ado* represent them. Internal dramas, I will argue, draw upon the antitheatrical literature to which Heywood responds in a way that both affirms and contradicts the criticism of the stage. On the one hand, the internal dramas of *Much Ado* show how spectators accept fiction as facts, witnessing to the Puritan critique of plays as an overpowering spectacle. On the other, this very response from spectators testifies to the lifelike qualities of personation, thereby affirming the theater's power. To see how Shakespeare presents well and poorly performed personations and how observers respond to such displays, I turn to those scenes from *Much Ado* that stage or describe deceptions within the fiction itself. In doing so, I hope to demonstrate how *Much Ado* is explicit about theatricality, and, in the subsequent sections, I will show how such dramatic illusions or meta-theater deepens character.

Pedro's charge to Leonato and Claudio "to practice" on Benedick creates a scene for Benedick to behold (*Much Ado*, 2.1.364). "What was it you told me of today," Pedro asks, "that your niece Beatrice was in love with Signor / Benedick?" (2.3.92–94). Claudio, who marks Benedick, next refers to him as a "fowl" (2.3.96), punning upon another definition of the term "gull," which could denote a young bird or gosling and, thus, became a metaphor for one easily deceived or led along. To be successful in deceiving Benedick, Pedro's gulling strategy first juxtaposes "all outward behaviors" of Beatrice (2.3.100) with her alleged internal thoughts and feelings. Next, Pedro must describe to Benedick all the outward signs that truly disclose Beatrice's secret love.

Pedro's company imparts these lessons to Benedick through a performance of their own, which assesses Beatrice's behavior in terms of credible signs of passion:

> Leonato: By my troth, my lord, I cannot tell what to think of it but that she loves him with an *enraged affection*; it is past the infinite of thought.

Pedro: Maybe she doth but *counterfeit*.
Claudio: Faith, like enough.
Leonato: Oh, God, *counterfeit*? There was never *counterfeit of passion* came so near *the life of passion* as she discovers it.
Pedro: Why, what *effects of passion* shows she? (2.3.103–11, my emphasis)

The dialogue discloses "the life of passion" in contrast to the "counterfeit" of one. The former signifies authenticity and the latter artful pretense. The juxtaposition of the two creates a Beatrice designed for Benedick's imagination, but the contrast also raises the question about the performance of passion.

The argument over Beatrice's behavior, in a theatrical sense, becomes how does Beatrice personate the role of a lover. Well-played passions, the gullers' argument suggests, are signs of "that within," providing an echo either of the rhetorical theory of acting for playing passions with verisimilitude or a distinction from it in the name of sincerity. An "enraged affection" could be a monstrous passion that signifies overacting, like "strutting and bellowing," or crude delivery and obvious pretense. Conversely, the gullers' presentation means that Beatrice manifests her passions so vehemently that they are true signs of her love. So, too, the term "counterfeit," as in my earlier discussion of *King Richard III*, might indicate playing a role in an artful fashion, but the gullers' use "counterfeit" in contrast with that "life of passion" experienced by Beatrice. The "enraged affection" of a lover, we infer, should be so "feelingly personated" that what appears exteriorly actually discloses authentic affection.

Pedro's small company not only speaks of "the life of passion" but also "counterfeits" for Benedick's sake. Instead of experts in the performance of passion, though, they are poor players. Like the Rude Mechanicals, Pedro's troupe appears to ignore cues and break character. They speak of the distinction between poorly feigned and true displays of passion while providing subpar theater themselves. As a result, Pedro's troupe ironizes the importance of representation. Benedick's gullibility, if extrapolated to all theater audiences, means that actors need only claim something to be true in order for an onlooker to accept it as such.

The gullers wish to present essential evidence about the "effects of passions" that Beatrice shows—what Claudio crucially introduces with the imperative, "bait the hook well; this fish will / bite" (2.3.112–13)—but Pedro's counterfeit stalls at precisely this point. Leonato fails to provide an account of Beatrice's passion, urging Claudio to do so because he must have learned details about Beatrice from Hero. Yet invention fails Claudio as well, who may only reply, "She did, indeed." So Pedro must intervene: "How, how, I pray you? You amaze me. I would have thought her spirit had been invincible against all assaults of affection" (2.3.116–17). Because Pedro's question of "how?" precedes his immediate answer of "you amaze me," directors typically insert some stage-business to clarify what otherwise appears as an illogical conclusion on Pedro's part. In both the 1971 and 1990 Royal Shakespeare Company (RSC) productions, Leonato communicates nonverbally to Pedro in an intervening silence. Kenneth Branagh's 1993 film adaptation provides a typical solution when Leonato simply whispers in Pedro's ear.[29] Even so, Pedro's leap in logic isn't an embedded stage direction but a demonstration of how he, Claudio, and Leonato are clumsy or unskilled. Like Quince's troupe of those players who have "unbreathed" memories, Pedro's accomplices forget the crucial description of "the effects of passion" that Beatrice must show, marring their performance.

Pedro refers to the gulling scene as a "practice," a designation that is conventionally glossed as a "stratagem," but the term "practice" invokes discussion of the place and import of the theater in Elizabethan England as well.[30] As Mary Thomas Crane has shown, the word "performance," our word for what the actors thought about their art, was not their word for the same trade of playing.[31] The word "practice" can denote the performance of plays, as well as an occupation, signifying "the carrying out or exercise of a profession."[32] Pedro addresses Claudio and Leonato in a manner that suggests how deceiving Benedick constitutes performing for him, a collective occupation in a very particular production: "And I, with your two / helps, will so *practice* on Benedick that, in despite of / his quick wit and queasy stomach, he shall fall in / love with Beatrice" (2.1.363–66). Next, Pedro calls his conspirators aside for on offstage conference so that his comrades will learn of his "drift" (2.1.369). In arranging a gulling scene, Pedro plans not simply to dupe Benedick but also to design a performance for his ears. To practice on Benedick means to manipulate him by practicing for him.

The same term is used to describe the action of staging Hero's infidelity in an important parallel to how Pedro employs and designs "practices." To briefly recall Don John's own scheme: In order to prove the charge that Hero, Claudio's betrothed, sleeps with Borachio, the Count receives the same sort of "ocular proof" that Othello demands but does not obtain. From a vantage point outside of Hero's bedroom window, Claudio observes Margaret, Borachio's actual mistress, impersonating Hero. This gulling of Claudio is supposed to corroborate the suspicion that Borachio has enjoyed Hero "a thousand times in secret" (4.1.94). Such a window scene is also termed a "practice." After Pedro learns how Hero was falsely accused, he questions Borachio: "But did my brother set thee on to this?" To which Borachio replies: "Yea, and paid me richly for the *practice* of it" (5.1.241–42, my emphasis). In this second instance of the term, the generic though now archaic sense of a "method of action or working" becomes refined into a mode of duping others, a gulling of them, but in the play it also signifies a performance that will influence spectators, like Claudio, in a morally harmful manner. Borachio's own practice, finally, doubly falsifies the truth about Hero by slandering her and by requiring that Margaret exchange her "true person" with Hero's "fictive role."

Though the scene outside of Hero's chamber window is not staged in *Much Ado*, Borachio's description of it is exactly the sort of "practice" that critics of the theater would pinpoint as needlessly titillating and inherently degrading. Borachio's account provokes questions of sexual fidelity and proposes the imagination of illicit pleasures; but the setting, more particularly, violates Elizabethan moral assumptions about the place of women as guarded and protected within the home.[33] Window scenes are places of elopement for Jessica's escape in *Merchant of Venice* and for the exchange of forbidden vows in *Romeo and Juliet*.[34] The very setting represents a variation upon this same theme of a woman's chastity and invites Claudio to assume sexual betrayal.[35]

Howsoever Pedro and Borachio differ in terms of malice, they both speak about "practices" after a similar fashion because of how deception and performance intertwine. The definition of practice as a "method of action" I cite above comes from the *Oxford English Dictionary* (*OED*), which gives Borachio's lines as exemplary, but Pedro's earlier usage of "practice" the *OED* includes as well, an entry that does not account for his good intentions. Pedro use of the term employs "practice" as a transitive verb: "to plot or plan (mischief, harm); to plan and carry out (a harmful course of action) upon a person; to conspire or plan (to do some evil or mischief)."[36] Both of these instances of "practice" in *Much Ado* occur in the context of the play's internal dramas. Shakespeare thereby associates plotting or acting for nefarious purposes with playacting or performance, even an art of trickery that harms observers, as in the case of Margaret's impersonation of Hero misleading Claudio.

The alliance of deception, moral harm, and performance clarifies why the term "practice" abounds in the writings of antitheatrical authors and those who oppose them. The word pervades the debate literature about the theater from 1576, the opening of commercial theaters, to 1613, the year when the Globe burns down. To cite a prominent and indicative example: In 1582, the most important critic of the theater and a former playwright, Stephen Gosson, refers to the "practice of playing," using the term like one applied to any other profession, such as the practice of law, though without any laudable connotations attached to the trade. Instead, the "practice of playing" refers to how performance and actors morally infect beholders because "vice is learned with beholding" and immoral "impressions of mind are secretly conveyed over to the gazers, which the players do *counterfeit* on the stage."[37] The "practice of playing" is the same as in the case of those who "counterfeit on the stage" and overwhelm or transmit "impressions of mind" to defenseless playgoers.

In an earlier use of "practice," John Northbrooke suggests more diverse though similar significations. "Let me understand your judgment as touching comedies," writes Northbrooke in *A Treatise against Dicing*,

Dancing, Plays, and Interludes, with Other Idle Pastimes (1577), a dialogue between "Youth" and "Age." The Youth refers to how scholars "practice" comedies "both in the universities and also in diverse other good schools." To which the voice of Age replies that such are teachers "not of learning, but of destroying children, which *practice* them in these interludes and stage plays."[38] In Northbrooke's first usage, "practice" signifies "performance," but in the second, rehearsal or study. Northbrooke's point is that to "practice" students in acting roles requires immoral behavior of them, such as lewd or lascivious gestures, a common Puritan complaint.[39]

In the antitheatrical tracts, the "practices" of the commercial theater are doubly damning: First, for falsifying the true nature of things through fiction; and, second, because of the lying actors, who lend credibility to the misrepresentation. The term corresponds to personation as well because "practice" can mean the enactment of a particular role, such as the "practice of a parasite" or "the practice of a diligent captain." The action indicative of a particular type-character may signify a "practice," revealing how the word can be used as term of literary characterization and theatrical personation.[40] Actors are twice condemned because, as Howard summarizes of "renaissance antitheatricality," they "present lies about reality and they counterfeit their true persons in the assumption of fictional role."[41]

The "practices" played for Benedick and Beatrice also represent antitheatrical discourse because opponents of the stage seem most concerned about the impact of plays upon audiences. Thus, Gosson pronounces: "So subtle is the devil that, under the color of recreation, in London, and of exercise of learning, in the universities, by seeing of plays, he maketh us to join with Gentiles in their corruption."[42] For Gosson, as we have seen, the practice of playing shows how "vice is learned with beholding" because "sense is tickled, desire pricked, and those impressions of mind are secretly conveyed over to the gazers."[43] If the concerns about the false nature of representation and personation are exemplified in Borachio's practice, Gosson's critique encapsulates the practices of Pedro's plans to gull Benedick and Beatrice. In both gulls, the spectators hear tales of desire, which may be understood as "those impressions of mind" that "are secretly conveyed over to the gazers." Beatrice and Benedick emerge as "tickled" or "pricked" with desire for one another as a result of what is counterfeited before them.

As designers of internal drama within the play, both Borachio and Pedro traffic in lies, fictions within the overarching fiction of Messina. In calling them "practices" they remind us of the conflation of lying and fiction that opponents of the theater leveled against the poets' office. Anthony Munday—another occasional playwright, even a coauthor with Shakespeare of the *Book of Sir Thomas More*—condemns the theater for its manifold production of deceits. Even so, "the notablest liar is become the best poet," complains Munday, because "he that can make the most notorious lie, and disguise falsehood in such sort that he may pass unperceived, is held the best writer."[44] Pedro and Borachio are not writers but authors of lies. Both the window and gulling scenes "disguise falsehold in such sort that they pass unperceived," what Munday identifies as a sign of corrupt playwrights. Borachio "practices" upon Don Pedro and Claudio; Pedro and Claudio "practice" upon Benedick.[45] Characters, like early modern audiences, are gulled into believing things that are fictive.

IMPRESSIONS OF THE MIND

Gulling scenes or internal dramas provoke questions about what is lifelike, who is in "earnest" or in "jest," and what constitutes a "trick." Shakespeare, I argued above, emphasizes these questions by dramatizing the language of antitheatrical tracts and those who reply to them. In this section, I will explore how the same debate literature presents audience responses to plays and how some dramatic persons in *Much Ado* occasionally imitate early modern playgoers. Because of how Shakespeare composes internal dramas within *Much Ado*, we shall see how characters emerge as overpowered spectators not unlike those vulnerable audience members described in antitheatrical tracts.

First, the reaction of Benedick to the "practice" of Pedro confirms part of the argument against the stage. For opponents of the theater, audiences fail to understand the difference between what is feigned and what is true, which puts them in a position of moral hazard because they may "act out" in earnest whatever the fiction conveys to their imaginations. Such an audience response is exactly what Benedick provides. After the gulling concludes, he comments:

> This can be no *trick*. The
> conference was sadly borne. They have the truth of
> this from Hero. They seem to pity the lady. It seems
> her affections have their full bent. Love me? Why, it
> must be requited. I hear how I am censured. (2.3.217–21)

In response to Pedro's internal drama—a jest and a trick, a practice, no matter the play's conclusion—Benedick reasons precisely as the antitheatrical authors claim an audience member would react to viewing a play. Benedick responds to Pedro's practice, to appropriate a description from Munday, "in earnest." He will take on the practices of a lover, or the stock traits of one from the stage, in the scenes that follow, wearing "civet" or cologne, shaving his beard, dressing finely, and turning all orthography.[46]

Benedick receives what Gosson calls "impressions of mind" by observing what Pedro arranges for him to behold, what is counterfeited.

Claudio refers to the transfer of these impressions in an aside during the gulling scene. He says of Benedick: "he hath ta'en the infection" (2.3.125). In fact, the "infection" Claudio seeks to pass on to Benedick accompanies the scene's emphasis upon Beatrice's "affection," thereby dramatizing the question of whether or not "enraged" passions may transfer from what is played upon the stage to those who observe dramatic action.[47] Claudio's metaphor of infection, in other words, demonstrates how Benedick falls in love.[48] As an echo of the same association between counterfeit passion and what, in turn, is described as an "infection," once Beatrice is gulled, she catches "the Benedick," which hangs upon one "like a disease" (1.1.81–85).

Thus, the focus upon theatricality in the gulling of Benedick exemplifies what Myhill calls the "vulnerability of the spectator."[49] Because of this same vulnerability, Munday uses the word "practice" to describe the "example of the stage player" who is beset by "much liking of another man's wife" in a production. Munday condemns how auditors, "having *noted* by what *practice*" seduction may occur, "have not failed to put the like effect in earnest, that was before shown in *jest*."[50] The use of words like "earnest" and "jest" are proverbial for the mediation of stage fictions and the playing by which such fictions are conveyed. Hamlet, too, defends his mousetrap play in terms similar to Munday's critique. He tells Claudius not to worry over the performance because the players do not act "in earnest"; instead "they do but jest, poison in jest" (*Hamlet*, 3.2.232–35). But Hamlet also asks about the audience, especially the reaction of Claudius to the stage. He badgers Horatio in an attempt to see whether his friend recognized Claudius's guilt. "I did very well note him" (3.2.288), Horatio replies. As Horatio notes Claudius, who observes the mousetrap play, audiences observe the stage whereupon Benedick notes the gullers. Yet Benedick claims what is performed "can be no trick."

Munday's phraseology about "noting practices" mirrors Shakespeare's usage in *Much Ado About Nothing* as well. The word "nothing" from the play's title was pronounced like "noting" in Elizabethan London and "to note" could be defined as to consider deeply, or to indicate with condemnation, or to observe with care.[51] For this reason, Stephen Greenblatt believes *Much Ado* is "obsessed with characters noting other characters" in a world where "watching and being watched" corresponds to the "social emotions" of "honor and shame."[52] Greenblatt's observation is true within the fiction of the play, but also in regard to debates about how Elizabethan audiences *noted* performances in general. A play's title often signifies its thematic content by way of proverbial turns of phrase, such as *Measure for Measure*. In punning upon the word "nothing," Shakespeare invites his audiences to think about the experience of attending the theater.

As part of that reflection, the title evokes Munday's general point about the dangers of "noting practices," a case against the theater that corresponds with the one made by Gosson. Plays impart paradigms of emulation, or object lessons in how to behave, to naïve audience members. In the antitheatrical literature, audience members are like Benedick or Beatrice from the gulling scenes: spectators who cannot grasp elementary distinctions between fiction and reality, practices as performances and real life, or representations of spectators who fail to protect themselves from the influence of those particular practices or personations they observe.

On the same point of overpowering spectators, Pedro and Claudio witness to the influence of "noting practices." When Claudio and Don Pedro are invited by Borachio "to see her / chamber window entered" on the night before Hero weds, Claudio replies: "If I *see* anything tonight why I should not marry her, tomorrow in the congregation, where I should wed, there will I *shame* her" (*Much Ado*, 3.2.106–7; 3.2.117–19). Sight as the basis for shaming Hero illustrates how Claudio conflates perception and judgment, making them one, a sign of Claudio's inability to recognize the distinction between practices and reality. Don Pedro concurs, replying "let the issue *show* itself" (3.2.123–24).[53] After Borachio's spectacle, Claudio and Pedro leave enraged. Claudio subsequently shames Hero with a bad pun on his wedding day for all Messina to hear, "O Hero, what a Hero hadst thou been / If half thy outward graces had been placed / About thy thoughts and counsels of thy heart!" (4.1.100–103). Like the gulling scenes of Benedick and Beatrice, Claudio is overwhelmed by what is performed for him.

Yet if acting practices corrupt audience members, especially in comedies, because of how spectators observe practices, Benedick and Beatrice's change in behavior could also represent the position of apologists of theater. For the infections they contract are salutary ones. Heywood models his own reply to arguments like those of Reynolds after Philip Sidney's own *Defense of Poetry*, which taught that comedy chastened or corrected behavior for the sake of improving audience members. Heywood summarizes Sidney's teaching: "We present men with the ugliness of their vices, to make them the more abhor them."[54] Sidney's original formulation was that "comedy is an imitation of the common errors of our life, which he [the playwright] representeth in the most ridiculous and scornful sort that may be, so as it is impossible that *any beholder* can be content to be such a one."[55] With both Heywood and Sidney's teaching in mind, Pedro's gulling of Benedick, as in the case of Ursula and Hero's condemnation of Beatrice's pride, proves to be corrective. Benedick becomes Sidney's "beholder," who hears how he is censured and changes. When Pedro concludes the gulling scene with an Elizabethan *sententia*—or a "sentence" that hints at "a motif underlying a scene"—he proclaims: "I love Benedick well, / and I could wish he would modestly examine himself, to see how much he is unworthy so good a lady" (2.3.205–7).[56] Benedick responds in soliloquy thereafter: "I must not seem proud; happy are they that hear their detractions and can put them to mending" (2.3.224–26). In these words, Benedick again represents an audience member who views performances as truthful representation because he takes Pedro's players to speak in earnest. Even so, Benedick's perception of what is staged allows him to grow in self-knowledge and to profess resolutions of amendment. Likewise, Beatrice follows the staged denunciation of herself, with questions: "What fire is in mine ears? Can this be true? / Stand I condemned for pride and scorn so much?" She already knows the answer and, therefore, will "tame" her "wild heart" to Bendick's "loving hand" (3.1.107–12). It is her question—"Can this be true?"—that captures my point. To accept as truth what was staged before her compares to Benedick's statement that his own gulling scene was "no trick." Both of these gulls suggest the argument that an audience member's inability to recognize the artifice of performance need not produce moral harm. The stage, like Prospero's island, is full of sounds that give delight and hurt not.

If Benedick and Beatrice, ultimately, enact defenses of the theater in terms of how they respond to gulling scenes, Don Pedro and Claudio emerge as counterpoints. The plot of Borachio, staging Hero's infidelity at the window, allies Claudio's perspective with that of early modern audiences and parallels the antitheatrical argument about how "practices" corrupt spectators. The essential question for Borachio's gambit to work is whether Margaret plays Hero convincingly, which is precisely what Conrade asks Borachio, "And thought they Margaret was Hero?" Borachio replies the Prince and Claudio did so, whether because of the "oaths" alleging infidelity already had partially convinced them or the darkness of the night aided the illusion (3.3.152–56). The crucial question about Margaret's appearance, it turns out, is one about lifelike personation. Modern directors answer it by mitigating the guilt of Claudio, staging the window scene with Margaret dressed in Hero's clothes, or casting Margaret as one who looks similar to Hero, or even having the same person play both Margaret and Hero.[57] Yet the point is that Claudio, like an audience member characterized in the antitheatrical tracts, represents a spectator easily overpowered by the stage's "practices."

Both in *Much Ado* and in the theatrical debate literature, spectators are overcome by the performance of passions, which they then assimilate. From a moral point of view, characters as beholders, perhaps, should take representation "in earnest," as in the cases of Benedick and Beatrice, yet beholders should also suspect it as feigning, as Claudius might have done in response to Borachio's ruse. In *Much Ado*, no matter how characters *should* note practices, they always find performance as credible or constitutive of real life rather than mere fiction. The internal dramas amplify and celebrate the theatre's importance precisely because stagecraft is capable of such *deceptio visus*, a deceptive vision that transforms audiences by infecting them with passions, just like those characters who are gulled on stage become infected. In this sense, the Puritan critique remains present in *Much Ado*, but is transformed into a simple affirmation of theatrical power upon spectators.

ONSTAGE AUDIENCES MEMBERS OR OFFSTAGE CHARACTERS

The affirmation of theatrical power in terms of an audiences' vulnerability makes the internal dramas of *Much Ado* slightly different from those that precede it in Shakespeare's canon. Similar to Shakespeare's earlier versions of plays within plays, like that of Pyramus and Thisbe from *A Midsummer Night's Dream* or the Nine Worthies in *Love's Labour's Lost*, internal dramas in *Much Ado* are "jests" that can pose so-called metatheatrical questions, which explore the significance of "counterfeiting" passions, motives, and action. In earlier playlets, however, the onstage audiences are limited to occasional comments and criticisms, which voice educated criticism or cutting humor in reply to amateur performances. Neither are these onstage audience members the focus of the internal drama. Bottom wishes to perform for Theseus, but Pedro wants his practice to transform Benedick. Holofernes might be proud of his elocution, but Borachio performs to move Claudio. Thus, the characters who represent onstage audiences in *Much Ado* pose an alternate representation of theater. Audience members are no longer aristocrats, who criticize productions according to refined aesthetics, but appear more like ordinary playgoers, "noting practices" that they take for truths.[58]

Once again, the influence of performance upon playgoers returns. "If both the Puritans and their adversaries were willing to argue publicly that a play could affect reality and the lives of its audience," Jeremy Lopez argues, "it seems more than safe that this kind of assumption playgoers would have brought with them to the playhouse."[59] With such "safe" assumptions in mind, Benedick, Beatrice, Pedro, or Claudio's responses to practices within the play represent the emotional contagions of persons because of the theater they witness, just like what supposedly occurs at the very Globe theater where *Much Ado* is performed. When Philip Stubbes attacks the performance of plays in his *Anatomy of Abuses* (1583), he decries the theater for "such wanton gestures, such bawdy speeches, such laughing and fleering . . . such winking and glancing of wanton eyes . . . as is wonderful to behold."[60] Though such a description might capture Borachio's idea for how to stage Hero's infidelity, as Anthony Dawson observes of early modern audiences, Stubbes's comments "make it difficult to distinguish playhouse behavior from on-stage impersonation; the two become so entangled that real and fictional are interwoven, and the stage spectacle curves around to include that within the house—both are 'wonderful to behold.'"[61] To curve the stage spectacle around so that it may include the house, Shakespeare dramatizes scenes of emotional transport, incorporating the points of antitheatrical polemicists by depicting their point of view in his characters who behold gulling scenes.

In scripting dramatic persons of Messina who represent the attributes of Elizabethan playgoers, *Much Ado* becomes an object lesson in what Brett Gamboa calls "Shakespeare's 'real'" or "the paradox of the audience." For Gamboa, actual audiences constitute the "locus of reality in the theatre" even though "its experience of the real is synonymous with its experience of instability." The experience of instability arises due to the fact that "Shakespeare repeatedly advertises the artifice of his actor/characters" and "risks metatheatrical references that may undercut any pretense at realism." At the same time, Shakespeare's scenes of explicit theatricality can result in "an audience ever more intensely engaged in a theatrical illusion as that illusion more vigorously confesses itself as one."[62] In *Much Ado*, the contrast between the internal dramas and those characters who judge or respond to these practices creates ruptures in the illusion of Messina by exposing how performances are deceptive and pointing out how untrue or feigned passions transfer to onstage audiences. Put differently, gulling scenes manage and direct audiences' attention such that what they see is a representation of what they may be doing as beholders.

The gulling scenes, as a result, offer us another vantage point from which to understand Shakespeare's composition of person-effects. Simon Palfrey remarks how the last twenty years of criticism resists identification between "a staged body and a correspondent individuality," a resistance he applauds. "We posit a unified individual 'behind' the words spoken and acts performed," and, in so doing, "we project our own presupposed idea of selfhood—our intuitive trust in a self-present 'I'—onto dramatic personae." For Palfrey, such projection contradicts "character as a textual or dramatic construct," a "network of signs," as "specific dramatic machinery takes the place of psychology, motivation, and self-image." Palfrey, in these contexts, rightly advocates that contemporary audiences and critics should "de-naturalise" the ways they think about characters.[63]

Yet even so, the extension of dramatic personhood beyond the stage need not invoke Cartesian ideas of selfhood but, instead, demonstrate how Shakespeare conflates onstage personations with particular and actual playhouse behaviors. Dramatic persons, in these select instances, are composed to appear from time to time as if they speak independently of the play's fictional locality or dramatic action. Such a person-effect, as in the case of *Much Ado*, is a function of gulling scenes and how Shakespeare's inscribes qualifies that imitate early modern audience members into some of his dramatic persons. By presenting characters with privileged positions of judgment in relation to the internal dramas of Pedro or Don John, Shakespeare invites audiences to think of onstage spectators as persons not unlike those standing or seated next them, people of the theater in the broadest sense, those gulled by counterfeit action and infected with passions. In the responses of Benedick and Beatrice or Claudio and Pedro to what is performed for their sakes, characters direct attention to fictionality upon the stage while speaking from the fictive world of Messina. In doing so, these characters possess a dual mimetic functionality—as playgoer and character, onstage audience member and offstage character—that enhances the illusion that there isn't a difference between the "staged body" and the "real" ones that behold the stage.

In cases like these, the supposition that a staged body exists apart from the materiality of the theater would not be an imposition of Cartesian thought upon the early modern period, but the result of how Shakespeare distances characters from fictionality in order to create the illusion that some characters speak and act in nontheatrical or nonrepresentational modes. In the debate over personation, whether it evolves in the late sixteenth century or not, *Much Ado* shows how Shakespeare does not need a new acting style apart from the rhetorical one because he designs his drama so that some dramatic persons might not appear like actors.

NOTES

1. See "personate" as a transitive verb, 4.a, in the *OED*, which means: "to act or play the part of (a character in a play, etc.)." The *OED* gives Florio's definition, cited above, as its example. On the dating of Shakespeare plays, see Michael Dobson, (ed.), *The Oxford Companion to Shakespeare* (Oxford: Oxford University Press, 2001), 533.

2. Nova Myhill, "Spectatorship in/of *Much Ado about Nothing*," *SEL Studies in English Literature 1500–1900* 39, no. 2 (1999): 294. For a historical overview and critical summary of the composition, tastes, and behavior of early modern audiences, see Siobhan Keenan, *Acting Companies and their Plays in Shakespeare's London* (London: Bloomsbury Arden Shakespeare, 2014), 133–57; and Andrew Gurr, *The Shakespearean Stage 1574–1642* (Cambridge, UK: Cambridge University Press, 2009), 258–85.

3. James Calderwood, *Shakespearean Metadrama: The Argument of the Play in Titus Andronicus, Love's Labour's Lost, Romeo and Juliet, A Midsummer Night's Dream, and Richard II* (Minneapolis: University of Minnesota Press, 1971), 5. Calderwood defines Shakespeare's representation of "dramatic art" in terms of "its materials, its media of language and theater, its generic forms and conventions, its relationship to truth and the social order." See, too, Pauline Kiernan's discussion in "'O'er-wrested seeming': dramatic illusion and the repudiation of mimesis. 'Love's Labour's Lost', 'A Midsummer Night's Dream' and 'Hamlet,'" in *Shakespeare's Theory of Drama* (Cambridge, UK: Cambridge University Press, 1996), 91–126.

4. All citations from Shakespeare are from *The Complete Works of William Shakespeare*, 5th ed., ed. David Bevington (New York: Longman, 2004). For the above, see *Twelfth Night*, 2.3.133–35. Hereafter cited internally.

5. See "gull," v.3 in the *OED*.

6. Jonson is cited from Gurr, *The Shakespearean Stage*, 118, who adds that acting "occasionally used a verbal form of the noun generally used for the 'action' of the orator, his art of gesture. What the common stages offered was mere 'playing.'"

7. Most critics today agree that acting theory evolves in the 1590s. Gurr, Jane Donawerth, Robert Weimann, and Douglas Bruster, all of whom are cited below, argue how Shakespearean characterization or personation grows in refinement or individualization over and against the practice of rhetorical *actio*.

8. Thomas Heywood, "An Apology for Actors (1612)," in *Shakespeare's Theater: A Sourcebook*, ed. Tanya Pollard (Oxford: Blackwell Publishing, 2004), 220.

9. Heywood, "An Apology for Actors (1612)," 221.

10. Robert Weimann and Douglas Bruster, *Shakespeare and the Power of Performance* (Cambridge, UK: Cambridge University Press, 2010), 143.

11. Gurr, *The Shakespearean Stage*, 99.

12. Andrew Gurr, "Elizabethan Action," *Studies in Philology* 63, no. 2 (1966): 144–56. Though Gurr recycles his 1966 argument in *The Shakespearean Stage* (2009), it still rests upon questionable assumptions that academic and commercial theater practices were isolated from one another or at variance. On the players and academic training, see John H. Astington, *Actors and Acting in Shakespeare's Time* (Cambridge, UK: Cambridge University Press, 2010), 39–75; see, too, Martin Wiggins, *Shakespeare and the Drama of his Time* (Oxford: Oxford University Press, 2000), 16–17: "However, it is all too easy to overemphasize the differences between the various institutions producing drama, at the expense of the associations between them." Wiggins argues for a close relationship between universities and playhouses.

13. Weimann and Bruster, *Shakespeare and the Power of Performance*, 145 and 160.

14. The distinction between "lively" and "lifelike" belongs to Jane L. Donawerth, "Shakespeare and Acting Theory in the English Renaissance," in *Shakespeare and the Arts: A Collection of Essays from the Ohio Shakespeare Conference, 1981 Wright State University, Dayton Ohio*, ed. Cecile Williamson Cary and Henry S. Limouze (Washington, DC: University Press of America, 1982), 169.

15. On the supposed differences between Edward Alleyn and Richard Burbage, the two leading actors of the Elizabethan stage, see A. J. Gurr, "Who Strutted and Bellowed?" in *Shakespeare Survey*, vol. 16 (Cambridge, UK: Cambridge University Press), 95–102.

16. Heywood, "An Apology for Actors (1612)," 227.

17. Compare Heywood's summary with the five canons of rhetoric from *Rhetorica Ad Herennium*, 1.2.3. For discussion, see Peter Mack, *Elizabethan Rhetoric: Theory and Practice* (Cambridge, UK: Cambridge University Press, 2002), 9–47.

18. Cicero, *De Oratore*, trans. E. W. Sutton and H. Rackha. (Cambridge, MA: Harvard University Press, 1996), 3.55.213.

19. Heywood, "An Apology for Actors (1612)," 228.

20. Heywood, "An Apology for Actors (1612)," 227.

21. John Rainolds, "The Overthrow of Stage-Plays (1599)," in Pollard, *Shakespeare's Theater*, 174.

22. Shakespeare's Julia, too, explicitly uses "lively" to indicate a "lifelike" performance, linking what she calls the "passioning" of a role with "lively" acting. If Rainolds focuses upon the impact to actors, Julia's words capture the connection between playing passion, lively acting, and how it would or should impact audiences:

> For I did play a lamentable part:
> Madam, 'twas Ariadne, passioning
> For Theseus' perjury and unjust flight;
> Which I so lively acted with my tears
> That my poor mistress, moved therewithal,
> Wept bitterly; and would I might be dead
> If I in thought felt not her very sorrow. (*The Two Gentlemen of Verona*, 4.4.165–71)

23. Gurr, "Elizabethan Action," 149, summarizes: "From the 1580's 'lively' was the simplest term of praise for acting, always meaning 'life-like,' the sense in which it applied to the sister-art of the miniaturist; and 'life' was the theatre's basic criterion."

His article documents this case often from authors who associate acting with oratory, thereby undercutting his thesis that personation constitutes a new form of lifelike performance.

24. For Heywood's teaching about personable men, see "Apology for Actors (1612)," 233. On the term "typecasting," I follow Simon Palfrey and Tiffany Stern, *Shakespeare in Parts* (Oxford: Oxford University Press, 2007), 44: "typecasting was a primary feature of the early modern theatre, in that actors were cast along the lines of personality 'type.' Thus the fat and exuberant had fat exuberant parts given them, while the lean and melancholy had lean melancholic types to perform. This is not quite the same as modern typecasting, where an actor has a character he is to play all the time."

25. Heywood, "Apology for Actors (1612)," 233. On how chief actors were cast in major parts, see T. J. King's evidence in *Casting Shakespeare's Plays* (Cambridge: Cambridge University Press, 1992), 17.

26. Heywood, "Apology for Actors (1612)," 233–34.

27. On imagination and "lively" acting, see Thomas Wright, *The Passions of the Minde in Generall: A Reprint Based on the 1604 Edition* (Urbana: University of Illinois Press, 1971), 124: "The rhetoricians likewise do not content themselves with the simple pronunciation of their orations, but also prescribe many rules of action, the which they hold so much the better, how much more *lively* it represents *the conceits and affections of the mind*." I have transliterated Wright's quotation into modern English. For early though still useful discussion of Wright's teaching in regard to rhetoric and to Shakespeare's acting style, see Bertram Joseph, "Action and the Word," in *Acting Shakespeare* (New York: Theatre Arts Books, 1969), 82–109; for recent analysis in light of poetics, see Luis Martínez Zenón, "Macbeth and the Passions' 'Proper Stuff,'" *SEDERI* 20 (2010): 71–101. Of importance and in contrast to critics who argue that personation is a new acting style, Bertram believes the rhetorical technique would supply naturalistic effects.

28. Heywood, "Apology for Actors (1612)," 226.

29. John F. Cox (ed.), *Shakespeare in Production: Much Ado About Nothing* (Cambridge, UK: Cambridge University Press, 1997), 2.3n101.

30. Hugh Macrae Richmond, *Shakespeare's Theatre: A Dictionary of his Stage Context* (London and New York: Continuum, 2004), 355.

31. Mary Thomas Crane, "What was Performance?" *Criticism* 43, no. 2 (2001): 169–87, especially her assessment at 175: "Words such as 'exercise,' 'practice,' and 'quality' tend to be used by defenders of the theatre, although its enemies also use them and contest their meanings."

32. See "practice" in the *OED*, n.1.

33. See Hanna Scolnicov, "The Woman in the Window: A Theatrical Icon," in *Spectacle and Image in Renaissance Europe: Selected Papers of the XXXIInd Conference at the Centre d'études supérieures de la Renaissance de Tours, 29 June–8 July 1988*, ed. André Lascombes, 281–305 (Leiden: Brill, 1993), 284.

34. Scolnicov discusses both examples in "The Woman in the Window," 287–93.

35. On how window scenes explore moral agency, see Cynthia Lewis, "'You were an actor with your handkerchief': Women, Windows, and Moral Agency," *Comparative Drama* 43, no. 4 (2009): 473–96.

36. For Borachio's lines in *OED* as an instance of "practice" as a noun, see 2.c; for Pedro's usage, see 9.a.

37. Stephen Gosson, "Plays Confuted in Five Actions (1582)," in Pollard, *Shakespeare's Theater*, 108–9, my emphasis.

38. John Northbrooke, "A Treatise Against Dicing, Dancing, Plays, and Interludes, with Other Idle Pastimes (1577)," in Pollard, *Shakespeare's Theater*, 15, my emphasis.

39. See, for example, Rainolds's admonition in "The Overthrow of Stage-Plays (1599)," 175: "Seeing that diseases of the mind are gotten far sooner by *counterfeiting* than are diseases of the body, and bodily diseases may be gotten so, as appeareth by

him, who, feigning for a purpose that he was sick of the gout, became (through care of *counterfeiting* it) gouty in deed. So much can imitation and mediation do."

40. For the "practice of parasites" and the "practice of a diligent captain," see Thomas Lodge, "A Reply to Stephen Gosson's School of Abuse, in Defence of Poetry, Music, and Stage Plays (1579)," in Pollard, *Shakespeare's Theater*, 55, 40.

41. Jean E. Howard, "Renaissance Antitheatricality and the Politics of Gender and Rank in *Much Ado About Nothing*," in *Shakespeare Reproduced: The Text in History and Ideology*, ed. Jean E. Howard and Marion F. O'Connor (New York: Methuen, 1987), 169.

42. Gosson, "Plays Confuted," 99.

43. Gosson, "Plays Confuted," 108.

44. Anthony Munday, "A Second and Third Blast of Retreat from Plays and Theaters (1580)," in Pollard, *Shakespeare's Theater*, 78.

45. Because of the play's emphasis upon self-conscious fictionality, commentators typically address *Much Ado about Nothing* in terms of ethical or epistemological categories, probing the importance of detecting illusions or deceptions. For examples in addition to Myhill, see Richard Henze, "Deception in *Much Ado about Nothing*," *Studies in English Literature, 1500–1900* 11, no. 2 (1971): 187–201; Carl Dennis, "Wit and Wisdom in *Much Ado about Nothing*," *Studies in English Literature, 1500–1900* 13, no. 2 (1973): 223–37; Carol Cook, "'The Sign and Semblance of Her Honor': Reading Gender Difference in *Much Ado about Nothing*," *PMLA* 101, no. 2 (1986): 186–202.

46. See 3.2.1–68 for signs of Benedick's transformation.

47. On the transfer of passions from the stage to those who observe performances, see Joseph R. Roach, *The Player's Passion: Studies in the Science of Acting* (Ann Arbor: University of Michigan Press, 1993), 27. Gulling scenes may function as an example of what Dawson calls "scopic management," which direct audiences' attention for the sake of "collective" engagement. For Anthony Dawson, "the primary medium for that management was the actor's body in concert with the poet's text; it was the 'player's passion,' i.e., the act of embodied personation leading toward an ethos of participation" [Anthony Dawson and Paul Yachnin, *The Culture of Playgoing in Shakespeare's England: A Collaborative Debate* (Cambridge, UK: Cambridge University Press, 2001), 96–97].

48. For an account of the "emotional collectivity" of early modern audiences in terms of the contagion of passions, see Allison P. Hobgood, *Passionate Playgoing in Early Modern England* (Cambridge, UK: Cambridge University Press, 2014), 28–30.

49. The "vulnerability of the spectator" was ubiquitous. As Siobhan Keenan summarizes "what evidence we have about audience responses tends to emphasize the communal nature of the theatrical experience, contemporaries often describing collective experiences" in Keenan, *Acting Companies and their Plays in Shakespeare's London*, 147.

50. Munday, "A Second and Third Blast," 76; my emphasis on "jest."

51. For a list of denotations for "noting" in regard to the play's title, see Marjorie Garber, *Shakespeare After All* (New York: Pantheon Books, 2004), 379–80.

52. Stephen Greenblatt, introduction to Stephen Greenblatt et al., *The Norton Shakespeare: Based on the Oxford Edition*, first edition (W. W. Norton & Company, 1997), 1409.

53. The emphasis is mine in both quotations.

54. Heywood, "Apology for Actors (1612)," 244.

55. Philip Sidney, "An Apology for Poetry (1595)," in Pollard, *Shakespeare's Theater*, 150.

56. The quotation on sententia is from Joseph, *Elizabethan Acting*, 63.

57. For analysis of Claudio's performance in light of modern productions, see Michael D. Friedman, "'Get thee a wife, get thee a wife!': *Much Ado About Nothing*," in *The World Must Be Peopled: Shakespeare's Comedies of Forgiveness* (London: Associated University Presses, 2002), 76–11.

58. Characters who play onstage audiences in *Much Ado* and seemingly invoke *platea* space do so while remaining in character. D. J. Hopkins, "Performance and Urban Space in Shakespeare's Rome, or 'S.P.Q.L.'" in *Rematerializing Shakespeare: Au-*

thority and Representation on the Early Modern Stage, eds. Bryan Reynolds and William N. West (New York: Palgrave Macmillan, 2005), 43–44, reminds us that the *platea* is "produced by early modern actors when they acknowledged the actual event of performance while performing in relation to a representational event." Speaking from the *platea*, therefore, allows playwrights and performers "opportunities to engage the audience, to comment ironically upon the action of the narrative, and (not unimportantly) to make a joke." Yet there is a crucial caveat or disqualification of *platea* discourse in the case of *Much Ado*. To illustrate by way of example, Benedick's monologue in response to Pedro's internal drama about Beatrice's love may recognize and engage audience members in direct address, but when and if the actor breaks "the fourth wall" I argue that he should do so in the voice of the character he plays. Such direct address of audiences, if and when it occurs, does not strictly constitute conventional *platea* discourse because the actor would employ such slippages on behalf of the play's fiction. The actor would not break character but enact Benedick in more than one role, that is, as a character who plays an audience member and vice-versa. On the point of identification in regard to the *platea*, see Robert Weimann, *Author's Pen and Actor's Voice: Playing and Writing in Shakespeare's Theatre*, ed. Helen Higbee and William West (Cambridge, UK: Cambridge University Press, 2000), 196, who explains that the *platea* is where actors, "more often than not" were "*not* entirely prepared to sink themselves into their roles" (my emphasis).

59. Jeremy Lopez, *Theatrical Convention and Audience Response in Early Modern England* (Cambridge, UK: Cambridge University Press, 2003), 31.

60. Philip Stubbes, "Anatomy of Abuses (1583)" in Pollard, *Shakespeare's Theater*, 121.

61. Dawson and Yachnin, *Culture of Playgoing*, 91.

62. Brett Gamboa, "'Is't real that I see?': Staged Realism and the Paradox of Shakespeare's Audience," *Shakespeare Bulletin* 31, no. 4 (2013): 676–77.

63. Simon Palfrey, *Doing Shakespeare* (London: Arden, 2011), 223, 321–22.

FOUR

Iago's Acting Style

The critical argument about early modern acting styles originates with the distinction between "naturalism" and "formalism"; an opposition that I would like to dispute by examining how Iago may be played as a type character.[1] The influence of typological character—passing through Menander, Plautus, Terence, and Cicero to poets in early modern England—has long been recognized, an influence that comes not only from playwrights, but also and especially from classical rhetoric, its figures of speech, and a variety of ethical or poetic treatises.[2] So, too, we are assured that characters based on early modern social roles, allegory, or types do not possess the "interiority" or "subjectivity" often attributed to them.[3] "Types" are not sufficiently "rounded" or multidimensional to capture a Hamlet or an Iago. If William Shakespeare began with types, he must have transformed them, "stretching character," creating a space for later and more complex representations of "subjectivity."[4] Hence, how one plays a character indicates how one theorizes character, but, more particularly, we encounter the implication that type should be considered distinct from more individual and natural portrayals. Type characters are not lifelike but cartoonish. Iago's malice, after all, strikes many as an incredible depiction of any real person.[5]

Even so, I will argue that type as an indication of a rhetorical or formal acting style does not adequately account for how type characters may be performed. "Modern concepts," argues Edward Burns, "like 'the stereotype'" or "E. M. Forster's 'flat characters'" involve a misunderstanding of the ancient traditions out of which typology emerges. Burns writes of the ancient "character sketch" that it "derives from its schematisation of the social codes of character—dress codes, typical behavior, common physical types, and so on—a flexible basis for the articulation of character as social interaction, as implicated in the knowledge of a particular world."[6]

As a flexible basis for the portrayal of specific traits, I will sketch one possible realization of the flatterer type by retracing the links between Plutarch's description of a flatterer and how that account could function as a resource for playing Iago. By first examining Shakespeare's Iago in light of Plutarch's explanation, and then reviewing how figures of "auricular defect"—"stops" or pauses—could aid a performance of *Othello* act 3, scene 3, I will propose how playing Iago according to type would contribute to the illusion of credible and sincere friendship between Othello and Iago. Though "stops" or silences are part of the conventional rhetoric of flatterers, even a strategy of "dilation" crucial to the play's narrative, they correspond with the later, distinctly modern directions and points of emphasis for playing Iago written by the famous Shakespearean actor, Edwin Booth.[7] As we shall see, both the figures of "auricular defect" and Booth's prompts are a function of how Shakespeare inscribes the flatterer's specific characterological attribute—the pretense of friendship—into Iago's dramatic person.[8]

FLATTERERS AND FRIENDS

In locating an important source behind the character of Iago, Paul Jorgensen recommends that Iago's "honesty" be looked for in "the widespread and urgent Elizabethan problem: How may one know the honest man from the knave?"[9] Warnings about knaves, dissemblers, and flatterers often particularly described their tactics, providing an itinerary of identifiable traits, which Iago would seem to represent. More recently, Robert Evans has focused attention on Iago in light of Plutarch's distinction between flatterers and true friends from Philemon Holland's translation of Plutarch's essay on how "To Discern a Flatterer from a Friend."[10] Rather than simply identifying the flatterer with comely, ingratiating speech, Plutarch amplifies the similarities between a true friend and a flatterer who plays one. It is a "hard matter" to "discern a flatterer from a friend" because it appears "there is no difference between them."[11] Plutarch means there is no difference in outward behavior between friend and enemy because the "right flatterer" employs covert sycophancy, practicing as "his own craftmaster, and can skill how to handle the matter artificially" (41).[12] Craft, skill, and artifice all indicate flattery as an art form, a performance of friendship.

Plutarch's assessment of covert sycophancy corresponds with other depictions in which the flatterer possesses what Christy Desmet calls the capacity to use "effectively the gestures and props of an actor," thereby playing a friend or advisor in a credible manner. Indeed, the flatterer's ability to deceive contributed to an early modern preoccupation with his "rhetorical gestures."[13] As Evans shows, Plutarch's flatterer *plays* a friend by pretending to find lies, comely discourse, and superficialities detestable; such a posture is necessary to conceal deception. The flatterer's "whole study is to win the name and reputation of a man that hateth vice" (63). Thus, Plutarch writes that flatterers "have learned forsooth to knit and bend the brows" and "look with a frowning face and crabbed countenance," mixing "glavering glozes" with "rough reprehensions and chiding cheeks." These histrionics are supposed to create a persona that is "rough, violent, and inexorable in all dealings with others," employing what we may think of as *display candor* for the purpose of deception.

Iago's own use of display candor is the most obvious element of his relationship to the flatterer type, epitomized best, perhaps, by his statement—"For I am nothing if not critical."[14] Iago makes this confession before exchanging "praises" with Desdemona about the nature of women, employing the "rough reprehensions" and "chiding cheeks" that indicate a man unafraid to speak harshly despite decorum. Even "deserving women," Iago ultimately claims, "suckle fools, and chronicle small beer" (2.1.159–60). Although Desdemona responds to Iago's words by calling him a "profane and liberal counsellor," Cassio interprets the matter differently. He parses Iago's harsh words: "He speaks home, madam, you may relish him more in the soldier than in the scholar" (2.1.165–66). E. A. J. Honigmann glosses "home" as "directly, to the point," which is a polite way of describing the "rough, violent, and inexorable" manner that Plutarch's flatterer takes up to "win the name and reputation of a man that hateth vice."[15] Iago uses display candor to suggest to others that he is in possession of a kind of virtue. Thus, A. C. Bradley writes of Iago: "In fact, he was one of those sterling men who, in disgust at gush, say cynical things which they do not believe, and then, the moment you are in trouble, put in practice the very sentiment they had laughed at. On such occasions he showed the kindliest sympathy and the most eager desire to help." Iago here represents a "blunt, bluff soldier" who "spoke his mind freely," though he was "not seldom rather rough and caustic of speech."[16] Iago's display candor, then, appears to have taken in at least partially Bradley himself. Bradley's response to Iago illustrates how a typological character's histrionic essence as a flatterer might strike character critics as novelistic or lifelike. He finds Iago's words a sign of "cynicism," which constitutes an outlook that disguises hidden, meritorious qualities like "sympathy." Yet the situation is almost the precise opposite. Iago plays the honest man of rough speech, a pretense Cassio mistakes for a candid and unlearned soldier. The reason why Cassio mistakes Iago's character is the same one that defines Iago's type: Flatters perform candor in a lifelike way.

For Plutarch, a flatterer behaves in a rough manner in imitation of the honesty that constitutes a true mark of friendship. Such a teaching on the importance of candor is an ancient commonplace, which both Aristotle and Cicero address along with the qualities of "good will" or "benevolence." Because the manifestation of candor, good will, and friendship contribute to appeals from *ethos* or *pathos*, each or any of these attributes are considered part of persuasion's arts. So, too, the same traits may become character-effects of the flatterer's use of persuasion.

In the *Rhetoric*, Aristotle distinguishes between good will and friendship, identifying good will as part of *ethos* and friendship as part of *pathos*. Good will emerges from speech that persuades an audience that its best interests are the speaker's aim; such benevolence inspires trust and thereby evokes assent.[17] Yet Aristotle also connects good will to an appeal from *pathos* that emphasizes friendship. He writes: "Good will and friendliness of disposition will form part of our discussion of the emotions, to which we must now turn."[18] Of significance, emotions are defined as "all those feelings that so change men as to affect their judgments."[19] In terms of flattery, appeals that manifest good will or friendship are a speaker's technical means of self-fashioning.

For Cicero, too, good will intrinsically relates to honesty, telling the truth without fear or favor.[20] "It is characteristic of true friendship both to give and to receive advice," writes Cicero, and to do so with "all freedom of speech"; as a result, "nothing is to be considered a greater bane of friendship than fawning, cajolery, or flattery."[21] Honesty, in this account, exists in tandem with the ability to give "good advice," but advice includes persuasion as well because it belongs to the orator's office to provide prudent and eloquent counsel. A speaker's projection of good will in giving advice, then, constitutes an ingredient of *ethos* as well as of friendship, an appeal from *pathos*. Within the Ciceronian tradition, an emphasis upon honesty in friendship finds its parallel in oratory because both friend and orator should enact the role of "good man."[22]

That persuasive, flatterer type—the pose of a "good man" and the practice of display candor—Plutarch combines with a specific area in which flatterers are prone to play the false friend and give harmful, though persuasive, advice: In matters of love. In a passage that Evans identifies as a "thumb-nail summary of the plot" of Iago's persuasion of Othello in act 3, scene 3, Plutarch writes that flatterers excel

> in amatorious and love matters . . . : there you shall have them most of all to come over those whom they flatter and lay on load; to them they will join close, and set them on flaming fire. For if they see brethren at some variance, or setting nought by their parents, or else to deal unkindly with their own wives, and to set no store by them, or to be jealous and suspicious of them; they never admonish, chastise, or rebuke them for it, that they may amend, but rather they will kindle more coals between, and increase their anger and discontentment on both sides. (66)[23]

In matters of love, Plutarch believes the flatterer will use the rhetoric of friendship in order to "set brethren at variance" or, more relevant, to "deal unkindly" with wives. That template, using friendship as persuasion to turn one against a spouse, not only is Iago's work, but also part of his genealogy as a flattering type. Yet to be persuasive, so Plutarch thought, the flatterer must appear credible, a person whose friendship would appear authentic to those whom he wishes to deceive.

RHETORICAL FIGURES AND FLATTERY

Flatterers introduce a division between seeming and being, inner and outer, what is intended and what is conveyed through speech, a set of oppositions that require attention for performance. In act 3, scene 3, Iago's own advising of Othello employs figures of "auricular defect," a rhetorical approach that enacts the wiles of false friendship described by Plutarch. Iago observes Cassio's departure from Desdemona with the exclamation, "Ha, I like not that." Othello replies, "What dost thou say?" And Iago rejoins: "Nothing, my lord; or if – I know not what" (3.3.34–36). Iago's initial "Ha" is a *praecisio*, which Thomas Wilson calls "A Stop, or Half Telling of a Tale." It occurs "when we break off our tale before we have told it."[24] That "half telling" George Puttenham describes as *aposiopesis*, "another auricular figure of defect," which occurs when "we begin to speak a thing and break off in the middle way, as if either it needed no further to be spoken of, or that we were ashamed or afraid to speak it out."[25] These figures of speech direct or cue the actor in performance of passions, like Puttenham's shame or fear, which in the context of the scene transforms Iago into a reluctant speaker. In fact, the rest of Iago and Othello's exchange displays a series of "stops" that indicate how performing a typological Iago could occur:

> Iago: I did not think he [Cassio] had been acquainted with her.
> Othello: O yes, and went between us very oft.
> Iago: Indeed?
> Othello: Indeed? Ay, indeed. Discern'st thou aught in that?
> Is he not honest?
> Iago: Honest, my lord?
> Othello: Honest? Ay, honest.
> Iago: My lord, for aught I know.
> Othello: What dost thou think?
> Iago: Think, my lord? (3.3.99–108)

Iago's interrogative stops above combine the display candor of the flattering type with conventional figures of persuasion, indicating a rhetorical acting style. Yet the figures that signal the withholding of information or speech also cue the performance of passions; the performance of such "withholding" because of feigned feelings of shame or fear in the speaker invite audiences and Othello to infer or imagine interior designs or motives that belong to Iago.

Tiffany Stern has added to the picture of this kind of rhetorical acting style by suggesting "study" — referring both to "private learning" and to "learning with a teacher" — as a term better suited than "rehearsal" to describe how a Shakespearean actor would prepare.[26] Study would be the means of suiting the word to the gesture, and here the actor followed "the classical rhetorical tradition," which emphasized "action," or the "physical side," including gesture and facial expression, and "pronunciation," including cadence and figures of speech.[27] "Study for early actors, as much as for those of the post-Stanislavski generations," comments John H. Astington, "necessarily meant the assumption of character and emotional temperature as they proceeded, rereading and checking back to the scrolls of paper which gave a map to compelling vocalization and embodiment, accent and action, the life of the stage characters they committed themselves to play."[28] More specifically, stops or pauses, speculates Stern with Simon Palfrey, were determined less by the punctuation observed in the actor's part-text, and more by that "private 'study' and 'instruction'" where the actor would determine how pauses would facilitate rhetoric's art of persuasion.[29] Pronunciation and gesticulation, too, were part of the process in which "passions" and "humors" — or transitions from one passion to another — would be identified.[30] Palfrey and Stern note how players "were famous," in particular, "for contrasting words and stops with magnificent grandeur."[31] Like new or long words, stops could provide opportunities for performative flourish, displaying "passion," and the players' rhetorical training or study made them keen observers of such chances.

The context provided by Stern and Palfrey helps explain the exchange between Iago and Othello cited above in which stops and directions for emotional expression are associated through figures of speech. In reply to Othello's questions, Iago says: "Nothing, my lord; or if – I know not what." That stop is the *aporia*. According to Puttenham, the *aporia* should be called "the doubtful." He explains: "because oftentimes we will seem to cast perils and make doubt of things, when by a plain manner of speech we may affirm or deny him."[32] Likewise, in reply to Othello's question — "Honest? Ay, honest" — Iago's rejoinder, "my Lord for aught I know," illustrates *epitropis*, a figure in which Puttenham describes speakers who for "manner sake," and to avoid troubling "the judge or hearer with all that we could say," rest content with "having said enough already."[33] In the uses of any or some of the tropes for suggestive stops, we find connections between linguistic feature, what we have seen is related to "pronunciation," and passion or emotion, all of which prescribe how an actor may play a character, such that Iago feigns doubt, or awkward embarrassment, or shame. When Marvin Rosenberg first explained his disagreement with rhetorical character, or "formalism," he thought actors would "exaggerate movement," use "inflated delivery" and "conventional posture." That proposal Rosenberg found too restrictive, especially considering the size of the Globe and other theaters, which were small enough to accommodate an "expressive face to help communicate the emotion the playwright intended."[34] Yet the figures prompt a feigning of emotion too. Statues do pretend doubt or friendly concern, but the flatterer type, and the tropes that correspond to its performance, prescribe just that.

Each of the emotional prompts from the figures, too, corresponds to the type of a flatterer, who plays the role of a friend. Stern and Palfrey argue: "rhetorical tropes and figures of speech, and the generic 'types' that underlie particular characters (e.g., the Vice in Iago or Richard III)" are matters "fundamental" for performance.[35] Type characters and figures, in particular, could have been associated together as early as Theophrastus, whose sketches, Desmet writes, may have been "intended as models for dramatic figures" or for providing "orators with a handy reference for gauging audiences."[36] The repetition of some words—such as "indeed," "honest," and "think"—call attention to themselves, not simply as cues or tropes of repetition, but as directions for performance according to type, detailing where Iago should feign good will and how he should show good will as part of the "honest advice" that may turn Othello from Desdemona. Because the flatterer feigns friendship, Iago attempts a pose of reluctance through his use of stops, hesitating to broach a topic that would bring pain to Othello; all the while, however, that reluctance "kindles more coals" in Othello, just as Plutarch describes. Reticence as insinuation combines with Othello's belief in Iago's "honesty," thereby increasing the significance of stops and illustrating how Plutarch's "candid" flatterer may perturb people in "amatorious and love matters." The withholding tactics of Iago, finally, work in conjunction with the display candor exhibited elsewhere by him to persuade Othello: "This honest creature," claims Othello of Iago, "sees and knows more— much more—than he unfolds" (3.3.246–47). The implication of Plutarch's flatterer was that he could play a friend with such authenticity that a difference between friend and knave was hard to determine, and that dilemma finds its way into performance by following Shakespeare's deployment of the figures of withholding.

In the same way that feigned friendship appears authentic, playing Iago according to the flatterer's type indicates a rhetorical acting style that aims at a lifelike depiction of honesty and good will. Already, we have seen how the figures above, though oratorical conventions, are precisely meant to cover artifice. As Polixenes claims in *The Winter's Tale*, "over that art / Which you say adds to nature is an art / That nature makes" (4.4.90–92).[37] Iago may feign doubts or anxieties in his withholding tactics in order to increase Othello's curiosity in what he (actually) wants to tell him, but there remains little distinction between persuasion and performance in such a case; either art includes the pretense of authentic concern for the sake of manipulating an auditor.

LIFELIKE TYPES: THEN, AND NOW

Though later stage portrayals of Iago approach Shakespeare's script according to the theatrical aesthetics of their own day, the prompts for dramatic action implicit in the figures of Wilson and Puttenham, like stage directions, still cue actors to perform or feign Iago's honesty. To take a prominent example, Edwin Booth wrote out directions for the Horace Furness *Variorum Othello* (1886), because Furness was of the opinion that "in the interpretation of Shakespeare's plays, our first appeal, and perhaps our last, should be made to the dramatic instinct, as it has been termed, with which eminent Actors are especially endowed."[38] We know Booth himself favored a romantic Othello, and his own directions encourage "reflections" that "help the actor to *feel* the character he assumes."[39] Booth's modern, naturalistic sense of identifying with the character stands in contrast to a performance based upon type and figures of speech, but his notes coincidentally explore the same rhetorical stops listed above.[40] In fact, Booth's instructions set beside the figures discussed above show more correspondence rather than deviation:

Iago: Indeed?

> [Puttenham: "we begin to speak a thing and break off in the middle way, as if either it needed no further to be spoken of, or that we were ashamed or afraid to speak it out."]
> [Booth: "Contract the brows, but do not frown,—rather look disappointed, and merely utter in surprise, 'Indeed'!"]

Othello: Indeed? Ay, indeed. Discern'st thou aught in that? Is he not honest?

Iago: Honest, my lord?

> [Puttenham: *Aporia*, "the doubtful"]
> [Booth: "Hesitatingly."]

Othello: Honest? Ay, honest.

Iago: My lord, for aught I know.

> [Puttenham: *Epitropis*, "this manner of speech is used when we will not seem, either for manner sake or to avoid tediousness, to trouble the judge or hearer with all that we could say . . . ."]
> [Booth: "With indifference."] (3.3.101–6)[41]

The final "Think, my lord?" of Iago from this exchange, Booth recommends, should be stated with "embarrassment." That embarrassment indicates the pain and awkwardness of Iago, performing like one of "exceeding honesty," a friend that, Othello believes, "knows all qualities, with a learned spirit, / Of human dealings" yet is not sharing that insight with him (3.3.262–64). Both the withholding figures and Booth's directions attempt to portray reticence as a part of friendship, which we have seen Plutarch describe as an identifying mark of the flatterer.

The unexpected similarities between Booth's directions, Puttenham's figures, and Plutarch's type, indicate where and how type provides a region of possibility—full of distinctive sayings, typical behaviors, gestures, feigned emotions, and so on—that the text particularizes, and which may function as cues for performance. Type remains the "flexible basis" for disclosing character, as Burns noted, but performance, even in vastly different approaches to and portrayals of the same character, will constitute an elaboration of those basic traits. Though Booth's approach to the performance of Iago's character differs from the early modern art of personation, his prompts are a reflection of the figural and oratorical design Shakespeare embeds into Iago's lines. For the typological character of the flatterer, even when unacknowledged or unknown, provides the linguistic framework for performances of Iago.

As with figures, or *pronuntio*, so, too, with gesture, *actio*: Booth's focus on the "contracted brow" above repeats Othello's own observation about Iago and Plutarch's description of a flatterer. After Iago responds—"Think, my lord?"—Othello wonders about Cassio, saying of him and then of Iago:

> And when I told thee he was of my counsel
> In my whole course of wooing, thou criedst "Indeed?"
> And didst *contract and purse thy brow together*
> As if thou then hadst shut up in thy brain
> Some horrible conceit. If thou dost love me
> Show me thy thought. (3.3.114–19, my emphasis)

"In a highly gestured theatre," writes Stern, "non-verbal byplay could significantly affect the way the audience responded to a drama: fools like Tarlton and Reade were famous for the facial additions they made to their parts."[42] Booth, as we have seen, thought the "contracted brow" should show "disappointment," as if Iago were disappointed to have confirmed, in part, his suspicions about Cassio and Desdemona. In Holland's translation, too, Plutarch teaches that flatterers "have learned forsooth to knit and bend the brows," especially as they perform the role of true friend; likewise, Othello wonders why Iago did "contract and purse thy brow together," concluding that the expression is the result of some "horrible conceit" that Iago will not share. For Plutarch, such a sign indicated false or pretended candor, the means by which a flatterer could assume the posture of a man who hated vice. If so, irritation, or indignation, would be the emotion feigned by Iago, as if he were angry over hearing confirmation of his suspicions, rather than Booth's more moderate "disappointment."

Yet either response reveals how the flattering type originates in manipulating or employing oratorical conventions. Thomas Wilson's *Art of*

Rhetoric (1560) considers "gesture" as a "certain comely moderation of the countenance and all other parts of the body," agreeing with Cicero, that the "gesture of man is the speech of his body." A persuasive body entails such things as "the head to be holden upright, the forehead without frowning, *the brow without bending*"; in short, all that a serene *ethos* would convey.[43] Plutarch's flatterer is the near opposite with a contracted brow. Even so, Othello remarks upon those brows, providing what we might think of as a stage direction for a lifelike delivery of Iago's "Indeed."

Elsewhere and in further contradiction to Rosenberg's concerns about a rhetorical style of acting, Shakespeare presents Iago as a master of how "gesture"—the art that binds both orators and actors together through *actio* or action—includes facial expressions. Iago instructs Othello to hide and observe Cassio's response to Iago's questions about an affair with Desdemona. Because Othello cannot hear the conversation, Iago easily manipulates the occasion; he asks about Cassio's mistress, Bianca, instead of Desdemona. Cassio's response—his "gestures and light behavior"— cause Othello's "unbookish jealous" to misconstrue the meaning of Iago and Cassio's exchange (4.1.102–4). Iago's instructions to Othello show how he arranges the deception precisely in terms of gesture:

> Do but encave yourself
> And *mark the fleers, the gibes and notable scorns*
> *That dwell in every region of his face*;
> For I will make him tell the tale anew
> Where, how, how oft, how long ago, and when
> He hath and is again to cope your wife.
> I say, but mark his *gesture*. (4.1.82–88, my emphasis)

"Fleers" are mocking looks, which encompass striking or easily noticed "gibes"—another term for scoffs or taunts—along with "notable scorns," all of which enact or entail what Iago calls "gesture." Iago teaches Othello how to judge a performance solely upon gesture even as he provides embedded stage directions for the performance of Cassio's part. "Individual modern actors," writes Astington of Iago's instructions, "might feel such gesture to be something of an overstatement, or cliché, but an audience would not find it unsuited to the word when skillfully performed." Early modern rhetorical delivery, even in a theater the size of the Globe, involves "the smaller and more subtle movements of the body, including the inclination and turn of the head, the intensity of the gaze, and the cast of the mouth, in speech or silence."[44]

Indeed, gazes seem particularly important in this play. After Iago instructs Othello about these sorts of gesture, his general attempts to deduce Desdemona's innocence or guilt by judging the look in her eyes. Othello orders her: "Let me see your eyes. / Look in my face" (4.2.25–26). Shakespeare scripts directions for such minute gestures as Cassio's fleers or Desdemona's gaze, but Iago's ability to direct the responses of Othello and to teach him the significance of gesture suggests his own expertise in how to portray and judge particular passions, not just vocally, but in terms of facial expressions.

In fact, variability in facial expression constitutes the flatterer's specialty. For Plutarch, uncomely expressions are necessary to counteract the "glavering glozes"—that hypocritical smooth speech—by which flatterers easily may be identified. The abilities to feign fleers, gibes, and notable scorns becomes necessary because, like display candor hides deceit, covert sycophancy requires something other than statuesque delivery, or a serene *ethos*, as a means of concealment. So Plutarch writes of the flatterer: "he carrieth himself like a grave tragedian, and not as a comical and satirical player, and under that visor and habit he counterfeiteth a true friend" (42). Performed accordingly, the "knit brows" of Iago would show seriousness of thought and authentic concern, a sign of his protective attitude toward and friendship with Othello. Covert sycophancy requires a credible or lifelike pretense of friendship. Put otherwise, the illusion of honesty, good will, and friendship are the result of particular forms of persuasion from the classical rhetorical tradition that Shakespeare has written into Iago's dramatic person.

Thus, Iago's words suggest that Othello is foolish for preferring Desdemona to his friend, but it is Iago's manner and delivery that Othello ultimately finds convincing. Before Othello turns against Desdemona, Othello confesses to Iago the reason why he finds him persuasive:

> I think thou dost [love me].
> And for I know thou'rt full of love and honesty
> And weigh'st thy words before thou giv'st them breath,
> Therefore *these stops of thine* fright me the more.
> For such things in a false disloyal knave
> Are tricks of custom, but in a man that's just
> They're close delations, working from the heart,
> That passion cannot rule. (3.3.120–27, my emphasis)

Othello specifically recognizes "these stops" of Iago as performative "tricks," but what are "tricks of custom" in a "false disloyal knave" become marks of truth in an honest man. "In a man that's just," Othello judges, such "stops" are "close delations, working from the heart, / That passion cannot rule." Othello, once again, directs our attention to Iago's capacity for lifelike performance: Iago does not play a part, using oratorical methods, but is true. The irony, of course, is that the knave plays the just man in a plausible way; that is the flatterer's type.

Such credibility emerges as essentially histrionic because Iago best enacts the flatterer's type when he speaks most like a friend. As act 3, scene 3 progresses, Othello warns Iago of making false insinuations: "If thou dost slander her and torture me / Never pray more, abandon all remorse" (3.3.371–72). As in Cicero, where hypocrisy was called "especially inimical to friendship since it utterly destroys sincerity, without which friendship can have no meaning," Othello values candid conversation in true friendship and believes he should be wary of hypocrites, who poison friendship with their lies.[45] Hence, in response, Iago will allude to Cicero's example about the friend who gave frank advice, but had it received unworthily. Iago's flattering discourse remains parasitic to that of friendship just as his type appropriates the gestures that best disguise his intentions.

Cicero's teaching on friendship further illumines Iago's flattering strategy. In *De Amicitia*, a companion tells the truth, even when it may be critical, out of love for his friend and in consideration of their mutual love of virtue. Cicero admits that this is a difficult area of friendship: "A troublesome thing is truth, if it is indeed the source of hate, which poisons friendship; but much more troublesome is complaisance, which, by showing indulgence to the sins of a friend, allows him to be carried headlong away."[46] Yet true friends will accept criticism, because "it is absurd that men who are admonished do not feel vexation at what ought to vex them, but do feel it at what ought not; for they are annoyed, not at the sin, but at the reproof." Thus, a virtuous person should "grieve for the offence and rejoice at its correction."[47] Iago echoes these teachings, telling Othello,

> O grace! O heaven forgive me!
> Are you a man? have you a soul, or sense?
> God buy you, take mine office. O wretched fool
> That lov'st to make thine honesty a vice!
> O monstrous world! Take note, take note, O world,
> To be direct and honest is not safe.
> I thank you for this profit, and from hence
> I'll love no friend, sith love breeds such offence. (3.3.377–83)

When Iago exclaims that the world should take note that "to be direct and honest is not safe," he reconfigures Othello into the "absurd" friend mentioned by Cicero, who takes offense at the criticism instead of the sin. What Othello calls "slander," then, becomes the language of a true friend, who speaks frankly even when it is difficult to do so. Iago's conclusion— "I'll love no friend, sith love breeds such offence"—shames Othello, and the flatterer's performance convinces his general, who responds, "Nay, stay, thou shouldst be honest" (3.3.384). Where Othello's words raise a Ciceronian objection to hypocrisy, Iago's own language incorporates Ciceronian prescriptions for friendly behavior in his defense.

These rhetorical contexts of friendship and flattery can seem far removed from an audience's experience of contemporary productions of *Othello* because, as Stephen Orgel reminds us, it is the actor who must turn "the lines into a credible simulacrum of human behavior," and what appears as "psychologically credible" is a function of variable theatrical tastes and the choices each actor makes.[48] Thus, an actor playing Iago for today's audiences may choose to follow those cues of the flatterer type that Othello recognizes, the raised eyebrow or the performance of stops, but he would do so, more like Booth's instructions, in a way that identifies the actor's own person with the character he plays. "Actors," writes Peter Lichtenfels, "always have to take active responsibility for the words and silences within the text to realize or 'play' the characters' actions." Shakespeare writes the "words and silences," Lichtenfels concludes, but "an actor has to choose them."[49] Lichtenfels writes in explanation of how contemporary actors approach Shakespearean drama, yet he suggests a model of performance wherein the playwright provides a framework for delivery, even for stops or silences, which corresponds to Booth's directions.[50] Like Booth, Lichtenfels might find Iago's stops as opportunities to add to performance. Though Booth doesn't acknowledge the formal rhetorical structure of Iago's dramatic person, his comments resonate with the performative nature of the flatterer. Thus, in consideration of Iago's manipulation of Cassio, Booth provides an overall recommendation applicable to the exchange between Othello and Iago above and consistent with Plutarch's description of flatterers: "The more sincere your manner," Booth writes, "the more devilish your deceit."[51]

Booth's view of the importance of sincerity in playing deceit, an echo and modern appropriation of Iago's original type, remains. Dan Donohue, reflecting upon his performance of Iago at the 2008 Oregon Shakespeare Festival, makes a similar statement: "Iago is known as 'Honest Iago' because he behaves that way."[52] Donohue believes the audience witnesses all of Iago's "illusions" as if the character were a magician. Audiences see Iago's illusions, he writes, "without seeing the mechanisms that make them work," providing a comment about contemporary performance that captures what the oratorical figures of deception—tricks of speech—were meant to accomplish as well. The impact on audiences results from how the actor approaches the role of Iago. Donohue writes:

> In a scene where there are moments of deception, it is best for me—Dan, the actor—to be simply "Honest Iago." I keep in my mind what Iago secretly wants, but I play the scene as if I were really trying to help the Moor. With that in mind, I would choose to play—*Protect my friend, Othello, from some painful news*—rather than playing—*Torture the person I want to destroy.*[53]

In these words, Donohue captures how Iago may provide a lifelike depiction of friendship with Othello while remaining his adversary, for "Iago pretends, but he does act like he is pretending. He acts, but he does not pretend like he is acting."[54] For Donohue, Iago's powers of manipulation mean that Iago is a "great actor." The challenge for an actor today who plays a great actor in this case is to make the audience think, as Donohue puts it, "*I would have believed Iago too.*"[55] That assessment of credulity explains and updates Booth's own recommendation for a "more devilish" deceit. Yet Booth and Donohue illustrate not only a modern actor's identification with character, but also how they recognize and recalibrate the display candor of a flatterer according to more contemporary theatrical tastes.

DUAL AWARENESS

An early modern performance of a persuasive and credible Iago would have ramifications in terms of audience response, which further suggests how typological character fashions a particular way for audiences to experience, or identify with, Othello's dilemma. As in the case of acting styles, audience response includes a sharp natural versus formal distinction, a divide that a typological Iago played with qualities of honesty and good will would challenge. Considering Iago, Peter Holland notes that the "vice figure" tradition includes a particular "dramatic trajectory that has strong similarities with the audiences' dynamic in its response to *Othello*." When type is employed, Holland acknowledges a "certain staginess, a conscious theatricality," a design which may indicate "the mode of Jacobean performance of such realist roles" like that of Iago is better referred to as "quasi-Brechtian *presentation*," rather than "Stanislavskian *representation*." Holland calls this a "participatory mode" for audiences, distinct from psychological or novelistic portrayals, where character is "prescriptively separate from and observed by the audience."[56] In opposition to Holland's account of the connection between formal acting style and audience participation, I would cite Harold Bloom as exemplifying the contrary tradition of audience isolation; he writes that "a Shakespearean audience is like the gods in Homer: we look on and listen, and are not tempted to intervene."[57] A formal versus a natural distinction in acting style emerges in correspondence to the division between audience participation and isolation.

Yet we have already seen how type may incorporate a rhetorical acting style that would not seem "unnatural" to early modern audiences because the appeal from friendship, though duplicitous, should appear as credible. The division between flattering type and displays of friendship, then, would entail subsequent distinctions, where Iago's soliloquies, for example, might retain some of Holland's "staginess," but the dramatic and deceptive dialogues, paradoxically, would be played as "authentic." In this way, rather than isolating audiences, or appropriating them through participation, playing a typological Iago would propose a version of what S. L. Bethell originally called "dual awareness." For Bethell, "the mixture of conventionalism and naturalism demands a dual mode of attention," which allows audiences a variety of responses to character, just as Falstaff, in Bethell's analysis, evokes "amusement" and is "morally reprehensible."[58] By analogy, audiences could find Iago "amusing" as stage villain, orchestrating and articulating his plots, but "morally reprehensible" in the enactment of his deceits.

Alternatively, because the flatterer type may include early modern signs of credible friendship and concern, audience awareness could extend not just to the illusion of the person over the conventions by which the illusion occurs, but also to the feigned persona of the type character. Deceiving types, flatterers like Iago, enact a persona as part of a type character, as a friend is played by a knave, with the persona of friend "read" by audiences. Flattering types show not just an actor playing a character, but an actor playing a character who plays *another* character, as a member of Shakespeare's acting troupe might play an Iago, an Iago who plays an honest friend for Othello. As audiences focus on the drama of courtship between Orlando and Rosalind, knowing Rosalind is dressed as Ganymede, that a boy actor plays a "girl" who plays a "boy" who then plays a "girl" in the performance, so, too, they attend to the drama of deceiving Othello, finding Iago's portrayals of friendship plausible, though they know he is other than his self-presentation, just as they know he is other from the actor's body who plays both flattering character and the corresponding role of "honest friend" that type employs.

In this last understanding, where Iago's persona of "friend" receives emphasis, Iago's relationship to the flatterer type becomes part of the dynamic of audience response, less as an interaction with a character's "staginess" and more in terms of the believability of his displays of friendship. An audience dynamic in response to a lifelike display of friendship would create for the playgoer the dilemma faced by Othello, who thinks his wife "honest" but finds Iago "just" as well (3.3.387–89).[59] Though such a theater experience would only occur in select places like act 3, scene 3 and suffer an obvious and great diminishment in those scenes where Iago's villainy becomes transparent, it would increase the ultimate anguish audiences experience on behalf of Othello. In those moments when Iago is particularly persuasive, audiences know what Othello does not about his putative friend, but they also see—and may even feel—the power of Iago's rhetoric and his performance of friendship at the same time. If at least some audience members are tempted to believe Iago, Shakespeare's play would dramatize the problem, to borrow from Plutarch, of how to discern a flatterer from a friend.[60]

NOTES

This chapter is a revision of my earlier essay, "'Stops' in the Name of Love: Playing Typological Iago," in *Shakespeare's Sense of Character: On the Page and From the Stage*, ed. Yu Jin Ko and Michael W. Shurgot (Burlington, VT: Ashgate Publishing Company, 2012).

1. Cf: Yu Jin Ko, *Mutability and Division on Shakespeare's Stage* (Newark: University of Delaware Press, 2004), 42–43: "The critical debate about early-modern acting styles still largely centers on, but remains divided about, the question of whether the acting leaned more or less towards one of two poles labeled long ago as 'naturalism' and 'formalism,' though related if not entirely interchangeable binary oppositions between 'inwardness' and 'rhetorical character,' 'representation' and 'presentation,' or 'identification' and 'alienation' come into play as well."

2. On Theophrastus's relation to classical rhetoric, and influence upon Shakespeare's England, see Benjamin Boyce, *The Theophrastan Character in England to 1642* (Cambridge, MA: Harvard University Press, 1947), 11–52; on figures and character, see Charles McDonald, *Rhetoric of Tragedy* (Amherst: University of Massachusetts Press, 1966), 87, 33n, who points out how grammar school exercises in *ethopoeia* are sufficient to present the idea of type. For a reading of a poetic treatise with reference to character, see Travis Cutright, "Sidney's Defense of Poetry: Ethos and the Ideas," *Ben Jonson Journal* 10 (2003): 101–15, where I address rhetorical and poetic objectives of type in Sidney's articulation of "character" and the "ideas."

3. See Barker, *The Tremulous Private Body: Essays on Subjection* (London: Methuen, 1984), 24–25, 31–32, 52, 59, 68; Catherine Belsey, *The Subject of Tragedy: Identity and Difference in Renaissance Drama* (New York: Methuen, 1985), 18, 26–34, 40; on roles over individual identity, Beatrice Gottlieb, *The Family in the Western World from the Black Death to the Industrial Age* (New York: Oxford University Press, 1993), 262.

4. For Belsey, *The Subject of Tragedy*, 32–33, "the half century before the revolution" presents the "intersection of the two modes, illusionist and emblematic," with Shakespearean characters like Iago "moving between the two modes." Similarly, E. A. J. Honigmann, *Shakespeare: Seven Tragedies Revisited: The Dramatist's Manipulation of Response*, second edition (Houndmills, UK: Palgrave Macmillan, 2002), 13, writes:

> Placing his tragic hero upon the rack, and thus making him act against his nature (as it was previously exhibited), Shakespeare achieved an effect that we may observe in his other plays as well. All the complex comic characters behave incongruously, from Petruchio's Kate to Caliban, as do the tragic heroes: arriving on the literary scene just as English drama advanced from Faustus, from type to individual, Shakespeare stretched character by exploring its inexhaustible diversity, and so prepared the way for later pluralistic theories.

Though Belsey and Honigmann have very different approaches, both believe a more modern sense of character emerges from type, especially by deviation from it.

5. Bernard Spivack's *Shakespeare and the Allegory for Evil* (New York: Columbia University Press, 1958), 3–27, for example, doesn't find Iago's motives as credible and defines Iago as a figure of vice. For a response to Spivack, see Stanley Edgar Hyman's *Iago: Some Approaches to the Illusion of His Motivation: A Study in Pluralist Criticism* (New York: Atheneum, 1970), 25–28.

6. Edward Burns, *Character: Acting and Being on the Pre-Modern Stage* (New York: St. Martin's Press, 1990), 32.

7. On the significance of "stops," see Patricia Parker, "Shakespeare and rhetoric: 'dilation' and 'delation' in *Othello*," in *Shakespeare and the Question of Theory*, ed. Patricia Parker and Geoffrey Hartman (London: Routledge, 1985), 54–74.

8. Cf. Honigmann, *Shakespeare: Seven Tragedies Revisited*, 22: "I wonder, indeed, whether Shakespeare could have created Iago's delicate skills without to some degree sharing his creature's artistic satisfaction, and without expecting the audience to share it too."

9. Paul A. Jorgensen, "Honesty in Othello," *Studies in Philology* 47 (1950): 557. In a note, Jorgensen writes "Probably the most nearly definite usage of honest or honest man was in its habitual antithesis to knave. Cf. Wilson's *The Pedlar's Prophecy* (1595)." Ibid., 557n3. To Jorgensen's *Pedlar*, Robert Evans adds eight books that are written before 1600, which "include essays dealing with character-types relevant to the issues

of flattery, false friendship, true friendship, and how to distinguish a flatterer from a friend." Robert Evans, "Flattery in Shakespeare's *Othello*: The Relevance of Plutarch and Sir Thomas Elyot," *Comparative Drama* 35 (2001): 39n22.

10. In proposing Holland's Plutarch as a source text for Shakespeare's *Othello*, Evans argues: "It is possible, in fact, that Holland's translation may have been in existence several years earlier than this date of publication [1603] would suggest, since a version of the text was entered on the Stationers' Register on 18 April 1600 by the publisher W. Ponsonby, while the same translation was later entered on the Register on 5 July 1602 by G. Bishop and others. When the book finally did appear in print in 1603, the publisher was A. Hatfield. It seems possible, then, that Holland's translation may have existed in manuscript several years before it finally appeared in print. Indeed, it may have existed in manuscript at least four years before our first recorded performance of *Othello* in November 1604." Evans, "Flattery in Shakespeare's *Othello*," 3.

11. Here and throughout I quote from Plutarch, *Plutarch's Moralia: Twenty Essays translated by Philemon Holland*, ed. E. H. Blakeney (London: Dent, 1911). For the lines cited, see 41. Hereafter, page numbers are cited parenthetically.

12. False friendship and flattery are interchangeable terms in Plutarch's essay.

13. Christy Desmet, "The Persistence of Character," in *Shakespeare Studies*, vol. XXXIV, ed. Susan Zimmerman (Cranbury, NJ: Associated University Presses, 2006), 52.

14. Here and throughout I refer to *The Arden Shakespeare: Othello*, ed. E. A. J. Honigmann (London: Thomson Learning, 2001). Hereafter cited internally. For the lines cited, see 2.1.119. See, too, Evans, "Flattery in *Othello*," 10, who demonstrates a connection between these lines and Thomas Elyot's treatment of flattery in *The Book Named the Governor*.

15. For Honigman's gloss of the word "home," see *The Arden Shakespeare: Othello*, 2.1.16 n.165.

16. A. C. Bradley, *Shakespearean Tragedy: Lectures on Hamlet, Othello, King Lear, Macbeth* (New York: Penguin Books, 1991), 201.

17. William W. Fortenbaugh suggests that "good will" should be thought of as an emotion: the speaker feels good will towards the audience and the audience feels the same way toward the speaker; such an emotional dynamic, of course, would aid the speaker in persuading his audience, moving them toward his point of view. See William W. Fortenbaugh, "Aristotle's Accounts of Persuasion through Character," in *Theory, Text, Context: Issues in Greek Rhetoric and Oratory*, ed. Christopher Lyle Johnstone (Albany: State University of New York Press, 1996), 147–68.

18. Aristotle, *Rhetoric*, trans. W. Rhys Roberts in *The Rhetoric and Poetics of Aristotle* (New York: The Modern Library, 1954), 1378a15–20.

19. Aristotle, *Rhetoric*, 1378a20–25. Maratha Nussbaum, "Aristotle on Emotions and Rational Persuasion," in *Essays on Aristotle's Rhetoric* (Berkeley: University of California Press, 1996), 303–4, writes: "In Aristotle's view, emotions are not blind animal forces, but intelligent and discriminating parts of the personality, closely related to beliefs of a certain sort, and therefore responsive to cognitive modification." She concludes: "Thus, rather than having a simple dichotomy between the emotional and the (normatively) rational, we have a situation in which all emotions are to some degree 'rational' in a descriptive sense—all are to some degree cognitive and based upon belief—and they must be assessed, as beliefs are assessed, for their normative status."

20. Cicero, *De Amicitia*, trans. William Armistead Falconer (Cambridge, MA: Harvard University Press, 1959), 6.20–22.

21. Cicero, *De Amicitia*, 25.91–92.

22. Cicero specifically relates *honestas* to friendship and giving advice in *De partitione oratoria*, trans. H. Rackam (Cambridge, MA: Harvard University Press), 25.88–90; see, too, *De Oratore*, trans. E. W. Sutton and H. Rackham (Cambridge, MA: Harvard University Press), 2.72.333; and *Rhetorica ad Herennium*, trans. H. Caplan (Cambridge, MA: Harvard University Press, 1954), 3.2.3. For the relationship between a "good

man" and oratory, see *Quintilian: The Orator's Education*, Bk 12, trans. Donald A. Russell (Cambridge, MA: Harvard University Press, 2001), 12.1.1ff, where a good man (*vir bonus*) is also skilled in speaking.

23. On act 3, scene 3 and Plutarch, however, Evans writes: "Indeed, the excruciatingly hesitant way in which Iago first plants a suspicion and then pretends to dismiss it suggests the process Plutarch describes when he remarks that the false friend's 'counterfeit liberty of plain dealing and plain speech may be very well likened to the wanton pinches and bitings of luxurious women who tickle and stir up lust and pleasure of men by that which might seem to cause their pain.' [Plutarch, 67]. There is, indeed, an almost erotic quality to Iago's seduction of Othello here, especially since the ensign is alternately coy and blunt in the ways he speaks." Evans, "Flattery in Shakespeare's Othello," 15. If "seduction" and an "erotic quality" are at work in Iago's words, Othello does not understand them in such a manner. As I argue, Othello is aware that the "stops" of Iago are "custom's tricks," and, therefore, they are signs of courtly rhetoric, not erotic seduction.

24. Thomas Wilson, *The Art of Rhetoric* (1560), ed. Peter E. Medine (University Park: the Pennsylvania State University Press, 1994), 205.

25. George Puttenham, *The Art of English Poesy: A Critical Edition*, ed. Frank Whigham and Wayne A. Rebhorn (Ithaca, NY: Cornell University Press, 2007), 250.

26. Tiffany Stern, *Rehearsal from Shakespeare to Sheridan* (Oxford: Clarendon Press, 2000), 64.

27. Stern, *Rehearsal from Shakespeare to Sheridan*, 72.

28. John H. Astington, *Actors and Acting in Shakespeare's Time* (Cambridge, UK: Cambridge University Press, 2010), 141.

29. Simon Palfrey and Tiffany Stern, *Shakespeare in Parts* (Oxford: Oxford University Press, 2007), 318–20.

30. On passions and performance, see Palfrey and Stern, *Shakespeare in Parts*, 311–17.

31. Palfrey and Stern, *Shakespeare in Parts*, 319.

32. Puttenham, *Arte of Poesie*, 311. The editors gloss *him* as *it*.

33. Puttenham, *Arte of Poesie*, 311–12.

34. Marvin Rosenberg, "Elizabethan Actors: Men or Marionettes?" *PMLA* 69, no. 4 (September 1954): 920.

35. Palfrey and Stern, *Shakespeare in Parts*, 9.

36. Desmet, "The Persistence of Character," 50.

37. I cite *The Winter's Tale* from *The Complete Works of Shakespeare*, fifth edition, ed. David Bevington (New York: Pearson Longman, 2004).

38. *A New Variorum Edition of Shakespeare: Othello*, new Dover edition, ed. Horace Howard Furness (New York: Dover Publications, Inc., 1963), vii.

39. *A New Variorum Edition of Shakespeare: Othello*, 27.

40. The divide between Booth and earlier performance holds for more modern acting styles as well. "The enactment of 'character,'" writes W. B. Worthen, "The Rhetoric of Performance Criticism," *Shakespeare Quarterly* 40, no. 4 (Winter, 1989), 455, may have been a more "collaborative or even collusive activity" than modern acting methods because "the seam between actor and character may have been visible"; hence, "to naturalize" the playing of parts according to "Stanislavskian attitudes" will obscure "certain potentialities of Shakespearean characterization" by negating the presence of an audience.

41. For Booth's notes, see *A New Variorum Edition of Shakespeare: Othello*, 167–69.

42. Stern, *Rehearsal from Shakespeare to Sheridan*, 105.

43. Wilson, *The Art of Rhetoric*, 243–44, my emphasis.

44. I follow Astington's analysis of Iago's instructions about gesture and cite his conclusion about its significance for performance from *Actors and Acting in Shakespeare's Time*, 22. Though Astington does not reference Othello's command to Desdemona to look into his face, he argues how "the face, in fact, is at the centre of the

business of suiting action to word, since its movement in speech is in organic relationship with what is being spoken" (idem.)

45. Cicero, *De Amicitia*, 25.91–92.

46. Cicero, *De Amicitia*, 24.89–90.

47. Cicero, *De Amicitia*, 24.90.

48. Stephen Orgel, "What Is a Character?" in *The Authentic Shakespeare: And Other Problems of the Early Modern Stage* (New York and London: Routledge, 2002), 12.

49. Peter Lichtenfels, "Shakespeare's Language in the Theatre," in *Reading Shakespeare's Dramatic Language: A Guide*, ed. Sylvia Adamson, Lynette Hunter, Lynne Magnusson, Ann Thompson, and Katie Wales (London: Thomson Learning, 2001), 162.

50. In addition to the passages cited above from Stern, *Rehearsal from Shakespeare to Sheridan*, see Ellen J. O'Brien, "Mapping the Role: Criticism and Construction of Shakespearean Character," in *Shakespearean Illuminations: Essays in Honor of Marvin Rosenberg* (Newark: University of Delaware Press, 1998), 13–32, who argues that character is the product of a player's labor, which is guided by the role found in the play text, a role "shaped by the nuances of every word, metrical feature, rhetorical structure, spatial arrangement, and so on"; she concludes that "mapping the role is a form of close reading."

51. *A New Variorum Edition of Shakespeare: Othello*, 146.

52. Dan Donohue, "Iago: In Following Him I Follow But Myself," in *Shakespeare's Sense of Character*, 141.

53. Donohue, "Iago," 150.

54. Donohue, "Iago," 150.

55. Donohue, "Iago," 141, 150

56. Peter Holland, "The Resources of Characterization in *Othello*," in *Shakespeare Survey Volume 41: Shakespearian Stages and Staging*, ed. Stanley Wells (Cambridge, UK: Cambridge University Press, 1989), 129–30.

57. Harold Bloom, *Shakespeare: The Invention of the Human* (New York: Riverhead Books, 1998), 7.

58. S. L. Bethell, *Shakespeare and the Popular Dramatic Tradition* (Westminster: P. S. King & Staples, 1944), 27.

59. Audiences went to the theater, write Palfrey and Stern, *Shakespeare in Parts*, 317, "to feel newly amazed, not only at an actor's or playwright's facility, but at their own capacity to feel apparently impossible 'contraries' at one time, as though the theatre was introducing its 'rapt' spectators to new possibilities of feeling."

60. The anxieties about dissimulation that early modern audiences brought with them to the theater are well documented. In addition to the work of Evans, Desmet, and Jorgenson on flattery, for a general statement on the ubiquity of concerns over flattery and dissembling, see Katharine Eisaman Maus, *Inwardness and Theater in the English Renaissance* (Chicago: University of Chicago Press, 1995), 5–8.

FIVE

Marina as Char*orator*

William Shakespeare's *Pericles, Prince of Tyre* (1607–1608) inaugurates the genre of romance into his canon in unusual ways.[1] Even if *Pericles* is a late play, its story emerges from an adaptation of the same plot that Shakespeare had used in one of his first comedies. As Robert Miola has shown, Latin New Comedy heavily influences *Pericles* and provides the play with its "localities" like the temple, sea, and brothel or its climactic revelation of a character's identity in order to facilitate reunion scenes. Heroines in Latin New Comedy, Miola argues, are saved from difficult situations by external interventions, but, in an important difference, Marina "saves herself."[2]

I don't think Marina saves herself, but she sounds like she does because of her use of forensic speech or judicial oratory, a rhetorical genre that adjudicates a question through debate with speeches of defense and accusation.[3] As we shall see, Marina's forensic speeches of self-defense comprise the linguistic essence of her dramatic person and demonstrate the influence of the classical rhetorical tradition on *Pericles*. Shakespeare used ancient and Renaissance sources on judicial rhetoric as late as *Othello*, written between 1601 and 1603, or *Measure for Measure* in 1604, or *All's Well That Ends Well*, composed between 1606 and 1607.[4] If Shakespeare coauthored *Pericles* with George Wilkins between 1607 and 1608,[5] the creation of Marina as a forensic speaker, Shakespeare's signature contribution to the play, would echo or continue his previous interest in the Roman tradition of judicial oratory.[6]

To claim that Marina embodies Shakespeare's ongoing fascination with forensic discourse in his composition of dramatic persons will challenge some relatively hegemonic views about *Pericles* as an exemplary late play or romance.[7] Criticism of *Pericles* privileges the play's narrative structure instead of its characters, a decision that is justified by Shakespeare's assumed changes in writing style or transition to a late style of composition more compatible with a new mode or genre of dramatic action. Anne Barton summarizes this position when she writes of the romance genre: "Shakespeare has adjusted his language and dramatic art to the demands of a new mode: one in which, on the whole, has become more vivid and emotionally charged than character."[8] In analyzing a character's speech from the romances, the mimetic or rhetorical qualities found in earlier plays should be put aside. Russ McDonald's *Shakespeare's Late Style* (2006) agrees, which claims that the "mature Shakespeare" emerges "about 1607 or so" when the playwright "begins to weaken the link between speech and speaker."[9] James Sutherland goes further and writes in addressing the beginning of *Cymbeline*, "the person who is thinking rapidly, breaking off, making fresh starts and so on, is not the character, but Shakespeare himself."[10] "Most late-play critics," as Gordon McMullan summarizes, "have read the language of the plays as, in one way or another, a tangible manifestation of their lateness," which follows from the "fundamental difference between late Shakespeare and everything that came before it." That difference is epitomized in the words of Philip Edwards, "the Romances are written in a form of other-speaking."[11] Dramatic persons, as other-speakers, reveal the unique qualities of romantic dramaturgy. Thus, characters are symbols of "patience" or "charity" or other romance attributes, or they voice the concerns of an aging playwright, or character makes known ideological or topical discourse about monarchical succession and the family of King James.[12]

Because of such longstanding and relatively unchallenged critical assumptions about Shakespeare's late style, scholars have ignored Marina's forensic or judicial oratory and, more generally, how her appeals from *ethos* function. Even Lorna Hutson's landmark study, *The Invention of Suspicion* (2007), which studied the presence and significance of forensic rhetoric for lifelike methods of characterization, draws upon the plays of the late sixteenth century but does not extend to the romances. Quentin Skinner's more recent *Forensic Shakespeare* (2014) uncovers the importance of judicial oratory in plays not only from 1594 to 1600 but also in "the early Jacobean plays," a designation that he extends to *Timon of Athens*, composed between 1605 and 1607. Of note, his analysis terminates with *Timon*, in part, because "Shakespeare's dramatic purposes had changed." To justify the change in "dramatic purpose" Skinner cites McDonald's argument "on the vagueness and intensity in Shakespeare's late style."[13] Neither Hutson nor Skinner, despite their expert historical excavations of classical rhetoric from Shakespeare's plays, ventures a claim that forensic discourse extends beyond the "late style" horizon.

Despite scholarly preoccupation with Shakespeare's late style, I will show how Marina's dramatic person illustrates connections between the composition of character-effects and rhetorical appeals from *ethos*, and how the strictures of judicial oratory could prompt vocal modulation or the performance of particular passions to an early modern actor.[14] In Marina's speeches to Leonine and to Pericles especially, Shakespeare provides us with a heroine who attempts to persuade others by disclosing her identity through a forensic mode of discourse that creates the dramatic illusions of purpose, continuity, and even self-knowledge. Rather than "other-speaking," Marina illustrates the forensic arts of self-fashioning. Correspondingly, from the standpoint of the rhetorical style of acting, Marina's forensic speech would direct an actor how to articulate specific words and lines with particular internal feelings, ranging from fear to indignation. Rather than accept the category of romance or late play as a special stylistic designation, I argue how Marina exemplifies the relationship between the classical oratorical tradition and the early modern style of acting known as personation.

MARINA'S SPEECH OF SELF-DEFENSE TO LEONINE

To recognize how Marina employs judicial oratory, we must begin with an examination of how she voices appeals from *ethos*. Though often viewed in light of Aristotle's *Poetics*, *ethos*, within the rhetorical tradition, takes on a different, though related, meaning. Trained in classical rhetoric, Shakespeare knew that *ethos* creates a perception of the speaker for audiences, forming a crucial aspect of persuasion.[15] Aristotle believed that "persuasion is achieved by the speaker's personal character when the speech is so spoken as to make us think him credible." Because we are more likely to believe "good men" generally, but absolutely in matters where "opinions are divided," *ethos* can be of decisive importance.[16] Similarly, both Cicero and the author of the *Ad Herennium* recommend that a speaker win "good will" from an audience by projecting a moral self from the speech's beginning.[17] *Ethos* was an important consideration for speakers in antiquity, whether Greek or Roman, and we find this teaching revived not only in Renaissance theory, but also in Shakespeare's Marina.[18]

In fact, Shakespeare enacts a textbook appeal from *ethos* in presenting Marina with an almost impossible—and certainly urgent—rhetorical task, persuading her assassin, Leonine, not to harm her. The dramatic circumstances of Marina's confrontation with Leonine call for an appeal from *ethos* that is fashioned from the commonplaces of forensic discourse, a speech of self-defense.[19] We have seen how Shakespeare inherits three genres of rhetoric: epideictic or demonstrative oratory, the speech of praise or blame; deliberative oratory, which persuades assemblies to take or refrain from certain courses of future action; and forensic or judicial oratory, which teaches how to argue opposing cases of prosecution and defense.[20] Though demonstrative speech seems obviously inappropriate, because Marina's situation revolves around what future action Leonine might take, she could invoke deliberative oratory. Shakespeare's choice of rhetorical genre, in other words, indicates not simply plot but also characterization. Marina will present her own defense against Leonine, and, thus, all of the techniques associated with an orator's defense of a particular cause or case become means of describing her dramatic person or voicing an appeal from *ethos*.[21]

To recall Roman oratory's general theory of judicial rhetoric, speakers consider some *quaestio iudicii*—a question to adjudicate—that two parties must resolve through debate. Such a question in regard to a particular person and an alleged crime would be termed a *causa*, referring to the case or the side of the question an orator would represent. Accordingly, rhetorical invention, or the discovery of arguments, is defined as "the devising of matter, true or plausible, that would make the case [*causam*] convincing."[22] The importance of an orator's cause or "case" imparts a design to the whole of a speech, especially in its beginning *exordium* or *prohoemium*. The clearest statement comes from *Ad Herennium*, which states: "Given the cause, in order to be able to make a more appropriate Introduction, we must consider what kind of cause [*genus causae*] it is." Though the author specifies four causes, the essential ones are antonyms of each other and provide central categories of analysis: the *causa honesta* and the *causa turpis*. The *Ad Herennium* explains: "A cause is regarded as of the honourable kind [*honestum causae genus*] when we either defend what seems to deserve defense by all men, or attack what all men seem in duty bound to attack; for example, when we defend a hero, or prosecute a parricide." Conversely, "a cause is understood to be of the discreditable kind [*turpe genus*] when something honourable [*honesta res*] is under attack or when something discreditable [*turpis*] is being defended."[23]

To show how such a distinction between "honest" and "discreditable" causes works in Shakespeare's plays, Skinner reviews Thomas Cooper's *Thesaurus Linguae Romanae and Britanniciae* (1565), John Vernon's *Dictionarie in Latine and English* (1575) and Thomas Thomas's *Dictionarium Linguae* (1587), all of which gloss both *turpis* and *honestus* according to a "strong measure of agreement." Each refers to *turpis* as "dishonest" or, by way of synonym, "foul," as in Hamlet's sense of unethical action or "foul play," while its opposite indicates "honest." The list of synonyms for *honestus* includes: "good: of good behaveour: of good reputation" from Cooper; and "laudable, virtuous" from Vernon; Thomas adds "good, kinde, noble, honourable, of good behaviour, well mannered."[24] The distinctions that Cicero makes between causes, therefore, are translated into English with connotations that extend beyond forensic rhetoric even as they disclose the moral nature of competing causes.

In her exchange with Leonine, Marina stands not just as the accused party—the one condemned to death—but also the advocate or orator on her own behalf; her person constitutes her "case." She will argue for her innocence, performing as orator and even witness to her own cause, which concerns her person. Within the fiction of the play, the ramifications are transparent: speak well or die. Yet rhetorically, the conflation of speaker and cause seems significant because her self-fashioning becomes not simply an attempt to appear well before a judge, as both Cicero and Quintilian recommend, but also Shakespeare's means of producing character-effects. For the very term, *causa*, denotes not just "cause" or "grounds," but also "motive" or "reason."[25] In Shakespeare's depiction, Marina's *causa* will constitute her case *and* the dramatic illusion of motivation because of how she argues on her own behalf. Put differently, her self-referential language of defense creates the person-effects of self-awareness and intelligent purpose.

Correspondingly, because forensic discourse requires orators to engage and manipulate auditors to their cause, Marina orchestrates how her listeners should understand her own person. To persuade an auditor, she redescribes the person and intentions of interlocutors like Leonine as contrary to their own stated purposes.[26] Whether she succeeds or fails in these cases, judicial oratory imparts the dramatic action of one character attempting to persuade other characters on the basis of their causes. If Marina self-fashions in her appeals from *ethos*, she other-fashions in her descriptions of her opponent or her auditors. In all of this, however, the dramatic illusion of Marina's designs and expectations and potential to manage or direct others are character-effects derived from Shakespeare's use of forensic speech.

Indeed, Shakespeare sets the scene of confrontation between Marina and Leonine in terms of Marina as *causa honesta* versus Leonine's case, which appears wholly *turpis* or "foul." After Dionyza reminds Leonine to slay Marina, they converse:

> Dionyza: Let not conscience
> Which is but cold, inflame love in thy bosom,
> Nor let pity, which even women have cast off,
> Melt thee, but be a soldier to thy purpose.
> Leonine: I will do't, but yet *she is a goodly creature*.
> Dionyza: The fitter then the gods should have her.
> *Here she comes weeping her only nurse's death.*
> Thou art resolved?
> Leonine: I am resolved. (4.1.4–12, my emphasis).

Leonine's resolve to slay Marina means that in his subsequent debate with her over whether or not she should live, his side will represent a *turpis causa*, despite his knowledge that Marina is a "goodly creature," which is to say she is *honestam*. Rhetorically, when Marina debates Leonine for her life, she will defend a *causa honesta* that is synonymous with her dramatic person.

Thus, the description of how Marina enters to confront Leonine — "here she comes weeping her only nurse's death" — constitutes an embedded stage direction for the actor playing Marina, which is another strategy of forensic rhetoric. Though usually reserved for the peroration, action or *actio* may always enhance a defense through an appeal to *pathos*. Quintilian testifies: "I know that the wearing of mourning and the presentation of an unkempt appearance, and the introduction of relatives similarly arrayed, has proved of value, and that entreaties have been of great service to save the accused from condemnation."[27] Though Marina's attire remains a question, her weeping entrance enacts a similar visual attempt to arouse pity, just like an expert orator should present the accused. Shakespeare uses the techniques of judicial oratory—the *causa honesta* and appeals from *pathos*—in order to establish Marina as innocently accused even before she assumes her self-defense.

Most important, as an orator, Marina should enact an essential strategy for securing the good will of judges by emphasizing her own person. The *Ad Herennium* advises: "From our own person [*nostra persona*], we shall secure goodwill . . . by setting forth our disabilities [*incommoda*], need [*inopiam*], loneliness [*solitudinem*], and misfortune [*calamitatem*]."[28] Such attributes, designed for forensic speakers, first appear in the very terms by which Marina describes her state. "Ay me, poor maid," she exclaims of herself, "born in a tempest when my mother died, / This world to me is as a lasting storm" (4.1.18). Though "tempest imagery" may stand for tragic outcomes, which the romance genre eventually overcomes, in the context of forensic rhetoric, Marina's statement signals what the *Ad Herennium* calls "our *incommoda* and *calamitas*." The same early modern Latin dictionaries translate the first term as "hurtful, troublous and noisesome" and the second as "destruction, miserie and adversity"; each or any of these descriptions could apply to Marina in her self-lamentation.[29] Dionyza, next, questions—"How now, Marina, why do you keep alone?" (4.1.20)—which explicitly draws attention to her *solitudo*. Marina's subsequent description of her birth—"When I was born / Never was waves nor wind more violent" (4.1.57–58)—iterates the other three attributes necessary for persuasive fashioning of the accused in a final instance. In summary, forensic rhetoric reveals a strategy to shape *ethos*, which presents Marina as "a goodly creature" less in terms of romance's symbolism or characterlogical archetypes and more according to those attributes necessary for persuasive appeals "from our own person."

Leonine, next, declares his intentions, which amounts to the *questio* for adjudication, whether or not Marina deserves death. After the *questio*, Leonine reveals that he is Marina's opponent and judge, and she gives her exordium:

> Marina: Why would you kill me?
> Leonine: To satisfy my lady.
> Marina: Why would she have me killed now?
> As I can remember, by my troth,

> I never did her hurt in all my life.
> I never spake bad word, nor did ill turn
> To any living creature. Believe me, la,
> I never killed a mouse nor hurt a fly.
> I trod upon a worm against my will,
> But I wept for't. How have I offended,
> Wherein my death might yield her any profit, or
> My life imply her any danger? (4.1.69–78)

Once the question for debate is clarified, Marina begins her exordium in the speech above, following the advice of Roman rhetorical teaching for forensic occasions. There are two ways to open a judicial oration, argues the *Ad Herennium*, the *principium*, "the Direct Opening," or the *insinuatio*, the "Subtle Approach." If your cause is of "the honourable kind"—again, what the Latin refers to as *sin honestum genus causae*—then the orator may employ the *principium*.[30] The "Subtle Approach," in contrast, not only requires dissimulation, but also is best for dealing with hostile judges. Cicero calls the *principium* a simple, direct address in "plain language," which makes the auditor "well-disposed, receptive, and attentive," whereas "insinuation is an address which by dissimulation and indirection unobtrusively steals into the mind of the auditor."[31] Leonine represents not only the opposing cause, but also Marina's judge so the manner with which she opens becomes Shakespeare's further means of distinguishing Marina's dramatic person. She might employ a "subtle approach," for her judge is hostile, yet she chooses the *principium*, which reveals how much Shakespeare wishes to emphasize her "honest" person and case. Just as Marina cannot "hurt a fly," she cannot speak a "bad word" or employ deceptive pretense.

So Marina appeals for mercy by creating a self-portrait of innocence, reminding Leonine of her past and, in doing so, inviting him to pity her. The exordium, as we have seen, is the very place to establish *ethos*. According to the *Ad Herennium*, *ethos* requires a speaker to create an impression of virtue without appearing arrogant, conveying an impression of modesty.[32] In describing an exordium, Cicero writes that an audience's good will may be acquired "from our own person if we refer to our own acts and services without arrogance"; the author of *Ad Herennium* concurs, adding that if a speaker reveals his or her past good conduct toward "parents, friends, or the audience," listeners become more receptive.[33] And for Quintilian, a speaker that projects a good self-image may prompt auditors into feeling calm or gentle, if not benevolent.[34] Shakespeare dramatizes the dilemma of establishing *ethos* in the passage above: Marina reviews her personal history in a modest, plain way, which reveals her past good conduct. Marina's *ethos* should appear exemplary in an *exordium* and in a way that is direct, according the rule of the *principium*, so that she may transform Leonine into a receptive auditor.

The rhetorical context of forensic speech and *ethos* becomes clearer when Marina speaks to Leonine of his person, attempting to touch his conscience. As in Aristotle's assessment, *ethos* affects the relationship between the speaker and the audience. An orator should "make his own character look right and put his hearers, who are to decide, in the right frame of mind" for "it adds much to an orator's influence that his own character should look right and that he should be thought to entertain the right feeling towards his hearers; and also that his hearers themselves should be in the right frame of mind."[35] In the context of Roman oratory, Aristotle's objectives should be met in an exordium that will induce a feeling of good will toward the speaker in the audience, which is caused by "discussion of the person of our hearers."[36] Along the same lines, Cicero defines the purpose of an introduction in terms of the "mind of the auditor," which the orator shapes "into a proper condition to receive the rest of speech." The orator, therefore, aims at making an auditor "well-disposed" (*benevolus*), "attentive" (*attentus*), and "receptive" (*docilis*).[37]

As with her appeal from *ethos*, Marina enacts the Roman instructions for creating "good will" in audiences. In reference to Leonine's threat to murder her, Marina says:

> You will not do't for all the world, I hope.
> You are well favored, and your looks foreshow
> You have a gentle heart. I saw you lately
> When you caught hurt in parting two that fought.
> Good sooth, it showed well in you. Do so now.
> Your lady seeks my life. Come you between
> And save poor me, the weaker. (4.1.80–86)

In this second part of her exordium, Marina focuses on her audience—the man who would kill her. As the pronoun "I" was used earlier to establish *ethos*, here "you" is repeated, drawing attention to Leonine, his moral identity and behavior. The *Ad Herennium* explains: "From the discussion of the person of our hearers goodwill is secured if we set forth the courage [*fortiter*], wisdom [*sapienter*], humanity [*mansuete*], and nobility [*magnifice*] of past judgments they have rendered, and if we reveal what esteem [*existimatio*] they enjoy and with what interest their decision is awaited."[38] Marina's words enact these instructions, suggesting that Leonine's previous wise and courageous action will continue with her survival: by sparing her, he confirms his practice of good judgment from before. By recalling the noble actions of Leonine, Marina's appeal includes the rhetorical prescription that a speaker should exhibit good will toward an audience. Marina does not merely want to survive, she wants Leonine to "show well" in deeds, if only he will save the weaker party, sparing his victim. Indeed, Shakespeare's use of "shows well" translates *existimatio*, what the Latin-English dictionaries of the time refer to as "esteem, good reputation, and even renown."[39]

In Marina's speech to Leonine, we should recognize how Shakespeare's attention to and enactment of an appeal from *ethos* within the context of judicial oratory reveals his composition of person-effects. For Aristotle, a persuasive *ethos* emerges from the projection of three qualities: good sense, good moral character, and good will.[40] Marina's words of self-defense create an impression of a speaker concerned with just conduct, exemplifying a moral *ethos*. By questioning the reasons for her murder, she shows good sense as well. In recalling the noble actions of Leonine, her appeal includes good will toward her auditor. More than that, Marina appears to self-fashion in defense of an innocent person and cause, which her person provides: Her language, in fact, cannot be separated from her character because her language is designed to reveal her character. Instead of abandoning classical rhetorical techniques or, more particularly, forensic speech for the late plays' new and more ambiguous style, Shakespeare uses them in his composition of Marina.[41]

Because Marina's person becomes her cause, an appeal from *ethos* concomitantly enacts her defense. Such a rhetorical combination would invite theatergoers to infer motivation and polemical purpose on her part, such as transforming Leonine's emotional perception of Dionyza's charge to kill her so that she may save herself. Marina's attempt at conveying *ethos* aims at preventing Leonine's further provocation, soothing her attacker rather than agitating him, perhaps saving her life, an imperative that constitutes her case and motivation in this scene. In the classical rhetorical tradition, persuasion occurs through a projection of self in speech, which encompasses the speaker's audience in an attempt to move them with feelings of pity and even emulation. From either the dramatic or forensic context, as Marina shapes Leonine's perception of herself, she attempts to fashion an identity for him. Her words suggests to Leonine how others could believe that he is noble and his intention to commit murder was merely an aberration from his usual conduct, a mistake that he may now retract. Any of these putative characterological designs, however, are actually person-effects that result from Shakespeare's use forensic discourse.

JUDICIAL ORATORY OR SHAKESPEARE'S LATE STYLE?

The same judicial oratory that Shakespeare employs to fashion person-effects would prompt or direct the early modern actor's impassioned delivery. In fact, many of the attributes that supposedly distinguish the late style may be understood as directions for playing passion. McDonald qualifies the late style in terms of rupture or displacement, including techniques such as irregularities within blank verse, convoluted syntax, parenthetical or additive speech, and, especially, the use of repetition.[42] Yet these very traits, as we saw in the last two chapters' examination of classical rhetorical techniques and early modern personation, provide "cues" for actors to play passions.[43] As Simon Palfrey and Tiffany Stern remind us:

> Passions were written into plays, identified by actors looking at parts, extracted by the audience: they were some of the major building-blocks that went to make up plays and defined what plays were. Consequently, it was one of the first jobs of the actor, upon receiving his part, to search out and animate his own "cues" for passion; and it was one of the first heady tasks of the playwright to write them.[44]

Here the term "part" indicates the portion of a script that an actor would receive, a written transcription of a particular character's lines and a brief cue. Actors would study their parts not only to identify passions from figural language or prosody but also for transitions between different passions—what the above passage labels as "one of the first jobs of actor"—because these skills were essential for "pronunciation," the articulation of individual words and lines.[45] Thus, Palfrey and Stern advocate a form of theatrical close-reading, an attentiveness to reading the part-texts or "parts," which connects language to character by way of personation. In contrast, the late style heuristic employs similar close-reading skills to separate language from character.[46]

To exemplify the differences, let us return to Marina's exordium in address to Leonine. Marina's words are in blank verse, though occasionally irregular and often interrupted by caesura. So the regular line—"I NEver DID her HURT in ALL my LIFE"—is followed by lines that afford opportunities for variation:

> I NEver SPAKE BAD WORD, nor did ILL TURN,
> To ANy LIVing CREAture. BeLIEVE me, LA. (4.1.72–73)

If the first line substitutes spondees for iambs on "bad word" and "ill turn" for emphasis, the second includes an extra syllable and the exclamation, "la," which would cue emphatic statement or a burst of feeling. McDonald criticizes mimetic accounts of verse as "an old-fashioned argument about character," but variations in stress are precisely the means actors would employ in order to identify passions.[47] Palfrey and Stern spotlight the importance of iambic verse for identifying particular words to stress in light of rhetoric's overall charge of persuasion as two essential guideposts for early modern pronunciation. "Though all remaining parts are lightly punctuated," just like plays in manuscript that remain, "that punctuation varies markedly from script to script."[48] Early modern actors, in other words, search for rhetorical signals about how to play vocal difference, articulating distinctions in voice or tone or passion between and among phrases and even individual words. So the choices about stress in the examples above should combine with the content or rhetorical purpose of forensic oratory. In this case, Marina reminds Leonine of her past good conduct by stressing the wickedness she refrained from doing, thereby projecting persuasive *ethos*. In doing so, she follows Cicero's recommendation that an audience's good will may be acquired "from our own person if we refer to our own acts and services without arrogance." What both prosody and rhetorical genre may illustrate, therefore, is how an early modern actor might understand the language of his part-text as the technical means for vivifying his performance of an appeal from *ethos*.[49]

So, too, within the mostly regular blank verse speech of Marina, interpolations like "by my troth," and "believe me," alternate with assertions such as "I never kill'd a mouse nor hurt a fly," followed by qualifications, "as I can remember," and "I trod upon a worm against my will, / But I wept for't." Interpolations, digressions, or "syntactical divagation" in the late plays, McDonald asserts, fail to demonstrate "an index of passion or mental confusion" on the part of character but, instead, illustrate "a kind of jagged music," revealing "shortcuts to meaning." The sentences' irregular manner in the late style instead corresponds to the adventurous, wandering romantic narrative. "The parallels between syntax and larger elements of structure," McDonald insists, "suggest unity of inspiration."[50] Though such a literary unity may exist, in terms of performance, the classical rhetorical tradition recognizes the "violent disruption of the natural order of words and ideas" as the "most unmistakable signs of violent feeling, because those who really are angry or afraid . . . come forward with one idea and then rush off to some other."[51] As in the case of prosody, these disruptions, what rhetoricians classify as *hyperbaton*, would cue the performance of passion under the auspices of persuasion.[52]

A second and more complex example of such a disruptive quality appears when Marina defends herself against Lysimachus's advances in an equally pronounced forensic occasion. Marina understands Lysimachus in terms similar to Leonine, as both hostile judge and opponent in a forensic debate over the nature of her person, whether she is guilty or innocent, in this instance, of prostitution. In the case of the brothel scene, her exchange with Lysimachus begins:

> Lysimachus: Now pretty one, how long have you been
> at this TRADE?
> Marina: What TRADE, sir?
> Lysimachus: Why, I cannot NAME'T but I shall OFFEND.
> Marina: I cannot be OFFENDED with my TRADE. Please you
> to NAME IT. (4.5.70–75)

My typographical adjustments visually illustrate words that could heighten passion through vocal modulation upon repeated terms. Marina's cue words—"trade" and "offend"—would echo in her own lines, after all. Even so, in this case, Marina well knows what "trade" her location signifies, and she finds both the brothel and what it advertises offensive even before Lysimachus arrives. In defying Lysimachus's allegations, she means to redefine herself as innocent against her surroundings just as she protested her innocence against Leonine's death sentence. In both instances, Marina represents the *causa honesta*, which aligns with her person, while her interlocutor will represent the *causa turpis* as well as a hostile judge. On this occasion, however, she makes her final and successful appeal not to be raped in a single sentence:

> For me
> That am a maid, though most ungentle Fortune
> Have placed me in this sty, where since I came
> Diseases have been sold dearer than physic—
> O, that the gods
> Would set me free from this unhallowed place,
> Though they did change me to the meanest bird
> That flies i'th'purer air! (4.5.90–106)[53]

Marina's short speech begins by emphasizing her person in the objective case but quickly turns to describing her location—the brothel, what she calls a "sty"—that she proceeds to elaborate upon until a sudden break in thought occurs, a prayer for freedom.

What proponents of the "late style" refer to as Shakespeare's digressive quality, therefore, emerges in both of Marina's forensic speeches. In the first defense against Leonine, Marina's thoughts roam from questioning whether she could kill any living creature to remembering what she did before forcibly excusing herself; in the second, Marina breaks from describing herself into a wish that she would return to "purer air." In each case, however, Marina employs what classical and early modern rhetoricians consider figures of interruption, referred to as *hyperbaton* or *epanorthosis*, which amend or correct thoughts for the sake of making a "more vehement" utterance.[54] These figures explicitly cue the playing of passions to the actor. Performed accordingly, signs of "violent passion" like "fear" would prompt the speaker to imitate the supposed psychological state of a person in danger.

If we observe what parts of an oration Shakespeare composes for Marina, the prompts for playing passion become easier to imagine. As Marina's first speech to Leonine enacts the instructions for an *exordium*, her last speech to Lysimachus above represents the *peroratio*, which should include an impassioned plea. In addressing Leonine, Marina's "shortcuts to meaning" are an attempt at the plain and direct approach of the *principium*. All of her digressive clauses follow Ciceronian prescriptions for developing *ethos*, presenting an upright character in self-defense, even if in a "jagged" manner. On the stage, however, Marina ostensibly searches for a reason why Leonine would put her to death and, given the stakes, speaks in distress, following the figures of disruption or amendment of thought. At the other end of an oration, Cicero teaches that after summarization, the peroration should divide into two parts, deploying the devices of amplification to incite feelings of hatred against adversaries and, second, feelings of sympathy for the speaker's point of view.[55] In the first part, the *indignatio*, the speaker uses commonplaces, such as a "display of passion," which reveals "who is affected by this act we are denouncing."[56] By mentioning "disease" and denouncing the brothel wherein she finds herself as a "maid," Marina's part-text would cue anger, which an actor playing her role would hope to incite in both his on and offstage auditors and against Marina's imprisonment. In the next section, Marina's final appeal to the gods could incite feelings of sympathy, enacting the *conquestio*, the last part of the peroration, for Cicero also recommends that presenting the misfortunes the accused has suffered will move auditors toward pity.[57] Whether by way of *exordium* or *peroratio*, the forensic genre imparts directions for the performance of passion, which corresponds with the deployment of figures and intensifies the appeal of Marina's *causa honesta* in both instances.

The recognition of playing "passions," as in my analysis above, may resolve critical controversy over Marina's peroration to Lysimachus, which is accused by critics of brevity or justified by others because of its powerful imagery.[58] Though Marina's final appeal appears truncated to some critics, Lysimachus replies to her words: "I did not think / thou couldst have spoke so well, ne'er dreamt thou / couldst" (4.5.107–9). In the figural context of *hyperbaton* and *epanorthosis* and with knowledge of what passions forensic discourse may arouse, Marina's lines to Lysimachus are persuasive because of how they allow for vocal modulation to reflect a sudden change in thought for the sake of creating a more vehement utterance. Marina's brevity, use of images, and plea to the gods for freedom are moving, in other words, precisely because of *how* she should speak, that is, with passion. Lysimachus's assessment of Marina's eloquence testifies just as much to Marina's delivery as to her content. Even so, the figures of "violent disruption" cue such a passionate performance for the actor playing the part of Marina.[59] Just as Stern and Palfrey observe, "passions were written into plays" in sections like this one.

Indeed, Marina's forensic speeches further and finally cue passion because of how they use word repetition.[60] The *Ad Herennium* calls the figure of *conduplicatio*, or the "repetition of one or more words," an "appeal to pity," because "the reiteration of the same word makes a deep impression upon the hearer and inflicts a major wound ... as if a weapon should repeatedly pierce the same part of the body."[61] And Renaissance rhetorician Thomas Wilson provides an approximate translation in maintaining that "the oft repeating of one word doth much stir the hearer and makes the word seem greater, as though a sword were oft digged and thrust twice or thrice in one place of the body."[62] Such "weapons" are tools of persuasion because of how they prescribe the performance of passion.

As with digressive syntax, Marina uses word repetition to blend appeals from *pathos* with the disclosure of her psychological state within the fiction. In her *exordium*, she says "I never" three times, twice in succession at the beginning of a line, using *anaphora* to list all the misdeeds she could never do.[63] The repetition of the word "I" continues throughout, employing the figure of *ploche*, which amplifies the appeal from pity as it emphasizes her innocent character.[64] In her peroration to Lysimachus, instead of "I," the word "me" occurs four times in a single sentence. Renaissance theorist George Puttenham explains that figures of repetition employ "sensible approaches" upon an audience's mind, using the ear as conduit. To rule the "mind of man" is the "greatest and most glorious conquest," but the mind is not "assailable" except by audible "sweetness of speech," which exhibits the "greatest force for instruction or discipline."[65] For Puttenham, figures of repetition help orators because speech enacts an incantatory quality that persuades auditors by manipulating their emotions. But in order to influence auditors, as we have seen, emotion must be present in the speaker first. As Quintilian advises: "The chief requisite, then, for moving the feelings of others is, as far as I can judge, that *we ourselves be moved*, for the assumption of grief, anger, and indignation will be often ridiculous, if we adapt merely our words and looks, and not our minds, to those passions."[66] In the classical rhetorical tradition, we discover the relationship between figures like *anaphora* and *ploche* to appeals from *pathos*, which become early modern theatrical cues for the actor to experience the passion he or she wishes to arouse in auditors.

In Marina's case, these figures may influence the ear of Leonine or Lysimachus. Her use of repetition amplifies her appeal, revealing the person-effect of innocence through self-referential discourse. The techniques for recognizing how to play passion, therefore, remain subordinated less to an overall narrative design of the play's entirety and more to the rhetorical purpose of an individual dramatic person and in accordance with conventional practices for pronunciation. More than that, as the rhetorical style of acting and linguistic self-fashioning converge, Marina's speech and her character become inseparable: Her repeated "I" is meant to persuade Leonine, just as her repeated "me" should sway Lysimachus, but to persuade them on the basis of who she is.

So, too, Marina uses these rhetorical occasions to inspire the perception of *her* "good will" toward her auditors, despite their causes or motives. In Marina's earlier exchange with Leonine, she pleads that she does not deserve death and, in the brothel, that her purity should not violated. With Leonine, she repeats the word "you" in an attempt to refashion her auditor's intentions, but she does the same with Lysimachus:

If YOU were born to honour, show it now;

> If put upon YOU, make the judgement good
> That thought YOU worthy of it. (4.5.96–98)

Thus, the same crucial advice for orators from the *Ad Herennium* for dealing with auditors who are judges—"from the discussion of the person of our hearers goodwill is secured . . . if we reveal what esteem [*existimatio*] they enjoy and with what interest their decision is awaited"—appears in Marina's focus upon the kind of noble judgment that she expects from both men. Though Leonine rejects her plea, Lysimachus responds:

> For me, be you bethoughten that I came
> With no ill intent, for to me the very doors
> And windows savour vilely. Fare thee well.
> Thou art a piece of virtue, and I doubt not
> But thy training hath been noble. (4.5.113–17)

When Lysimachus claims that he had not entered the brothel with bad intentions, he doesn't simply misrepresent his original purpose. Rather, in the context of judicial oratory, he testifies to how much he wishes to "show well" in *her* judgment, which is perhaps Shakespeare's foreshadowing of why, ultimately, Lysimachus will be a better spouse for Marina than he otherwise first appears. What occurs in his change of purpose represents the success of Marina's judicial oratory, a victory which arises from her appeal from *ethos*, what Lysimachus refers to in calling Marina a "piece of virtue" and from her corresponding display of "good will" toward her auditor.

Because forensic discourse weds together metrical effect, syntax, repetition, and *ethos* in Marina's oratory, the division between speaker and language in the late plays should be questioned. Addressing the metrical and syntactic schemes in Leontes's tantrums, McDonald writes, "such instances of poetic mimesis, satisfying as they may be, are for the most part anomalous."[67] Language in the late plays, instead, shows "meanings reflecting not the character's frame of mind but the larger 'design' of the play."[68] To the question of Marina in particular, Anne Barton likewise argues for character as narrative device: "Shakespeare appears to be using Marina less as a character than as a kind of medium, through which the voice of the situation can be made to speak."[69] Yet my analysis indicates more of rhetoric's art than romance's design. As a result, the divisions between character and language, persuasion and repetition, a character's emotional state and syntax, all of these assumed oppositions, become tenuous.

Though the romance tradition of criticism encourages an either/or dilemma between character and plot, or character and authorial purpose, or character and the disclosure of ideology, Shakespeare did not appear to compose Marina's dramatic person with such disjunctives in mind. Instead of a modal contestation between tragedy and romance, which Marina and her disputants ostensibly dramatize, we discover judicial oratory's central feature: its focus on *controversiae* or debates between opposing sides, accuser and defendant, in this case, *causa turpis* and *causa honesta*.[70] Judicial oratory, instead of a bygone practice, provides the essential material for Shakespeare's presentation and impassioned delivery of Marina's dramatic person and speech.

THE RECOGNITION SCENE AND MARINA'S *NARRATIO*

So far, I have demonstrated how Marina performs as advocate of and even witness to her own *cause*, and her own cause, in turn, concerns and discloses her person. For this reason, all of Marina's forensic debates turn upon her opponents' recognition of Marina's person, as well as her cause, as "honest." The most climactic instance of this recognition, of course, occurs in Marina's reunion with Pericles.

In forensic terms, the rhetoric of self-defense connects the language of self-fashioning with an attempt to appear well before a judge—and these circumstances mirror those under which Marina appears before both her king and father. We have seen how the *Ad Herennium* advises such speakers. In order to win over judges, an orator should appeal from his "own person," and emphasize his "disabilities, need, loneliness, and misfortune."[71] To envision these qualities in Marina's reunion with Pericles, Shakespeare follows forensic instructions for a *narratio*—a chronological, clear, and brief description of events—that in this case or cause will detail the personal history of Marina. So when Marina shares the tale of her birth and life to Pericles, she delivers a *narratio*, what she refers to as "my history" (5.1.108), demonstrating once again how her cause and her person are the same.

Appropriately enough for an appeal from Marina's own person, she uses *martyria* throughout her discourse with her father, a rhetorical figure that confirms a question by one's own experience. *Martyria* signifies proof because it provides testimony, or the "character of witnesses, which carries the force of argument"; it is also a figure employed to establish *ethos*.[72] Of course, in a general sense, *ethos* is the question under consideration: Who is this girl, called before Pericles? As the recognition scene unfolds, Shakespeare shows the power of Marina witnessing to her own story while Pericles, like a judge interrogating a witness, responds by explicitly calling for the *narratio* with his commands, "report thy parentage" (5.1.120) and "tell thy story" (125). Pericles reassures Marina: "I'll hear you more, to th' bottom of your story, / And never interrupt you" (155–56).[73]

As Marina's earlier speeches provide paradigms of either an *exordium* or a *peroratio*, and both in relation to forensic argument, Shakespeare now provides her with a *narratio* for the reunion scene, indicating how the design of a dramatic person corresponds with oratorical partitioning of discourse.[74] In judicial oratory the end of an *exordium* transitions to the *narratio*, a statement of facts that concerns a particular case. As Thomas Wilson's *The Art of Rhetoric* (1560) summarizes: "After the preface and first entrance, the matter must be opened and everything lively told, that the hearers may full perceive what we go about." Such a statement of facts Wilson refers to as a "report," the "substance of the tale" or "narration," or the "reporting our tale," echoing Pericles's own terms above.[75] Wilson follows the *Ad Herennium* in this section of his *The Art of Rhetoric*, and so both texts suggest how brevity remains essential for lucidity. "Our statement of facts will be clear if we set forth the facts in the precise order in which they occurred, observing their actual or probable sequence and chronology," represents the Roman version. The author adds that "the shorter" the narrative, "the clearer will it be and the easier to follow."[76] And Wilson echoes the teaching: "And therefore to make our matter plain, that all may understand it, the best were first and foremost to tell everything in order, so much as is needful, observing both the time, the place, the manner of doing, and the circumstances thereunto belong."[77] In Marina's "story," she enacts these directions, articulating a sequence of events that observes time, place, and circumstances.

More artfully, the emphasis upon "story" reveals the character-effect of patience in Marina that critics wrongly assume to be the sole result of the play's romantic genre. The *narratio* described above constitutes Marina's personal history and anticipates Pericles's suspicions by urging "patience" upon him. Self-history and proactive refutation align in patience, a virtue transformed through *notatio* into a distinctive quality of Marina's own character. In the *Ad Herennium*, this figure means "character delineation," which lies in "describing a person's character by the definite signs, which, like distinctive marks, are attributes of that character"; in so doing, *notatio* describes "the qualities proper to each man's character."[78] Accordingly, Pericles will come to think of Marina in terms of patience because of how she deploys *notatio* in reference to herself. When Pericles claims he is mocked by Marina's story, she responds, "Patience, good sir," and Pericles replies, "nay, I'll be patient," for he already notices that Marina's story of shipwreck and loss shows her character to be "like Patience gazing on kings' graves and smiling / Extremity out of act" (5.1.129–37).[79]

Pericles hears Marina's story but discovers his daughter. In Marina's *narratio*, the strictures of forensic rhetoric become the means of Pericles's restoration. "A narrative," advises the *Ad Herennium*, that is based on "persons" ought to provide specific "traits of character," such as "gentleness" or "hope and fear, distrust and desire"; but most important, the narrative also ought to include responses to "the vicissitudes of life, such as reversal of fortune, unexpected disaster, sudden joy, and a happy outcome."[80] Like a good Ciceronian orator and a heroine of Shakespearean romance, Marina discloses her person by describing how she was born at sea, how she escaped murder in Tarsus, how pirates captured her and placed in a brothel against her will, where she was separated from her father, a king named Pericles, and all because of a series of misfortunes (5.1.147–69).

In another rhetorical sense, Marina's approach to Pericles is simply a version of the ingratiating means used to establish *ethos* reviewed earlier, but the emphasis upon "her story" now directs attention to a particular virtue; in this way, Marina speaks of herself and to Pericles's distraught state. She states this dual purpose, indicating how her story should change Pericles, by referring to herself in the third person: "She speaks, / My lord, that may be hath endured a grief / Might equal yours, if both were justly weighed" (5.1.77–79). Because Marina's words define patience as her foremost quality, she rebukes Pericles from his self-induced silence, for in dealing with trials, if Marina's tales are true, Pericles must confess to his daughter, "thou art a man, and I / Have suffered like a girl" (5.1.127–28).

The use of *martyria* and *notatio* within Marina's narration again reveals the problems with subordinating character to romance typology or its generic restraints. Though Marina may have been patient in undergoing her trials, she is not patience personified, a virtue speaking through a character; her speech identifies her person as the daughter of Pericles, whose wanderings fit with Pericles's own recollection of leaving Marina in Tarsus.[81] Patience is a foremost attribute within the rhetorical context of *ethos*, Marina's account of herself to Pericles, not within the poetical or narrative context of character, indicating typology. For similar reasons, Marina's self-presentation does not simply show the design of romantic narrative, such that her words convey a "mathematical problem," another riddle for Pericles to unravel, which invokes the themes of "clarifying the obscure" or "understanding the elliptical."[82] The emphasis upon either Marina's patience or the discovery of her identity may correspond with the narrative structure of the play, but the recognition scene derives from another rhetorical display, enacted by a speaker who manages to praise herself without conveying arrogance, thereby establishing *ethos*, and, in that process, she revives Pericles. As Jeanne Grant Moore writes of Marina, "she also appears to have an education in classical rhetoric; she is the educated aristocratic lady of Renaissance humanism." For Moore, Marina's "education and intelligence, as much as her virtue" saves the heroine from the brothel; her "eloquence even redeems others."[83] Eloquence, too, restores Marina's father.

Indeed, the recognition of Marina's eloquence provides nuance to the critical reception history of her dramatic person. First, both mythological and more historical analyses might be reexamined as unknowingly recording the influence of appeals from *ethos*, which they confuse with typology or allegory, as in the following statements: Marina "incorporates an eternal essence of personified Truth and Justice." Or, because of how her words and person seemingly heal others, in Jungian terms, "Marina is an Anima figure, a feminine presence presiding over renewal or rebirth." Or, within the historical context of Shakespeare drawing upon medieval religious drama, Marina "culminates a long and popular tradition of incorruptibly virtuous heroines going back to the saint's legend of St. Agnes."[84] Yet what Pericles eventually comes to believe—that Marina "seem'st a place / For the crowned Truth to dwell in" (5.1.112–13)— actually testifies to how powerfully her appeals from *ethos* and expert use of forensic discourse functions within the play's dramatic action.

The importance of the classical oratorical tradition in Shakespeare's development of Marina means that sentimental accounts of her character should be reevaluated as well. Inga-Stina Ewbank believes truth telling is the "technique" of Marina, a technique that is shown through the "the completely naturalistic strain" of her words. Remarking on Marina's style, Ewbank calls it "language which mediates between the strange and the true, often by simply stating the impossible, as the truth which it is."[85] In this reading, "the real miracle lies in what and who she is, and to determine this he [Pericles] need only ask a factual question and receive a simple answer, which is felt now, at this point in the structure, with as much impact as any poetic image: 'My name is Marina.'"[86] Here the reunion scene amounts to a transparent revelation of a miracle, as naturalism and romance theme merge. Ewbank is obviously right that Marina's words are an accurate account of all she underwent, but the highest virtue of the expression of *ethos*, argues Quintilian, consists "in making it seem that all that we say derives directly from the nature of the facts and persons concerned and in the revelation of the character of the orator in such a way that all may recognize it."[87] Marina's "statement of facts"— her narrative—manifests another appeal from *ethos*. What appears as spontaneous candor is the person-effect of how Shakespeare crafts Marina's sophisticated appeals from *ethos*.

Even in a dramatic context, Marina would be aware of her charge. Summoned before a king whose silent despair results from the loss of wife and daughter, she attempts to assuage his pain by presenting her own story of woe.[88] Significantly, Marina's "story" shows courage in the face of suffering, thereby restoring her father in a double sense. As his daughter is returned to him so returns his will to live. The latter, we may speculate, was the intended effect of her speech, and the former a serendipity that makes the play called a romance. Ewbank emphasizes the coincidence but ignores Marina's art. The reunion of Pericles and Marina is not a mere matter of question and answer, but the fruit of persuasion and chance. Miracles attend the use of eloquence as much as unlikely occurrences in plot development. Rather than the absence of rhetoric, the reunion scene highlights its importance.

Critics assume the rhetorical tradition does not apply to the romance genre, but Shakespeare employed it in several late plays. "The thematics of the romances," John Porter Houston writes, "are not those of tragedy, and although the conventions of romance are old enough, rhetorical theory did not bother with this kind of writings."[89] Yet Marina's speeches consistently disprove that idea. So, too, the same judicial oratory delineated in the case of Marina appears in other late plays, ranging from Alcibiades's defense of his friend from *Timon of Athens* (ca. 1607) to Leontes and Paulina's debate over whether or not Hermione is a "good Queen" from *The Winter's Tale* (1609), and including Fletcher and Shakespeare's composition of Queen Katherine's honest "cause" against King Henry VIII, another hostile judge, in *All is True* (1613).[90] Shakespeare's use of forensic speech in the late plays challenges what critics would otherwise and too often label another "romantic episode," with an unrealistic or miraculous sense of causality, a passage that only a narratological view of the dialogue may fully justify.[91]

The significance of Marina's eloquence, finally, returns us to the question of whether Shakespeare's dramatic persons could embed the character-effect of a coherent self. In an argument that "the category of 'character' has been justly disparaged by historicists and theorists of various persuasions," Alan Sinfield stipulates that there may be intermittent signs that "the characters experience themselves as *continuous subjectivities*."[92] Elsewhere, however, Sinfield explains that the impression of a character's "subjectivity" emerges from the interplay of different discourses in which a character swerves "between divergent possible selves."[93] Yet Marina's forensic speech cannot be relegated to a discrete moment of interior disclosure unrelated to the presentation of her dramatic person elsewhere in the play. The use of both *martyria* and *notatio* within her "story" demonstrate the person-effect of self-understanding in regard to the actions of the play in which she participated, requiring us to view Marina as a character who experiences and explains herself as a "continuous subjectivity," a dramatic person who consciously recollects and reflects upon all that she underwent. The events that Marina "experienced" become the means of Pericles's crucial restoration. In Shakespeare's design, Marina's story indicates a coherence of self, not a moment where she may diverge between possible identities. Such character-effects, we have seen, result from Shakespeare's ongoing use of classical oratory.

After Pericles recognizes Marina, he may refer to her as "Thou that beget'st him that did thee beget," and soon after, he hears the music of the spheres (5.1.185, 217). The restoration of Pericles, like the "resurrection" of a lost daughter, occurs through Marina's artful use of persuasion. The use of *ethos* in *Pericles* reflects Shakespeare's so-called "early" practices of characterization, though speakers typically used this art, as Luciana instructs Antipholus in *The Comedy of Errors*, to "apparel vice like virtue's harbinger."[94] Perhaps most prominently, the words of Richard from *The Third Part of Henry VI* illustrate how Shakespeare used *ethos* to reflect the acting style of personation. As I reviewed in chapter 1, Richard says of himself:

> Why, I can smile, and murther whiles I smile,
> And cry "Content" to that which grieves my heart,
> And wet my cheeks with artificial tears,
> And frame my face to all occasions.[95]

The capacity to frame a face, suggests Barton, reveals the distinction between tragedy and romance: "Duncan had lamented that 'there's no art / To find the mind's construction in the face,' but in the Last Plays it seems to be true more often that no art is required." In the last plays, Barton writes, "faces tell all."[96] Barton's distinction captures the different ends to which characters like Richard and Marina employ *ethos*, but Shakespeare's skillful use of it seems the same.

NOTES

This chapter is an expanded and revised version of my earlier article, "'Falseness Cannot Come from Thee': Marina as Character and Orator in Shakespeare's *Pericles*," *Literary Imagination* 11, no. 1 (2009): 99–110.

1. On "late Shakespeare" and *Pericles*, see *Pericles: Third Series (Arden Shakespeare)*, ed. Suzanne Gossett (London: Methuen, 2004), 54: "the 'lateness paradigm is inadequate to describe a play which is not entirely by Shakespeare; on which Shakespeare worked when he was not yet forty-four years old; which reworks a plot that had already served as a frame for one of his earliest comedies; and which he may have been writing simultaneously with or shortly before Coriolanus, a play with ties to an entirely different section of Shakespeare's *oeuvre*." All subsequent citations from the play are from this edition and cited internally by act, scene, and line numbers. Gossett believes planning and writing on Pericles begins as early as the autumn of 1607; in February of 1608, Shakespeare takes over the play's composition, beginning with the third act and (coincidentally) during the same month when Susanna Shakespeare delivers a daughter. By March of 1608, Shakespeare pens the father/daughter reunion scene of the fifth act. The play is entered in the Stationers Register on 20 May 1608 and staged about the same time. See *Pericles*, 57–58, 61. On Shakespeare and late writing, see Gordon A. McMullan, *Shakespeare and the Idea of Late Writing: Authorship in the Proximity of Death* (Cambridge, UK: Cambridge University Press, 2008), 5: "The idea of 'late Shakespeare,' in other words, contributed to what I will call a discourse of lateness—that is, a construct, ideological, rhetorical and heuristic, a function not of life or of art but of the practice of reading or appreciating certain texts within a set of predetermined parameters. The history of Shakespearean criticism foregrounds the attribution to late style of the status of a kind of apotheosis, an almost mystical seal attached to the life of a genius . . . for the construction by others of modern and postmodern creative selfhoods."

2. On the influence of New Comedy on *Pericles*, see Robert S. Miola, *Shakespeare and Classical Comedy: The Influence of Plautus and Terence* (Oxford: Oxford University Press, 1994), 143–49. The quote above about "localities" is at 143 and on Marina at 148.

3. On the definition and importance of judicial oratory in England, see Quentin Skinner, *Forensic Shakespeare* (Oxford: Oxford University Press, 2014), 21–47.

4. On composition dates and Shakespeare's canon, see the "Timeline" appendix in *The Norton Shakespeare*, third edition, ed. Stephen Greenblatt (New York: W.W. Norton & Company, 2016), A35. On Shakespeare's use of judicial oratory in *Othello*, *Measure for Measure*, and *All's Well That Ends Well*, see Skinner's *Forensic Shakespeare*, 60–63. By

late 1607, Shakespeare completed *King Lear*, *Macbeth*, and *Antony and Cleopatra*. For a biographical account of this period, see James Shapiro's *The Year of Lear: Shakespeare in 1606* (New York: Simon & Schuster, 2015).

5. *Pericles* was first performed after the King's Men reopened at the Globe in 1608 and up to a year before the lease of the Blackfriars. The title page from the First Quarto of 1609 advertises that the play "hath been divers and sundry times acted by his Majesty's Servants" at "the Globe." For the title page, see *Pericles*, 2. For a recent reassessment of the importance of the indoor theatre for the development of a late style, see Bart van Es, "Reviving the Legacy of Indoor Performance," in *Moving Shakespeare Indoors: Performance and Repertoire in the Jacobean Playhouse*, ed. Andrew Gurr and Farah Karim-Cooper (Cambridge, UK: Cambridge University Press, 2014), 237–51.

6. On coauthorship and *Pericles*, the definitive study is MacDonald P. Jackson, *Defining Shakespeare: Pericles as Test Case* (Oxford: Oxford University Press, 2003); but see also Brian Vickers, *Shakespeare, Co-Author: A Historical Study of Five Collaborative Plays* (Oxford: Oxford University Press, 2008), 291–332. Consensus holds that, in general, the first two acts belong to Wilkins and the last three to Shakespeare. All the Marina speeches examined in this chapter would be Shakespeare's creation.

7. The romance or late plays typically include *The Winter's Tale* (1611), *Cymbeline* (1610), *The Tempest* (1611), and this chapter's focus, *Pericles, Prince of Tyre* (1607-8). See the "Timeline" appendix, *Norton Shakespeare*, 3rd ed., A35–36.

8. Anne Barton, "Leontes and the Spider: Language and Speaker in Shakespeare's Last Plays," in *Shakespeare's Styles: Essays in Honour of Kenneth Muir*, ed. Philip Edwards, Inga-Stina Ewbank, G. K. Hunter (Cambridge, UK: Cambridge University Press, 1980), 149. By taking exception with several excellent critics of style in the name of classical rhetoric, I show that "close reading" does not constitute a homogenous or an ahistorical practice. A secondary aim of this chapter's approach is to indicate the importance of "new formalism." For qualifications of and demurrals from the term, as well as examples of its practice, see Mark David Rasmussen (ed.), *Renaissance Literature and Its Formal Engagements* (New York: Palgrave, 2002); for a look at "the changing profession," see Marjorie Levinson, "What is New Formalism," *PMLA* 122, no.2 (2007): 558–69.

9. Russ McDonald, *Shakespeare's Late Style* (Cambridge, UK: Cambridge University Press, 2006), 33–34.

10. James Sutherland, "The Language of the Last Plays," in *More Talking of Shakespeare*, ed. John Garrett (London: Longmans, 1959), 146.

11. Philip Edwards is quoted from McMullan, *Shakespeare and the Idea of Late Writing*, 110. "Other-speaking" places character (and action) in a movement away from realism and toward symbolism.

12. "Patience" and "charity" are from Robert Uphaus's proposal that Pericles may be viewed as a figure for patience, or Cerimon for charity, and Gower as a symbol of the storyteller, an image of figural consciousness, which witnesses to the play's entire narratological design. See Robert Uphaus, "*Pericles* and the Conventions of Romance," in *Beyond Tragedy: Structure and Experience in Shakespeare's Romances* (Lexington: University Press of Kentucky, 1981), 34–48. For an overview of late play criticism, see Kiernan Ryan's introduction to *Shakespeare: The Last Plays* (London: Longman, 1999), 1–21.

13. Skinner, *Forensic Shakespeare*, 60–65. Skinner mentions Shakespeare's late "dramatic purposes" at 65 and refers to McDonald on the same page at n74.

14. On "cues" and how early modern actors approached the performance of passions, I follow Simon Palfrey and Tiffany Stern, *Shakespeare in Parts* (Oxford: Oxford University Press, 2007), 311–27.

15. Shakespeare's knowledge of rhetoric is not disputed. In addition to those sources cited in the previous chapters, see Brian Vickers, *Classical Rhetoric in English Poetry* (Carbondale: Southern Illinois University Press, 1989); for an introduction to the theoretical aspects of Renaissance rhetoric with some attention to Shakespeare, see Neil Rhodes, *The Power of Eloquence and English Renaissance Literature* (New York: St.

Martin's Press, 1992), 3–65. On Shakespeare's use of rhetoric, see especially Heinrich R. Plett, "Poeta Orator: Shakespeare as Orator Poet," in *Rhetoric and Renaissance Culture*; and Scott Crider, *With What Persuasion: An Essay on Shakespeare and the Ethics of Rhetoric*, Studies in Shakespeare, vol. 18, ed. Robert F. Willson, Jr. (New York: Peter Lang, 2009).

16. Aristotle, *Rhetoric*, in *The Rhetoric and Poetics of Aristotle*, trans. W. Rhys Roberts (New York: The Modern Library, 1954), 1356a4–10. For a general treatment of how Renaissance scholars combined Roman and Aristotelian rhetoric, see Brian Vickers, "Rhetoric and Poetics," in *The Cambridge History of Renaissance Philosophy*, ed. Charles B. Schmitt (Cambridge, UK: Cambridge University Press, 1988).

17. For the Roman tradition of rhetoric, the relationship between a speaker's character and persuasion was crucial. See *Ad Herennium*, 1.4.6–1.7.11; Cicero's *De Inventione*, 1.15–18; *De Oratore*, trans. E. W. Sutton and H. Rackham (Cambridge, MA: Harvard University Press, 1949), vol. 1, 2.78–80.

18. On Shakespeare's use of *ethos*, see Miriam Joseph, *Shakespeare's Use of the Arts of Language* (New York: Hafner Publishing Company, 1966), 272–86; on classical teachings on *ethos* and reception in Renaissance England, see Skinner, *Reason and Rhetoric in the Philosophy of Hobbes* (Cambridge, UK: Cambridge University Press, 1996), 127–33.

19. Forensic debate comprises the most influential sections of the *Ad Herennium* upon the Elizabethan revival of classical rhetoric. On the importance of judicial oratory in England, see Skinner, *Forensic Shakespeare*, 11–47. Skinner traces the dissemination of the *Ad Herennium* at 29–33.

20. For an outline of classical rhetoric with attention to its genres, see BrianVickers, *In Defense of Rhetoric* (Oxford: Oxford University Press, 2002), 52–82.

21. Aristotle's *Rhetoric* makes it clear that "any one is your judge whom you have to persuade" (1391b10–16).

22. *Ad Herennium*, 1.2.3. Cf., Cicero, *De Inventione*, 1.6.9: "Invention is the discovery of valid or seemingly valid arguments to render one's cause [*causam*] plausible"; and see Skinner, *Forensic Shakespeare*, 25.

23. *Ad Herennium*, 1.3.5.

24. Skinner, *Forensic Shakespeare*, 70–71.

25. See *causa* in John C. Traupman, *The New College Latin and English Dictionary*, second edition (New York: Bantam Books, 1995), 88. The first four entries—"cause, grounds, motive, reason"—may include both characterological and legal connotations.

26. I address the cases of Leonine and Lysimachus above; for Marina's persuasion of Bolt, see 4.5.160–203. Marina only fails to persuade Leonine, but her results should not impact any assessment of her as an orator. As Quintilian writes, rhetoric is the *science of speaking rightly*, which may occur independently of unfortunate results. For Quintilian's definition, see *Institutio Oratoria*, trans. H. E. Butler, (Cambridge, MA: Harvard University Press, 1977), 2.15.35; his discussion of fortune is at 2.15.12.

27. Quintilian, *Institutio Oratoria*, trans. Butler, 6.1.33–34.

28. *Ad Herennium*, 1.5.8

29. Early modern definitions of *incommoda* and *calamitas* are cited from Skinner, *Forensic Shakespeare*, 83.

30. *Ad Herennium*, 1.4.6.

31. *De Inventione*, 1.15.20.

32. *Ad Herennium*, 1.5.8.

33. Cicero's *De Inventione*, 1.15–18; *Ad Herennium*, 1.4.6–1.7.11.

34. On the effects of *ethos* upon the emotions of audiences, see *Institutio Oratoria*, trans. Butler, 6.2.13–19.

35. Aristotle's *Rhetoric*, 1377b21–1378a5. For Quintilian's version of this teaching, see *Institutio Oratoria*, trans. Butler, 6.2.13–19. Skinner, *Reason and Rhetoric in the Philosophy of Hobbes*, 129, summarizes Quintilian: "The orator's aim in establishing his ethos will not be to invent arguments, but rather to embark on the complementary task of manipulating the emotions of his audience."

36. *Ad Herennium* 1.5.8.

37. *De Inventione*, 1.15.20: "An exordium is a passage which brings the mind of the auditor [*exordium est oratio animum auditoris*] into a proper condition to receive the rest of the speech. This will be accomplished if he becomes well-disposed, attentive, and receptive."

38. *Ad Herennium*, 1.5.8. And see Thomas Wilson, *The Art of Rhetoric*, ed. Peter E. Medine (University Park: Pennsylvania State University Press, 1994), 136.

39. The Latin-English dictionaries are cited from Skinner, *Forensic Shakespeare*, 85.

40. Aristotle's *Rhetoric*, 1378a5–20.

41. The recognition of how judicial oratory works in disclosing Marina's character adds context to why Victorian critics celebrated Marina's character as well. Much of what David Skeele calls "Marinolatry" testifies to the power of Marina's appeals from *ethos* and the effects of her forensic speech in producing readers and playgoers who find Marina not only "lifelike" but pristine, showing how Marina's words convinced Victorian critics if not Leonine about her moral nature. See David Skeele, "Pericles Meets the Victorian Critics," in *Thwarting the Wayward Seas: A Critical and Theatrical History of Shakespeare's Pericles in the Nineteenth and Twentieth Centuries* (Newark: University of Delaware Press, 1998), 17–38, and compare Victorian praise of Marina's character with my analysis above. George Brandes and Algeron Swinburne, to elaborate upon representative examples, praise Marina's character on the basis of the same scene with Leonine and unknowingly witness to the influence of Shakespeare's wedding of Marina's person and the traits of the *causa honesta*. For Brandes, "it is not until the birth of Marina in the third act that Shakespeare really takes the play in hand." And the reason why is "the development of this character, this tender image of youthful charm and noble purity, which attracts him to the task." Next, Brandes turns to Marina's appearance before Leonine, focusing on her "simple words" about being "born in a tempest." Brandes's argument parallels that of Swinburne, who writes:

> No one among Shakespeare's women makes the entrance on his stage with a more wonderful charm about her than does Marina. Her flowers, her tears, the fond fidelity and simplicity of tenderness in mourning win us . . . instantly and thoroughly. . . . There is hardly anything in Shakespeare more wonderfully and *beautifully life-like* than her innocent tour with the intending assassin when they are left together on the shore. (my emphasis)

What actually constitutes the marks of a *causa honesta*—in this case, Marina's *incommoda* and *calamitas* and *solitudo*—subsequently justifies "Marinolatry," revealing the potential of forensic discourse for delivering the person-effects of "wonderfully and beautifully like-like" depictions of character. For the qutations above, see George Bandes, "*Pericles*: A Critical Study" in *Pericles: Critical Essays*, ed. David Skeele (New York: Routledge, 2000, 69–70; and Algernon Swinburne, *Plericles and Other Studies* (London: Private Circulation, 1914), 12–15.

42. For McDonald's complete list, see his *Shakespeare's Late Style*, 33.

43. See my earlier analyses of rhetorical acting and of Iago's performance of "stops." To recall Cicero's original teaching, the very nature of the speaker's language itself—*ipsa natura orationis eius*—will stir passions in the speaker, first, and in the audience as a result. See Cicero, *De Oratore*, 2.46.191–92.

44. Palfrey and Stern, *Shakespeare in Parts*, 317. I follow Palfrey and Stern, 313–27, in this paragraph, which discusses "passions" and how parts may prompt their performance.

45. See Palfrey and Stern, *Shakespeare in Parts*, 68–69, on "instruction" in *pronuntio* or "speech."

46. McDonald, *Shakespeare's Late Style*, attacks character criticism often, arguing against mimetic accounts of verse (99); dividing syntax from character (113–15); and concluding that "the relationship between listener and poet supervenes that between listener and speaker: we sense that the characters, like their words, are pointers to something beyond themselves" (228). Yet the emphasis upon style is supposed by William Poole to show that character criticism should be revived. See William Poole,

"'Unpointed Words': Shakespearean Syntax in Action," *Cambridge Quarterly* 32 (2003), 27–42.

47. McDonald, *Shakespeare's Late Style*, 99.

48. Palfrey and Stern, *Shakespeare in Parts*, 318.

49. Cf., Harley Granville-Barker, *Prefaces to Shakespeare, Vol. 1* (Princeton, NJ: Princeton University Press, 1946), 11–12: "Shakespeare himself, intent more and more upon plucking out the heart of the human mystery, stimulated his actors to a poignancy and intimacy of emotional expression—still can stimulate them to it—as no other playwright has quite learned to do."

50. McDonald, *Shakespeare's Late Style*, 112–13, 138–39, 147.

51. Longinus, "On Literary Excellence," in *Literary Criticism: Plato to Dryden*, ed. A. H. Gilbert (Detroit: Wayne State University Press, 1967), 174. Longinus is defining *hyperbaton*.

52. For discussion of figures and emotional states, see Brian Vickers, "The Theory of Rhetorical Figures: Psychology and Emotion," in *Classical Rhetoric in English Poetry*, 93–121. For a detailed account of how figures were circulated in England, see Peter Mack, *Elizabethan Rhetoric: Theory and Practice* (Cambridge, UK: Cambridge University Press, 2002), 76–102.

53. Jackson, *Defining Shakespeare*, 232, confirms "the thoroughly Shakespearian quality of Marina's short speech to Lysimachus" in his study of attribution.

54. On *epanorthosis*, see its definition in Gideon O. Burton's *Silva Rhetoricae* at http://rhetoric.byu.edu: "Amending a first thought by altering it to make it stronger or more vehement."

55. *De Inventione*, 1.52.98.

56. *De Inventione*, 1.53.101.

57. The *conquestio* is a "lament or complaint," which arouses pity. Each of its commonplaces should "set forth the power of fortune over all men and the weakness of the human race." See *De Inventione* 1.54.106.

58. On Marina's words to Lysimachus, Anna Kamaralli writes: "Shakespeare wrote many plays in which his heroines are praised by other characters for speaking so well, but never with such paucity of reason as Marina's meager seven lines" (Anna Kamaralli, *Shakespeare and the Shrew: Performing the Defiant Female Voice* [New York: Palgrave Macmillan, 2012], 173). MacDonald P. Jackson, however, argues that Marina's "fine poetic images" could "provoke" Lysimachus's approval of her words in *Defining Shakespeare*, 232.

59. Though anachronistic, I submit Laura Rees's comments on playing Marina in this scene from the 2005 Globe production of *Pericles*: "It was an emotional scene to play and had to remain completely real in order for it to work. I remember one performance pleading to the gods to "set me free from this unhallow'd place, / Though they did change me to the meanest bird / That flies i'th'purer air!" at which moment an extremely scruffy pigeon that had been wandering about on the corner of the stage took flight and circled once around the auditorium of the Globe until escaping into the night sky. About 1,500 people gasped as one." Shakespeare couldn't rely upon pigeons, but the passion with which actors play the scene still registers. For Rees's comment, see *Pericles*, ed. Jonathan Bate and Eric Rasmussen (New York: The Modern Library, 2012), 157.

60. In contrast, see McDonald, who argues that repetition of all kinds in the late style constitutes "fundamentally a dramatic pleasure" of "recognition." Once more, the relationship between repetition and genre appears: "these musical effects induce aurally in the audience a sense of wonder corresponding to the aims and effects of the romantic or tragicomic mode" because "the effect is dreamlike." McDonald, *Shakespeare's Late Style*, 209, 211.

61. *Ad Herennium*, 4.28.38.

62. Wilson, *The Art of Rhetoric*, 225.

63. George Puttenham, *The Arte of English Poesie: A Facsimile Reproduction* (Kent, OH: Kent State University Press, 1970), 208, defines *anaphora*: "Repetition in the first degree

we call the figure of Report according to the Greek original, and is when we make one word begin, and as they are wont to say, lead the dance to many verses in suite." I have modernized all quotations taken from Puttenham.

64. Puttenham, ibid., 211, calls *ploche* the "doubler" because it consists of "speedy iteration" of a single word.

65. Puttenham, *The Arte of English Poesie*, 207.

66. *Quintilian's Institutes of Oratory*, trans. Watson, 427, my emphasis.

67. McDonald, *Shakespeare's Late Plays*, 29.

68. McDonald, *Shakespeare's Late Plays*, 30.

69. Barton, "Leontes and the Spider," 138.

70. *Ad Herennium* asserts that judicial oratory is based in *controversia* at 1.1.2.

71. *Ad Herennium*, 1.5.8.

72. Joseph, *Arts of Language*, 323.

73. On the grammar school training of boys in the *narratio* in general, see Mack, *Elizabethan Rhetoric*, 36–37; on its connection to dramatic mimesis and lifelike effects on stage, see Lorna Hutson, *The Invention of Suspicion: Law and Mimesis in Shakespeare and Renaissance Drama* (Oxford: Oxford University Press, 2011), 122–45.

74. The parts of an oration are listed in the *Ad Herennium*, 1.3.4.

75. Wilson, *Art of Rhetoric*, 139.

76. *Ad Herennium*, 1.9.15.

77. Wilson, *Art of Rhetoric*, 139.

78. *Ad Herennium*, 4.49.63, 65.

79. Michael Taylor refers to the "obvious inspiration for the image in carved figures of Patience on tombs," but makes an important qualification: "Although both statue and personification, Patience takes on here the active humanity necessary to repair the workings of extremity, the difference between merely 'gazing on,' and 'smiling . . . out of.'" Hence, Pericles's words praise "an active, uncloistered patience," a quality Taylor applies to Marina, writing that she "once more smiles extremity out of act" in waking her father. Taylor is cited from "'Here is a Thing Too Young for Such a Place': Innocence in *Pericles*," *Ariel* 13 (1982): 17. Taylor ultimately sees Marina as an exemplification of innocence.

80. *Ad Herennium*, 1.8.13.

81. For Annette C. Flower, Marina should be identified with "superhuman power," especially justice, truth, and patience, "virtues which she has come to represent." See Annette C. Flower, "Disguise and Identity in Pericles Prince of Tyre," *Shakespeare Quarterly* 26, no. 1 (1975): 41. For review and critique of patience in Pericles's character, see Thelma N. Greenfield, "A Re-examination of the 'Patient' Pericles," *Shakespeare Studies* 3 (1967): 51–81.

82. McDonald, *Shakespeare's Late Style*, 101–2. See, too, Phyllis Gorfain, "Puzzle and Artifice: The Riddle as Metapoetry in *Pericles*," in Skeele, *Pericles: Critical Essays*, 133–46.

83. Jeanie Grant Moore, "Riddled Romance: Kingship and Kinship in *Pericles*," *Rocky Mountain Review of Language and Literature* 57, no. 1 (2003): 41.

84. The quotes above are from G. Wilson Knight, *The Crown of Life* (1947); C. L. Barber and Richard Wheeler, *The Whole Journey: Shakespeare's Power of Development* (1986); Howard Felperin, *Shakespearean Romance* (1972). Each is cited from Skeele, *Pericles: Critical Essays*, 103, 158, 124.

85. Inga-Stina Ewbank, "'My Name Is Marina': The Language of Recognition," in *Shakespeare's Styles: Essays in honour of Kenneth Muir*, edited by Philip Edwards, Inga-Stina Ewbank, and G. K. Hunter (Cambridge, UK: Cambridge University Press, 1980), 118–19.

86. Ewbank, "'My Name Is Marina,'" 120.

87. Quintilian, *Institutio Oratio*, trans. Butler, 6.2.13.

88. Cf., Marianne Novy, "Multiple Parenting in *Pericles*," in Skeele, *Pericles: Critical Essays*, 242: "I could imagine a Marina who has been told that this is Pericles and

deliberately takes her time in leading him to this recognition, but has a purpose in introducing herself by talking about her ancestry and the loss of her parents."

89. John Porter Houston, *Shakespearean Sentences: A Study in Style and Syntax* (Baton Rouge: Louisiana State University Press, 1988), 209.

90. For Alcibiades's use of forensic speech, see *Timon of Athens*, 3.5; Queen Catherine discusses her "cause" in *All Is True*, 3.1; Leontes and Paulina's exchange is from *The Winter's Tale*, 2.3. For discussion of Alcibiades and Leontes, see Skinner, *Forensic Shakespeare*, 63–65. For date of composition and introduction to *All Is True*, see *The Norton Shakespeare*, second edition, ed. Stephen Greenblatt (New York: W.W. Norton & Co., 2008), 3119–28.

91. Barton, "Language and Role," 551.

92. Alan Sinfield, "From Bradley to Cultural Materialism," in *Shakespeare Studies, Volume XXXIV*, ed. Susan Zimmerman (Cranbury, NJ: Associated University Presses, 2006), 27.

93. Alan Sinfield, "When Is a Character Not a Character? Desdemona, Olivia, Lady Macbeth, and Subjectivity," in *Faultlines: Cultural Materialism and the Politics of Dissident Reading* (Berkeley: University of California Press, 1992), 64–65.

94. William Shakespeare, *The Comedy of Errors*, *The Norton Shakespeare*, second edition, 3.2.12.

95. I cite *3 Henry 6* from *The Riverside Shakespeare*, second edition, ed. G. Blakemore Evans (Boston, MA: Houghton Mifflin, 1997), 3.3.182–85.

96. Barton, "Leontes and the Spider," 143.

Conclusion

Direct Address as an "Original Practice"

How could actors trained in oratory provide audiences with lifelike dramatic action? *Shakespeare's Dramatic Persons* addressed this question by examining the close relationship between the classical rhetorical tradition and the early modern acting style known as personation. In this book, I have argued for the correspondence between typological character and theatricality in *Richard III*; the significance of formal declamation and delivery for understanding Kate's last speech from *Taming of the Shrew*; how figural language could direct performance in *Othello*; and explored connections between the aims of eloquence and how actors personate characters, whether in *Much Ado About Nothing* or in *Pericles*. Throughout, I have investigated the mimetic possibilities of a rhetorical style of acting.

I would like to conclude with a different, albeit related question. How may an early modern and theatrical understanding of persuasion's arts bear upon contemporary productions of William Shakespeare's plays? Too often, critical concerns about anachronistic naturalism lead to an overemphasis upon historicizing character. Such inquiry is crucial, but it privileges our distance from the plays, and, if followed by today's theater practitioners, would render character into an artifact rather than a role or artistic opportunity for actors to explore.

Indeed, the divide between scholarly investigation and theatrical practice constitutes a so-called "fifth wall" of separation within Shakespeare studies with few exceptions.[1] Perhaps the most recognizable exception is the ongoing collaboration between theater historians and practitioners in productions that feature "original practice(s)" (OP).[2] The term arises from the London Bankside Globe and its performance style but applies to other venues, such as the Blackfriars theater in Staunton, Virginia, where the American Shakespeare Center (ASC) performs.[3] OP productions are known for universal lighting, live and acoustic music, Renaissance or medieval costumes, and sometimes for the doubling of roles or all-male casts, and eschewing all sets. Less discussed, however, is the emphasis they place upon character as a manifestation of formal rhetoric.[4]

To explore one possible bridge between contemporary performance and early modern techniques of personation, then, I call upon today's "Elizabethanists."[5] In particular, I will focus on the "original practice" of speaking with and to audiences in modes of direct address. Early modern performances at Shakespeare's own Globe, of course, would include direct address, but these did so, in part, because of how the classical oratorical tradition had instructed speakers to address auditors, especially in the form of rhetorical questions. In a comparison and analysis of three recent though very different approaches to the question of direct address in the context of playing the role of Hamlet, I will show how today's actors either deliberately modernize or illustrate a contemporary attempt at recapturing an essential practice of the rhetorical style of acting.[6] At the end, I envision how Richard Burbage, Shakespeare's original Hamlet, might approach direct address as both a "grave orator" and an "excellent actor."

TODAY'S ELIZABETHANS

OP practitioners value direct address because the technique seems unavoidable upon thrust stages. "What happens to the space of playing and the space of the audience," questions Pauline Kiernan, "when this physical configuration of the actor and audience as centre and circle is recreated, as it has been at the reconstructed Globe on Bankside?" Kiernan, drawing upon the experience of actors in early productions, shows how the new Globe "prompts re-examination of the actor-audience relationship" and the "reconsideration" of the "boundaries of the fiction."[7]

Likewise, Ralph Cohen, co-artistic director of the ASC, explores the "boundaries of the fiction," but he does so in terms of the use of stage light. Cohen runs a professional theater that performs Shakespeare's plays in a 2001 building that is modeled after the Blackfriars Playhouse. "At the ASC," Cohen writes, "we try to approach the stagecraft of the period with minimal chronological or technological chauvinism." The ASC trumpets how, unlike in the "proscenium space" found "at a movie," actors and audiences share the same light.[8] The mottos for their productions range from "Shakespeare: Straight Up" to "We do it with the lights on."[9]

Cohen isn't interested in any replication of "olde England" but, instead, what he refers to as the sense of "awareness" that Shakespeare writes "for a certain environment." That "certain environment," above all, requires "leaving the lights up during a performance so that *spectators are visible to one another and to the actors*."[10] This "lights up" approach invests in "the fundamental theatrical transaction" between actor and audience, creating the "the joy of collaboration."[11]

The stress upon "collaboration" repeats the longstanding teaching of many theater historians and other OP directors. Shakespeare critics such as J. L. Styan emphasize "the immediately felt contact with the spectator" because of "the absence of an inflexible 'fourth wall' of darkness to which actors play in a modern theatre." Styan chides, "the audience was not there to counterfeit its participation in the play, like that watching a Victorian melodrama." Instead, "it was caught up in an act of creative collaboration."[12] And that same spirit of "creative collaboration," Mark Rylance, the former artistic director of the new Globe, confirms because "you and the audience are together in a creative process rather than you presenting an artifact to them for appreciation."[13]

Such collaboration with an audience returns to the importance of the thrust stage and the sense of realism it begets. In Styan's own early though influential account of *Shakespeare's Stagecraft* (1967), he singles out audience involvement:

> Strange arguments have been put forward to suggest that a platform jutting out into the house encourages an undesirable proximity to the actors, one which dispels "a sense of reality." This might have a slim element of truth in it, but only if that reality is thought of in a non-Shakespearian way, a reality of a kind which the audience had only to sit and observe externally, a make-believe reality. The reality in which Shakespeare trades is that which arises from involvement, and which therefore exists in part in the spectator before the performance begins, and wholly after it is finished.[14]

To think of reality in a "non-Shakespearian way" means to consider mimesis in terms of proscenium stage productions. For "the proscenium stage," as Jacalyn Royce elaborates in the current edition of *The Oxford Handbook of Early Modern Theatre* (2009), "aggressively discourages naturalistic characters from 'stepping out' of the frame." In contrast, acting at the Globe is grounded "in the actor's embodiment of character and not dependent on the pretense of a fourth wall." For Royce, the Globe's conventions of personation indicate how "audiences knew what to expect from the Chamberlain's and King's Men, and they learned to play the game," which consisted of following the actors' pretense "that the people and events were 'true,' 'real,' and 'now.'" Such Shakespearean realism, Styan would agree, emerges even when actors 'step out' in order to interact with or speak to audiences.[15]

In practical terms, Rylance's instruction about an actor and audience's shared "creative process" follows one of Cohen's "rules" for directing OP: "Actors who are in contact with the audience must always stay in character, serve the story, and listen to their fellow actors."[16] Actors and directors at the Globe, accordingly, emphasize the importance of actors playing the story even in moments of audience interaction. "The story has to come first," says Globe actor Matthew Scurfield, because "if you play out to the audience there's a danger of bringing them too much into the present, when you need to bring them into the presence of their imagination, where the story is taking place."[17]

Are these theatrical terms of collaboration between character and audience predicated upon modern ideas of naturalism or a return to Shakespearean authenticity or some combination of the two? From the standpoint of theater history, Royce reminds us, the original Globe would offer audiences "a three-dimensional perspective" of a large acting space with a variety of sightlines. The Globe's thrust stage, therefore, "capitalized upon and increased the theatrical potential of the English tradition of talking to audiences." Royce, like Styan and OP practitioners, believes such a stage configuration would free early modern actors "to move and speak without artificiality" and allow them "to stay 'in character' and, even, conversational when addressing the audience."[18]

The historical significance of the Globe's putative impact upon direct address, however, differs from the OP stress upon "story," which entails character consistency in a way that suits contemporary actors' training in post-Stanislavski techniques of playing or finding a character's motivation. As Tiffany Stern and Simon Palfrey have demonstrated and we have seen in chapter 5, early modern actors played passions on the basis of their "parts," what is often referred to today as "sides" or "cue scripts," which contained the lines of just their character in addition to a speaking cue from another character of one to three words. "Part," thus, signifies not only "character," but also "it stood for the written paper, often made into a roll, on which that part was transcribed." Actors would memorize their lines and cues, more often than not, in private and without the benefit of ensemble rehearsals.[19] Because actors didn't receive the complete text they were to perform, Stanislavski's notion of building character from a careful study of the whole emerges as a later rather than an original practice.

For OP actors today, "remaining in character" and privileging the "story" ultimately mean that character will have priority over any particular or spontaneous audience-response. Audiences are ancillary to the dramatic action. Contemporary playgoers, as a result, cannot be "collaborative" in the sense of equally creative partnerships with the actors.[20] To speak lines to audiences may be an early modern practice that blossoms because of a particular stage or theatrical space, but the acting techniques used by today's OP actors are not necessarily "original" or "Elizabethan" just because they perform on similar, or even historical reconstructions of, Shakespeare's own thrust stages.[21]

TO BE OR NOT TO BE HAMLET?

Rylance's own approach to direct address illustrates how modern the practice has become in OP productions. To show why this is so, I will situate his instructions for playing Hamlet's "to be or not to be" soliloquy between two other prominent examples of playing the same character.

Each actor's choice will illustrate how direct address—whether or not to use it and how it should be employed—correspondingly shapes the relationship between actor and audience. As we shall see, Kevin Kline's 1990 Hamlet rejected direct address in favor of playing Hamlet's inner sense of suffering wrong, whereas Adrian Lester's 2001 Hamlet relied upon audience-responses to shape much of his performance. Rylance's Hamlet, however, projects the interiority of his character upon audience members, addressing them as personifications of Hamlet's own conscience. As a theatrical choice, Rylance's Hamlet represents a middle position between Kline and Lester's decisions, but it also illustrates how OP performance combines with a contemporary acting technique.

Rylance begins with a distinction between storytelling and playing a part. "I had to become a storyteller as well as a part inside the story," Rylance explains.[22] In the distinction between "storyteller" and "part," he uses terms suggestive of "formal" and "natural" acting styles, what early and later twentieth-century theater historians typically have understood as contradictory or opposed ways of performing roles. Yet Rylance would align these two styles with two dramatic functions that nevertheless constitute the contemporary actor's performance of a single character. The reason why is this: In Rylance's view a fluid disclosure of character need not oppose the narrative and descriptive moments that an actor plays for the sake of an audience's comprehension of plot or action.

Accordingly, Rylance teaches that the actor should break up Hamlet's "to be or not to be" soliloquy into smaller units and to play each one in dialogue with the audience. Rylance describes his own approach in terms of conversational exchange: "But if you actually take it step by step, you know, 'to be or not to be, that is the question'; then, imagine the audience saying, 'What do you mean, that is the question? And go on, 'Whether 'tis nobler in the mind to suffer the slings and arrows of outrageous fortune.'"[23] Thus, the actor plays a character who addresses and informs the audience about the play's action in the function of storytelling but does so from the context of a particular point of view, which comes from his or her part or role.

Conversely, Kline abandoned his first attempt at the role in 1986 under director Liviu Ciulei because the "presentational style, directly addressing the audience," he felt, required him to lecture audience members. Such a Hamlet convinced Kline that he was "explaining the words rather than saying them."[24] Kline, therefore, rejects Rylance's alliance of "storytelling" or "explaining" with playing a "part" or "saying" lines that indicate a character's point of view. The decision *not* to speak with audiences and to reject "storytelling," in other words, allows Kline to immerse himself in his "part."

Kline also doesn't concern himself with audience responses because so many view him through the lens of his previous and famous cinematic roles. "You want to be the character you need to be that night and not think about what the audience expects from you," he says. So Kline approached the "to be or not to be" soliloquy, as Donald McManus describes, in a "tone" that "was so steeped in stream-of-consciousness that the audience had to lean forward to make sure they could hear the overfamiliar words." McManus reports how Kline "entered entirely into his own thoughts" and his tears on "to die, to sleep" were "so spontaneous that a sensitive viewer almost felt guilty for being privy to such private confession."[25]

Instead of private confession, Adrian Lester's 2001 Hamlet under director Peter Brook features impromptu audience interaction. Such audience involvement is crucial because, as Lester states, "character is simply how you react," but that reaction is "something the audience does, not me." By reversing the responsibilities for characterization from actor to audience, character emerges in improvised action. So when Lester caught an audience member with an edition of the play, he took the text from her before continuing the show with her script. Because Brook's version of the play was abridged, as Jonathan Holmes recalls, "Lester's reading restored dialogue that had been cut, causing other cast members to have to read from the same edition to keep up." Holmes claims Lester practiced a "constant displacement of characterization onto the audience." Such a "Hamlet was decentred and constantly changing, never where or who he was assumed to be."[26]

Though Lester's performance might seem to suit OP well, Rylance justifies his own approach to Hamlet's soliloquy because "there is a sense of dialogue with the audience who are *playing the role of Hamlet's conscience* at that moment."[27] Direct address, in this instance, combines with contemporary psychological realism because Rylance casts audiences as part of his character's interiority, transforming them into "Hamlet's conscience." Instead of Lester's practice of character "displacement," Rylance's use of direct address turns "the modern British actor's preoccupation with the invented inner lives of characters outward, to the audience," as Bridget Escolme rightly claims.[28]

More specifically, Rylance's instructions for the performance of Hamlet are other words for the technique of "actioning," which is predicated upon Stanislavski's teaching. Marina Caldarone and Maggie Lloyd-Williams explain: "Actioning provides the stimulation for the actor to directly play each line of the text and develop alternative ways of bringing their character to life."[29] To discover "alternative ways" of playing character in soliloquies, actors must distinguish between "externalizing the actions" and "internalizing" them. Thus, an actor may speak the same line—"to be or not to be"—by "imagining the space inhabited with people from the character's life and direct each complete thought to those people." Caldarone and Lloyd-Williams suggest that Hamlet might address "to be or not to be" to his absent father with the action of daring his ghostly visitor to reply. Alternatively, an actor may use the same question to address "different aspects of oneself," dividing a character "into his or her own lower and higher self, each having a different identity."[30]

Rylance's addressee, "conscience," would appeal to Hamlet's "higher self," thereby "internalizing" action. So Hamlet could speak to his own conscience, perhaps playing the action, "to awaken." In this scenario, though, direct address seems increasingly indirect because Rylance refuses to acknowledge audience members as people who have come to watch a play. In the case of internalizing action, as Caldarone and Lloyd-Williams recommend, the actor addresses "different aspects of oneself, as if talking to a separate person."[31] Instead of apostrophe or personification, though, Rylance imagines that audiences are a projection of his character's interior life. In performance, the difference between personification of and direct address to audiences might go unnoticed by playgoers. Yet in terms of the actor's technique, Rylance transforms audiences into a manifestation of his character's fictive selfhood.

To be or not to be Hamlet? With Kline, only the actor speaks for character, which the audience overhears like a "private confession." For Lester, the audience "reacts" and therefore creates the character he plays. In Rylance's case, everyone is Hamlet because of the actor's projection of a character's interiority. Escolme rightly judges that Rylance's "most powerful legacy" at the Globe "is a direct relationship between performer and audience."[32] Yet what emerges in Rylance's OP of direct address is Elizabethan convention tailored to contemporary tastes about theatrical realism. Alternatively, Rylance's method may be categorized somewhat ironically as "non-traditional theatre," which Susan Bennett broadly defines in terms of a "recreated" and "flexible actor-audience relationship and a participatory spectator/actor."[33] Elizabethanism, it turns out, becomes modern but nontraditional theater.

WHAT IS THE QUESTION?

Characters are, as Stephen Orgel defines them, "elements of linguistic structure" that provide the actor or actress with the mandate of transforming "the lines into a credible simulacrum of human behavior."[34] Credible behavior or lifelike dramatic action remains within the purview of the actor's choices, including whether or not to employ, or how to use, direct address. The question of how to perform with or speak to audiences, in other words, belongs to the actor.

Indeed, the choices described above provoke a question about how early modern actors would approach direct address from within the classical rhetorical tradition.[35] To argue an example from the same character but from a passage that the new Globe education team itself spotlights, Hamlet's "Who calls me coward?" soliloquy seems written to invite audience contact with all of its questions.[36] If this speech poises character between the possibilities of melodrama and internal disclosure for actors today, its rhetorical questions would have posed similar alternatives for early modern performers.

In fact, Hamlet's character is often marked by the praises lavished upon Richard Burbage's original performance of the role, yet this same soliloquy would have required Burbage to make choices about how to engage the audience. [37] After Hamlet condemns himself as a "rogue," he asks the following questions: (1) "Is it not monstrous that this player here, / But in a fiction, in a dream of passion, / could force his soul so to his own conceit . . . ? (2) What's Hecuba to him, or he to her, / That he should weep for her? (3) What would he do / Had he the motive and the cue for passion / That I have? (4) Am I a coward? (5) Who calls me villain . . . who does me this?"[38] Any of these rhetorical questions could become an occasion for Burbage to play dialogically with audiences, or to disclose his character's interiority, or to spur audiences into a reaction.

Though we tend to discount the figure, rhetoricians claim that affirming points through questions is powerful. *Interrogatio*, from the *Ad Herennium*, signifies our sense of questions that require no answers from the audience for the purpose of inquiry is to reinforce "the argument that has just been delivered."[39] Peacham uses *erotema* for the Latin term and teaches its effects. *Erotema* is a "form of speech" by which a speaker will either "affirm or deny something strongly." The figure imparts "life and motion" because Peacham assumes it is an appeal from *pathos* and of such power that "it may be compared to the point or edge of a weapon." As a result of its efficacy, "this figure is most commonly abused" either by "accusing falsely" or "denying shamelessly," but it is "much commended in the supporting of good causes."[40]

By way of extrapolation or application to Hamlet's speech, *erotema* would cue a display of passion in the speaker, especially when he questions in order to condemn his own cowardice, a question that appeals from *pathos* like the "edge of a weapon." If Burbage recognized and played *erotema* in delivery of Hamlet's soliloquy, the audience would be cast in roles not unlike those of judges, an audience that a speaker seeks to persuade through forensic speech.[41] What, though, would be the result of an oratorical Hamlet who could successfully appeal to audiences in condemnation of himself? Instead of audiences that emotionally identify with character, as in most proscenium stage productions, they would be distanced from this Hamlet because of the character's appeal to judge him.

No matter how audiences respond, Burbage would remain in character in condemning Hamlet's faults. The "part" itself and the formal rhetorical structure it contains would be enough to guide the actor. As in the cases of theatrical representations of declamatory speech that I reviewed in chapter 2, speakers play fictive roles, animating set speeches with their own voice, gesticulations, and pronunciation. The example of Marina from chapter 5 added to that picture of rhetorical exercise by demonstrating how forensic speech may accuse or excuse past conduct. Marina's self-defense contrasts with Hamlet's self-condemnation, but both are from the same rhetorical genre. *Erotema* suits a forensic speech by directly appealing to judges. By the same token, the figure cues the actor to address the audience.

Interrogatio, though, emerges as a general category, which other figures delineate with different points of emphasis and purpose. Peacham himself illustrates the tonal potentialities and manifold purposes of rhetorical questions. Speakers who ask questions, like Iago's inquiries I reviewed in chapter 4, may also employ *aporia*, which is "a form of speech by which the speaker showeth that he doubteth." Peacham includes how feigning or performing doubt involves "what to do or say in some strange and doubtful thing." *Aporia* serves "deliberation" and "to note the perplexity of the mind." The marginalia elaborates: "to signify perplexity."[42] With *aporia*, directly questioning an audience manifests the speaker's confusion, prompting an actor's performance of an internal or mental state.

Instead of escalating a passion of self-rebuke, as in the case of what could result with *erotema*, a choice to play *aporia* would produce a tonally and substantially different Hamlet. Even though the language of any given question from the soliloquy would justify the choice of either figure, the differences between figures correspondingly provide alternative prompts for the actor's performance. If Burbage played *aporia*, for example, he could earnestly wonder at the paradox between the players Hamlet ruminates upon and his own character, using the moment to interrogate Hamlet's ostensible lack of passion. Whether or not Burbage himself enjoyed the irony—he is a player who, as a character, compares himself to players—*aporia* would not mandate that he play such an illumination. Similar to the dynamic between Kline's Hamlet and his audiences, *aporia* configures early modern auditors as the character's addressees, as playgoers who witness a "confession" or, in this case, listen to Hamlet's doubts or perplexity. Audiences, even if they are demanded to condemn Hamlet, are freer to identify or empathize with the actor who plays *aporia* instead of *erotema*.

Peacham further proposes *anacoenosis* as a form of rhetorical question after the manner of dialoguing with audiences. In this case, "the orator *seemeth to ask* counsel of his adversary, or to deliberate with the judges what is to be done, or what ought to have been done."[43] To pretend to ask for counsel requires a performance of sincerity, which cues speakers to play earnest inquiry. As in the case of *erotema*, the audience is cast as jurors with the choice of *anacoenosis*, though the speaker does not ask questions to affirm a point directly but rather to invite auditors to make any reply.

In the pretense at dialogue, *anacoenosis* anticipates Rylance's own approach to audiences. When Rylance casts audiences as Hamlet's "conscience" and imagines that his character converses and deliberates with them, he echoes Peacham's recommendation in this sense: Both jurors and conscience fulfill the same function of judgment and, in this instance, will either exonerate or condemn the speaker for his past conduct.

Audiences, like conscience, often do pronounce judgment upon those characters who petition them to do so. Contemporary actors report how Hamlet's question—"Am I a coward?"—provokes audiences to deliver a reply. David Warner describes how a heckler answered his Hamlet with a resounding "Yes," which segued into his response, "who does me this?" That question of Hamlet also received a reply from the house, the heckler's name. After the audience member identified himself, Warner replied, "Hah, 'swounds, I should take it."[44] Warner, like with other actors who have experienced similar replies from playgoers, thought that Hamlet's lines seem as if they were written for such a dialogue.[45]

Warner's example not only adds credibility to Lester's position that character emerges in how audiences react to performance, but also it shows how early modern figures are designed to persuade audiences. In his addendum to *anacoenosis*, Peacham advises: "In using this figure, it is necessary and good to have an honest and upright cause, so true that the adversary may not deny it, and so just that the judges may not condemn it."[46] If jurors condemn causes, they may also approve arguments. Hamlet's question—"Am I a coward?"—brings to a climax his point that he is one. If the actor delivers a persuasive indictment, petitioning the audience for a verdict should serve as confirmation. Either Shakespeare as author or Burbage as actor could anticipate replies like those that Warner received because of how Hamlet's speech persuades audiences with the use of rhetorical questions.

EARLY MODERN ACTIONING

Analogous to, though not identical with, the contemporary practice of "actioning," *erotema*, *aporia*, and *anacoenosis* would stimulate actors to "develop alternative ways of bringing their character to life." *Erotema*, like the process of "clarifying what your character wants," would require an early modern actor to take questions to people in the audience in order to persuade them of the justice of Hamlet's self-condemnation and self-rebuke. The figure, as an appeal from *pathos*, also suggests emotional context to the articulation of the line, what the method of "actioning" would label as a means of "enlivening the performance."[47] *Aporia*, however, offers a different constellation of "actions" by prompting the performance of incredulity, wonder, or doubt. *Anacoenosis*, finally, prods audiences by pretending at dialogue with them. Hamlet's questions lead playgoers toward responses that an actor like Burbage might expect to hear, but, if they do reply to him, he may retort with lines already penned for his character. For the figure, in this case, incites or provokes audiences in seeking to convince them. Of course, today's method of "actioning" derives from a later and modern approach to the stage, but figures of speech prescribe a range of behaviors and passions to early modern actors that are more abundant and sophisticated than theatre historians often recognize.

In terms of rhetorical genre, all the above forms of *interrogatio* could qualify as techniques of forensic discourse and would invite actors to appeal to audiences like advocates addressing judges. These forms of direct address manifest the classical oratorical tradition found within Shakespeare's own habits of composition and direct attention to the rhetorical style of acting I have defined as personation. As Marina self-fashions to those characters she hopes to persuade in *Pericles*, Hamlet argues with audiences about whether or not he is a coward. Once again, forensic speech affords and accommodates dramatic action. Yet now audiences, like judges, must decide whether to excuse or accuse Hamlet's conduct because of the practice of direct address. Rylance's vision of audience members who represent Hamlet's conscience isn't "Elizabethan," but his approach resonates as it readjusts the idea that an audience should sit in judgment upon a character.

Direct address, finally, suggests something more. It signifies a lifelike encounter with a particular dramatic person because a script's role—its "linguistic structure"—demands that an actor's vivification of character occur through and when speaking with audience members. In these moments, the actor should communicate his or her character's point of view, argument, or assessment of the play's action or other characters. With such persuasion or commentary addressed to playgoers and delivered during a live performance, dramatic persons are born. For the same reason, the choices today's OP actors make about direct address have the potential, in a special manner, to impart presence. The dramatic persons these actors embody will appear lifelike because they talk to us.

NOTES

1. For discussion of the "fifth wall," see Lynette Hunter and Peter Lichtenfels (eds.), *Shakespeare, Language and the Stage, The Fifth Wall: Approaches to Shakespeare from Criticism, Performance and Theatre Studies* (London: Thomson Learning, 2005).

2. Jeremy Lopez writes of the ASC that "there is nowhere in North America—or arguably, even in the United Kingdom—where there are so many productions of the works of Shakespeare and his contemporaries going on and, at the same time, so much intimate, productive contact between scholars who study early modern drama and a company of actors performing that drama," in "John Harrell," *The Routledge Companion to Actors' Shakespeare*, ed. John Russell Brown and Kevin Ewert (New York: Rout-

ledge, 2012), 79. Lopez, ibid., explicitly mentions the "original practices" mandate of the ASC.

3. See Alan C. Dessen, "'Original Practices' at the Globe: A Theatre Historian's View," in *Shakespeare's Globe: A Theatrical Experiment*, ed. Christie Carson and Farah Karim-Cooper (Cambridge: Cambridge University Press, 2008), 45–53.

4. On rhetoric, characterization, and performance, see Giles Bloch, *Speaking the Speech: An Actor's Guide to Shakespeare* (London: Nick Hern Books, 2013).

5. With the term "Elizabethanist," I follow Joe Falocco's "A Note on Terminology," in *Reimagining Shakespeare's Playhouse: Early Modern Staging Conventions in the Twentieth Century* (Cambridge, UK: D.S. Brewer, 2010), viii. Falocco uses "Elizabethan staging," the "Elizabethan Movement" and "Elizabethanist(s)" in reference to "twentieth-century attempts to emulate some of the performance conditions under which Shakespeare's plays were originally produced." Such terms, he argues, are not historically precise because OP are used by the reconstructed Blackfriars theater, which is "Jacobean in inspiration." Even so, the imprecision is acceptable when the "primary goal" is analysis of recent theater practitioners and "Elizabethan accurately describes the approaches of these more recent people of the theatre."

6. See Lopez's articulation of ASC actor John Harrell's challenge: an actor must "assess both the scholarly underpinnings of an 'original practices' playhouse and the mystified ideals of late-modern naturalistic acting" in "John Harrell," *Actors' Shakespeare*, 79. On original practices and post-Stanislavski methods of acting, see Cary M. Mazer, "Historicizing Spontaneity: The Illusion of the First Time of 'The Illusion of the First Time'" and Tiffany Stern, "(Re:)Historicizing Spontaneity: Original Practices, Stanislavski, and Characterization," in *Shakespeare's Sense of Character: On the Page and From the Stage*, ed. Yu Jin Ko and Michael W. Shurgot (Burlington, VT: Ashgate, 2012), 85–110.

7. Pauline Kiernan, *Staging Shakespeare at the New Globe* (New York: Palgrave, 1999), 9.

8. Ralph Cohen, "Panel Discussion: The Mirror Image: Shakespeare in Authentic Style," in *Holding Up the Mirror: Authenticity and Adaptation in Shakespeare Today*, ed. Stephen Kuehler, John Frick, Nancy Friedland, and Martha S. LoMonaco (New York: Theatre Library Association, 2014), 50–51.

9. These mottos have appeared on ASC merchandize like sunglasses, t-shirts, coffee mugs, or bumper stickers, which are offered for sale in the gift shop outside of the theatre along with scholarly editions of plays and ASC study guides that feature OP techniques.

10. Cohen, "Panel Discussion," 50–51, my emphasis.

11. Ralph Alan Cohen, "Directing at the Globe and the Blackfriars: Six Big Rules for Contemporary Directors" in Carson and Karim-Cooper, *Shakespeare's Globe*, 218.

12. J. L. Styan, *Shakespeare's Stagecraft* (Cambridge, UK: Cambridge University Press, 1967), 17.

13. Mark Rylance, "Research, Materials, Craft: Principles of Performance at Shakespeare's Globe," in Carson and Karmi-Cooper, *Shakespeare's Globe*, 106. This is an interview with Christie Carson and the quote is her characterization of Rylance's practice, which he affirms by responding, "yes, exactly."

14. Styan, *Shakespeare's Stagecraft*, 230.

15. Royce, "Early Modern Naturalistic Acting: The Role of the Globe in the Development of Personation," in *The Oxford Handbook of Early Modern Theatre*, ed. Richard Dutton (Oxford: Oxford University Press, 2009), 492.

16. Cohen, "Directing at the Globe and the Blackfriars," 211, my emphasis.

17. Scurfield is cited from Kiernan, *Staging Shakespeare*, 23.

18. Royce, "Early Modern Naturalistic Acting," 491–92.

19. Simon Palfrey and Tiffany Stern, "Introduction" and "Rehearsal," *Shakespeare in Parts* (Oxford: Oxford University Press, 2007), 1, and see 70–73. See, too, Simon Palfrey, "Performance Cues" in *Doing Shakespeare* (London: Arden, 2011), 133–149.

20. On talking with audiences at today's new Globe, see Christie Carson's assessment of "interactivity" between actor and audience that emphasizes a "playful relationship" with audiences and the "consciously variable nature of the performance" from "Democratising the Audience?" in Carson and Karim-Cooper, *Shakespeare's Globe*, 118, and consider in light of Kiernan Ryan, *Shakespeare's Universality: Here's Fine Revolution* (London: Bloomsbury, 2015), xiv: "What is universal about Shakespeare's drama is not the plights and fates of his characters, but the perspective from which they are depicted, and from which we are invited to view them."

21. See, Styan, *Shakespeare's Stagecraft*, 230: "So many of Shakespeare's established techniques—the invitation to the actor to play to the audience, the 'attacking' north-to-south entrances, the intimate soliloquy, choric speaking to the audience, the use of the aside, the grouping of characters for liaison or repulsion—show the effort on his part to break down the barrier between actor and spectator; a proscenium arch artificially raises another barrier of which Shakespeare knew nothing."

22. Rylance, "Principles of Performance," in Carson and Karim-Kooper, *Shakespeare's Globe*, 106. Carson qualifies the distinction between part and storytelling as "shifting from psychological realism to storytelling."

23. Ibid., 107.

24. Kline is quoted from Donald McManus's "Kevin Kline" in Brown and Ewert, *Actors' Shakespeare*, 121.

25. McManus's "Kevin Kline, 121."

26. Lester's quotation and Jonathan Holmes's assessment are from Holmes's "Adrian Lester" in Brown and Ewert, *Actors' Shakespeare*, 137. "Hamlet's intimacy was with the audience, as Lester often addressed us directly and even physically interacted with spectators," confirms Kenneth J. Cerniglia, "Performance Review: *The Tragedy of Hamlet*," *Theatre Journal* 54, no. 1 (2002): 158.

27. Rylance, "Principles of Performance," 107, my emphasis.

28. Bridget Escolme, "Mark Rylance," in *The Routledge Companion to Directors' Shakespeare*, ed. John Russell Brown (London: Routledge, 2008), 411.

29. Marina Caldarone and Maggie Lloyd-Williams, *Actions: The Actors' Thesaurus* (Hollywood, CA: Drama Publishers, 2004), xiii.

30. Caldarone and Lloyd-Williams, *Actions*, xxii–xxiii.

31. Caldarone and Lloyd-Williams, *Actions*, xxiii.

32. Escolme, "Mark Rylance," 411.

33. Susan Bennett, *Theatre Audiences: A Theory of Production and Reception*, second edition (London: Routledge, 1997), 19.

34. Stephen Orgel, "What Is a Character?" in *The Authentic Shakespeare: And Other Problems of the Early Modern Stage* (New York: Routledge, 2002), 8, 12.

35. On an actor's choices and what is "psychologically credible" in the performance of character, see Orgel, "What Is a Character?", 12, and Joseph L. Roach, *The Player's Passion: Studies in the Science of Acting* (Ann Arbor: University of Michigan Press, 1993), 23–57.

36. Fiona Banks, *Creative Shakespeare: The Globe Education Guide to Practical Shakespeare* (London: Bloomsbury Publishing, 2013), 25.

37. See James P. Bednarz, *Shakespeare and the Poets' War* (New York: Columbia University Press, 2001), 252 and 321n46, for a succinct summary and bibliography of what Bednarz calls "the play's unique emphasis on the theatrical nature of human experience" (252). For recent examples critics who link Hamlet with Burbage for the purposes of analysis, see Bart van Es, *Shakespeare in Company* (Oxford: Oxford University Press, 2013), 238–41, and James Shapiro, *A Year in the Life of William Shakespeare: 1599* (New York: HarperCollins, 2005), 289–90.

38. *Hamlet: Third Series (Arden Shakespeare)*, ed. Ann Thompson and Neil Taylor (London: Thomson Learning, 2007), 2.2.484–511. This text is the Second Quarto (1604–1605).

39. Cicero, *Rhetorica Ad Herennium*, trans. H. Caplan (Cambridge, MA: Harvard University Press, 1954), 4.15–22.

40. Henry Peacham, *The Garden of Eloquence* (1593), 105. I have modernized all quotations from this text.

41. On early modern theater audiences as juries, see Joel Altman, *Tudor Play of Mind: Rhetorical Inquiry and the Development of Elizabethan Drama* (Berkeley: University of California Press, 1978), 280–82; and Hutson, *Invention of Suspicion: Law and Mimesis in Shakespeare and Renaissance Drama* (Oxford: Oxford University Press, 2011), 69–70. See, too, Aristotle's *The Rhetoric and Poetics of Aristotle*, trans. W. Rhys Roberts (New York: The Modern Library, 1954), which claims that "any one is your judge whom you have to persuade" (1391b10–16).

42. Peacham, *The Garden of Eloquence*, 109.

43. Peacham, *The Garden of Eloquence*, 110.

44. Mary Z. Maher, *Modern Hamlets and Their Soliloquies: An Expanded Edition* (Iowa City: University of Iowa Press, 2003), 41, 55.

45. Samuel West's 2008 Hamlet experienced the same response from audiences. See Holmes, "Adrian Lester," 138.

46. Peacham, *The Garden of Eloquence*, 110.

47. Caldarone and Lloyd-Williams, *Actions*, xviii–xix.

Bibliography

Adamson, Sylvia, Lynette Hunter, Lynne Magnusson, Ann Thompson, and Katie Wales, eds. *Reading Shakespeare's Dramatic Language: A Guide.* London: The Arden Shakespeare, 2001.
Adelman, Janet. *Suffocating Mothers: Fantasies of Maternal Origin in Shakespeare's Plays.* New York: Routledge, 1992.
Altman, Joel. *The Tudor Play of Mind: Rhetorical Inquiry and the Development of Elizabethan Drama.* Berkeley: University of California Press, 1978.
Aristotle. *The Rhetoric and Poetics of Aristotle.* Translated by W. Rhys Roberts. New York: The Modern Library, 1954.
Armitage, David, Conal Condren, and Andrew Fitzmaurice, eds. *Shakespeare and Early Modern Political Thought.* Cambridge, UK: Cambridge University Press, 2009.
Astington, John H. *Actors and Acting in Shakespeare's Time.* Cambridge, UK: Cambridge University Press, 2010.
Auslander, Philip. *Liveness: Performance in a Mediatized Culture,* second edition. London: Routledge, 2008.
Baldwin, T. W. *William Shakspere's Small Latine and Lesse Greeke.* Urbana: University of Illinois Press, 1944.
Banks, Fiona. *Creative Shakespeare: The Globe Education Guide to Practical Shakespeare.* London: Bloomsbury, 2013.
Barber, C. L. and Richard Wheeler. "Excerpt from 'The Masked Neptune.'" In *Pericles: Critical Essays,* edited by David Skeele, 147–63. New York: Routledge, 2000.
Barker, Francis. *The Tremulous Private Body: Essays on Subjection.* London: Methuen, 1984.
Barrol, J. Leeds. *Artificial Persons: The Formation of Character in the Tragedies of Shakespeare.* Columbia, SC: University of South Carolina Press, 1974.
Barton, Anne. "Introduction to *Much Ado about Nothing.*" In *The Riverside Shakespeare,* edited by G. Blakemore Evans, 361–65. Boston: Houghton, 1974.
———. "Leontes and the Spider: Language and Speaker in Shakespeare's Last Plays." In *Shakespeare's Styles*: *Essays in Honour of Kenneth Muir,* edited by Philip Edwards, Inga-Stina Ewbank, G. K. Hunter, 131–50. Cambridge, UK: Cambridge University Press, 1980.
Baumlin, Tita French. "Petruchio the Sophist and Language as Creation in *The Taming of the Shrew.*" *Studies in English Literature, 1500–1900,* no. 2 (1989): 237–57.
Bednarz, James P. *Shakespeare and the Poets' War.* New York: Columbia University Press, 2001.
Belsey, Catherine. *Shakespeare in Theory and Practice.* Edinburgh: Edinburgh University Press, 2008.
———. *The Subject of Tragedy: Identity and Difference in Renaissance Drama.* New York: Methuen, 1985.
Bennett, Susan. *Theatre Audiences: A Theory of Production and Reception,* second edition. London: Routledge, 1997.
Bentley, Gerald Eades. *The Profession of Player in Shakespeare's Time, 1590–1642.* Princeton, NJ: Princeton University Press, 1986.
———. "Shakespeare and the Blackfriars Theatre," *Shakespeare Survey* 1 (1948): 38–50.
Berger, Harry Jr. "Discourses and Psychoanalysis." In *Making Trifles of Terrors: Redistributing Complicities in Shakespeare,* edited by Peter Erickson. Stanford, CA: Stanford University Press, 1997.

Bergeron, David M. *Shakespeare's Romances and the Royal Family.* Lawrence: University Press of Kansas, 1985.
Bessell, Jacquelyn. "The Performance Research Group's *Antony and Cleopatra* (2010)." In *Shakespeare on the University Stage,* edited by Andrew James Hartley, 185–200. Cambridge, UK: Cambridge University Press, 2015.
Bethell, S. L. *Shakespeare and the Popular Dramatic Tradition.* Westminster: P. S. King & Staples, 1944.
Blake, Anne. "'The Humour of Children': John Marston's Plays in Private Theatres." *Review of English Studies* 38, no. 152 (1987): 471–82.
Bloch, Giles. *Speaking the Speech: An Actor's Guide to Shakespeare.* London: Nick Hern Books, 2013.
Bloom, Harold, ed. *Major Literary Characters: Iago.* New York: Chelsea House Publishers, 1992.
———. *Shakespeare: The Invention of the Human.* New York: Riverhead Books, 1998.
Bly, Mary. "The Boy Companies: 1599–1613." In *The Oxford Handbook of Early Modern Theatre,* edited by Richard Dutton, 147–49. Oxford: Oxford University Press, 2009.
Booth, Stephen, ed. *Shakespeare's Sonnets.* New Haven, CT: Yale University Press, 1977.
Boyce, Benjamin. *The Theophrastan Character in England to 1642.* Cambridge, MA: Harvard University Press, 1947.
Bradbrook, M. C. *Elizabethan Stage Conditions: A Study of Their Place in the Interpretation of Shakespeare's Plays.* Cambridge, UK: Cambridge University Press, 1932.
Bradley, A. C. *Shakespearean Tragedy: Lectures on Hamlet, Othello, King Lear, Macbeth.* New York: Penguin Books, 1991.
Brady, Frank, and W. K. Wimsatt, eds. *Samuel Johnson: Selected Poetry and Prose.* Los Angeles: University of California Press, 1977.
Brandes, George. "*Pericles*: A Critical Study." In *Pericles: Critical Essays,* edited by David Skeele, 63–74. New York: Routledge, 2000.
Brinsley, John. *Ludus Literarius (1612): A Scolar Press Facsimile.* Menston, England: The Scolar Press Limited, 1968.
Bristol, Michael. "How Many Children Did She Have?" In *Philosophical Shakespeares,* edited by John J. Joughin, 18–33. New York: Routledge, 2000.
Brockbank, J. P. "History and Histrionics in *Cymbeline.*" *Shakespeare Survey* 11 (1958): 42–49.
Brooke, Nicholas. "Marlowe as Provocative Agent in Shakespeare's Early Plays." *Shakespeare Survey* 14 (1961): 34–44.
Brown, John Russell, ed. *The Routledge Companion to Directors' Shakepeare.* London: Routledge, 2008.
———. *Studying Shakespeare in Performance.* Basingstoke, UK: Palgrave Macmillan, 2011.
Brown, John Russell and Kevin Ewert, eds. *The Routledge Companion to Actor's Shakepeare.* London: Routledge, 2012.
Bullough, Geoffrey, ed. *Narrative and Dramatic Sources of Shakespeare.* New York: Columbia University Press, 1960.
Burke, Peter. "Tacitism, Skepticism, and Reason of State." In *The Cambridge History of Political Thought 1450–1700,* edited by J.H. Burns, 479–84. Cambridge, UK: Cambridge University Press, 1991.
Burns, Edward. *Character: Acting and Being on the Pre-Modern Stage.* New York: St. Martin's Press, 1990.
Burrow, Colin. *Shakespeare and Classical Antiquity.* Oxford: Oxford University Press, 2013.
———. "Shakespeare and Humanistic Culture." In *Shakespeare and the Classics*, edited by Charles Martindale and A. B. Taylor, 9–27. Cambridge, UK: Cambridge University Press, 2004.
Burton, Gideon O. *Silva Rhetoricae.* http://rhetoric.byu.edu.
Caldarone, Marina and Maggie Lloyd-Williams. *Actions: The Actors' Thesaurus.* Hollywood, CA: Drama Publishers, 2004.

Calderwood, James. *Shakespearean Metadrama: The Argument of the Play in Titus Andronicus, Love's Labour's Lost, Romeo and Juliet, A Midsummer Night's Dream, and Richard II*. Minneapolis: University of Minnesota Press, 1971.
Cantor, Paul. "Shakespeare's *The Tempest*: The Wise Man as Hero." *Shakespeare Quarterly* 31, no. 1 (Spring 1980): 64–75.
Carson, Christie. "Democratising the Audience?" In *Shakespeare's Globe: A Theatrical Experiment*, edited by Christie Carson and Farah Karim-Cooper, 115–26. Cambridge: Cambridge University Press, 2008.
Carson, Christie, and Farah Karim-Cooper, eds. *Shakespeare's Globe: A Theatrical Experiment*. Cambridge, UK: Cambridge University Press, 2008.
Cerniglia, Kenneth J. "Performance Review: *The Tragedy of Hamlet*." *Theatre Journal* 54, no. 1 (2002): 156–58.
Chambers, E. K. *The Elizabethan Stage, Vol. I–IV*. Oxford: Clarendon Press, 1923.
———. *William Shakespeare: A Study of Facts and Problems*, vol. 1. Oxford: Clarendon Press, 1930.
Chambers, R. W. *Thomas More*. Ann Arbor: University of Michigan Press, 1958.
Cicero. *De Amicitia*. Translated by William Armistead Falconer. Cambridge, MA: Harvard University Press, 1959.
———. *De Inventione, De Optimo Genere Oratorum, Topica*. Translated by Harry Mortimer Hubbell. Cambridge, MA: Harvard University Press, 1949.
———. *De Oratore*. Translated by E. W. Sutton and H. Rackham. Cambridge, MA: Harvard University Press, 1996.
———. *De Partitione Oratoria*. Translated by H. Rackham. Cambridge, MA: Harvard University Press, 1942.
———. *Rhetorica Ad Herennium*. Translated by H. Caplan. Cambridge, MA: Harvard University Press, 1954.
Clark, Donald Lemen. *John Milton at St. Paul's School: A Study of Ancient Rhetoric in English Renaissance Education*. Hamden, CT: Archon Books, 1964.
Cohen, Ralph. "Panel Discussion: The Mirror Image: Shakespeare in Authentic Style." In *Holding up the Mirror: Authenticity and Adaptation in Shakespeare Today*, edited by Stephen Kueler, John Frick, Nancy Friedland, and Martha S. LoMonaco, 44–70. New York: Theatre Library Association, 2014.
Cohen, Ralph Alan. "Directing at the Globe and the Blackfriars: Six Big Rules for Contemporary Directors." In *Shakespeare's Globe: A Theatrical Experiment*, edited by Christie Carson and Farah Karim-Cooper, 211–25. Cambridge: Cambridge University Press, 2008.
Cook, Carol. "'The Sign and Semblance of Her Honor': Reading Gender Difference in *Much Ado about Nothing*." *PMLA* 101, no. 2 (1986): 186–202.
Cox, John F., ed. *Shakespeare in Production: Much Ado about Nothing*. Cambridge, UK: Cambridge University Press, 1997.
Crane, Mary Thomas. "What Was Performance?" *Criticism* 43, no. 2 (2001): 169–87.
Crewe, Jonathan. "Reclaiming Character?" in *Shakespeare Studies* XXXIV (2006): 35–40.
Crider, Scott. *With What Persuasion: An Essay on Shakespeare and the Ethics of Rhetoric: Studies in Shakespeare, Vol. 18*. Edited by Robert F. Willson, Jr. New York: Peter Lang, 2009.
Crystal, David and Ben Crystal. *Shakespeare's Words: A Glossary and Language Companion*. [http://www.shakespeareswords.com/Glossary] and London: Penguin Books, 2004.
Curtright, Travis. "'Falseness Cannot Come from Thee': Marina as Character and Orator in Shakespeare's *Pericles*." *Literary Imagination* 11, no. 1 (2009): 99–110.
———. *The One Thomas More*. Washington, DC: Catholic University of America Press, 2012.
———. "Sidney's *Defense of Poetry*: Ethos and the Ideas." *Ben Jonson Journal* 10 (2003): 101–15.
———. "Thomas More on Humor." *Logos: A Journal of Catholic Thought and Culture* 17, no. 1 (Winter 2014): 13–35.

Daitz, Stephen G. "Tacitus' Technique of Character Portrayal." *American Journal of Philology* 81, no. 1 (January 1960): 52–97.
Danner, Bruce. "Speaking Daggers." *Shakespeare Quarterly* 54, no. 1 (Spring 2003): 29–62.
Dawson, Anthony B. "Performance and Participation: Desdemona, Foucault, and the Actor's Body." In *Shakespeare, Theory, and Performance*, edited by J. C. Bulman. London: Routledge, 1996.
Dawson, Anthony and Paul Yachnin. *The Culture of Playgoing in Shakespeare's England: A Collaborative Debate.* Cambridge, UK: Cambridge University Press, 2001.
Dean, Leonard F. "Literary Problems in More's *Richard III*." *PMLA* 58, no. 1 (March 1943): 22–41.
Dennis, Carl. "Wit and Wisdom in *Much Ado about Nothing*." *Studies in English Literature, 1500–1900* 13, no. 2 (1973): 223–37.
Desmet, Christy. "The Persistence of Character." In *Shakespeare Studies, vol. XXXIV*, edited by Susan Zimmerman, 46–55. Cranbury, NJ: Associated University Presses, 2006.

———. *Reading Shakespeare's Characters: Rhetoric, Ethics, and Identity.* Amherst: University of Massachusetts Press, 1992.

Desmet, Christy and Robert Sawyer, eds. *Harold Bloom's Shakespeare.* New York: Palgrave, 2001.
Dessen, Alan C. "'Original Practices' at the Globe: A Theatre Historian's View." In *Shakespeare's Globe: A Theatrical Experiment*, edited by Christie Carson and Farah Karim-Cooper, 45–53. Cambridge, UK: Cambridge University Press, 2008.
Detmer, Emily. "Civilizing Subordination: Domestic Violence and *The Taming of the Shrew*." *Shakespeare Quarterly* 48, no. 3 (1997): 273–94.
Dickey, Stephen. "Language and Role in *Pericles*," *English Literary Renaissance* 16, no. 3 (1986): 550–66.
Dobson, Michael, ed. *The Oxford Companion to Shakespeare.* Oxford: Oxford University Press, 2001.
Dodd, William. "Character as Dynamic Identity: From Fictional Interaction Script to Performance." In *Shakespeare and Character: Theory, History, Performance, and Theatrical Persons*, edited by Paul Yachnin and Jessica Slights, 62–79. New York: Palgrave Macmillan, 2009.
Dollimore, Jonathan. *Radical Tragedy: Religion, Ideology, and Power in the Drama of Shakespeare and his Contemporaries*, third edition. Durham, NC: Duke University Press, 2004.
Donawerth, Jane L. "Shakespeare and Acting Theory in the English Renaissance." In *Shakespeare and the Arts: A Collection of Essays from the Ohio Shakespeare Conference, 1981 Wright State University, Dayton, Ohio*, edited by Cecile Williamson Cary and Henry S. Limouze, 165–78. Washington, DC: University Press of America, 1982.
Donohue, Dan. "Iago: In Following Him I Follow But Myself." In *Shakespeare's Sense of Character: On the Page and From the Stage*, edited by Yu Jin Ko and Michael Shurgot, 141–50. Burlington, VT: Ashgate, 2012.
Dowden, Edward. *Shakespeare: A Critical Study of His Mind and Art.* London: Henry S. King & Co., 1876.

———. *Shakespeare Primer.* London: Macmillan, 1877.

Driscoll, James P. *Identity in Shakespearean Drama.* London: Associated University Presses, 1983.
Dubrow, Heather. *Captive Victors.* Ithaca, NY: Cornell University Press, 1987.
Dusinberre, Juliet. *Shakespeare and the Nature of Women* , third edition. New York: Palgrave Macmillan, 2003.

———. "*The Taming of the Shrew*: Women, Acting, and Power." In *The Taming of the Shrew: Critical Essays*, edited by Dana Aspinall, 168–85. New York: Routledge, 2002.

Edwards, Philip, Inga-Stina Ewbank, and G. K. Hunter, eds. *Shakespeare's Styles: Essays in Honour of Kenneth Muir.* Cambridge, UK: Cambridge University Press, 1980.

Enterline, Lynn. *Shakespeare's Schoolroom: Rhetoric, Discipline, Emotion*. Philadelphia: University of Pennsylvania Press, 2011.
Erasmus, Desiderius. *Collected Works of Erasmus: Literary and Educational Writings, Vol. 2: De Copia / De Ratione Studii*. Edited by Craig R. Thompson. Translated by Betty I. Knott. Toronto: University of Toronto Press, 1978.
———. *The Praise of Folly*. Translated by Clarence H. Miller. New Haven, CT: Yale University Press, 1979.
Escomle, Bridget. *Talking to the Audience: Shakespeare, Performance, Self*. New York: Routledge, 2005.
Evans, G. Blakemore. *Elizabethan Jacobean Drama: The Theatre in Its Time*. New York: New Amsterdam Books, 1990.
Evans, Robert. "Flattery in Shakespeare's *Othello*: The Relevance of Plutarch and Sir Thomas Elyot." *Comparative Drama* 35 (2001): 1–41.
Ewbank, Inga-Stina. "'My name is Marina': The Language of Recognition." In *Shakespeare's Styles: Essays in Honour of Kenneth Muir*, edited by Philip Edwards, Inga-Stina Ewbank, and G. K. Hunter, 111–30. Cambridge: Cambridge University Press, 1980.
Falco, Raphael. "Introduction." In *Shakespeare Studies*, Vol. XXXIV, edited by Susan Zimmerman, 21–24. Cranbury, NJ: Associated University Presses, 2006.
Falocco, Joe. "A Note on Terminology." In *Reimagining Shakespeare's Playhouse: Early Modern Staging Conventions in the Twentieth Century*. Cambridge, UK: D. S. Brewer, 2010.
Felperin, Howard. "This Great Miracle: Pericles." In *Pericles: Critical Essays*, edited by David Skeele, 114–46. New York: Routledge, 2000.
Flower, Annette C. "Disguise and Identity in *Pericles, Prince of Tyre*." *Shakespeare Quarterly* 26, no. 1 (1975): 30–41.
Fortenbaugh, William W. "Aristotle's Accounts of Persuasion through Character." In *Theory, Text, Context: Issues in Greek Rhetoric and Oratory*, edited by Christopher Lyle Johnstone, 147–68. Albany: State University of New York Press, 1996.
Friedman, Michael D. *The World Must Be Peopled: Shakespeare's Comedies of Forgiveness*. London: Associated University Presses, 2002.
Frye, Northrop. *A Natural Perspective: The Development of Shakespearean Comedy and Romance*. New York: Columbia University Press, 1955.
Gamboa, Brett. "'Is't Real that I See?': Staged Realism and the Paradox of Shakespeare's Audience." *Shakespeare Bulletin* 31, no. 4 (2013): 669–88.
Garber, Marjorie. *Shakespeare After All*. New York: Pantheon Books, 2004.
Gay, Penny. *As She Likes It: Shakespeare's Unruly Women*. London: Routledge, 1994.
The Geneva Bible: A Facsimile of the 1560 Edition. Peabody, MA: Hendrickson Publishers, 2007.
Gosson, Stephen. "Plays Confuted in Five Actions (1582)." In *Shakespeare's Theater: A Sourcebook*, edited by Tanya Pollard, 84–114. Oxford: Blackwell Publishing, 2004.
Gosson, Stephen. "The School of Abuse." In *Shakespeare's Theater: A Sourcebook*, edited by Tanya Pollard, 19–33. Oxford: Blackwell Publishing, 2004.
Gottlieb, Beatrice. *The Family in the Western World from the Black Death to the Industrial Age*. New York: Oxford University Press, 1993.
Gorfian, Phyllis. "Puzzle and Artifice: The Riddle as Metapoetry in *Pericles*." In *Pericles: Critical Essays*, edited by David Skeele, 133–46. New York: Routledge, 2000.
Granville-Barker, Harley. *Prefaces to Shakespeare, Vol. 1*. Princeton, NJ: Princeton University Press, 1946.
Greenblatt, Stephen. *Renaissance Self-Fashioning: From More to Shakespeare*. Chicago: University of Chicago Press, 1984.
———. *Shakespearean Negotiations*. Berkeley: University of California Press, 1988.
———. *Will in the World: How Shakespeare Became Shakespeare*. London: Jonathan Cape, 2004.
Greene, Thomas M. *The Light in Troy: Imitation and Discovery in Renaissance Poetry*. New Haven, CT: Yale University Press, 1982.

Greenfield, Thelma N. "A Re-examination of the 'Patient' Pericles." *Shakespeare Studies* 3 (1967): 51–81.
Greer, Germaine. *The Female Eunuch*. New York: MacGraw-Hill, 1971.
Gurr, A. J. "Who Strutted and Bellowed?" In *Shakespeare Survey*, vol. 16. Cambridge, UK: Cambridge University Press, 2002.
Gurr, Andrew. "Elizabethan Action." *Studies in Philology* 63, no. 2 (1996): 144–56.
———. *The Shakespeare Company, 1594–1642*. Cambridge, UK: Cambridge University Press, 2006.
———. *The Shakespearean Stage, 1574–1642*. Cambridge, UK: Cambridge University Press, 2009.
Hapgood, Robert, ed. *Shakespeare in Production: Hamlet*. Cambridge, UK: Cambridge University Press, 1999.
Harbage, Alfred. "Elizabethan Acting." *PMLA* 54, no. 3 (September 1939): 685–708.
Hartwig, Joan. *Shakespeare's Tragicomic Vision*. Baton Rouge: Louisiana State University Press, 1972.
Heilman, Robert. "The Taming Untamed, or, The Return of the Shrew." *Modern Language Quarterly* 27 (1966): 147–61.
Heninger, S. K. *Sidney and Spenser: The Poet as Maker*. University Park: Pennsylvania State University Press, 1989.
Henze, Richard. "Deception in *Much Ado about Nothing*." *Studies in English Literature, 1500–1900* 11, no. 2 (1971): 187–201.
Heywood, Thomas. "Apology for Actors (1612)." In *Shakespeare's Theater: A Sourcebook*, edited by Tanya Pollard, 213–54. Oxford: Blackwell Publishing, 2004.
Hillebrand, Harold Newcomb. *The Child Actors: A Chapter in Elizabethan Stage History*. New York: Russell and Russell, 1964.
Hobbes, Thomas. *The English Works of Thomas Hobbes of Malmesbury*, vol. 8. Edited by William Molesworth. London: J. Bohn, 1839–1845.
Hobgood, Allison P. *Passionate Playgoing in Early Modern England*. Cambridge, UK: Cambridge University Press, 2014.
Holland, Peter. "The Resources of Characterization in *Othello*." In *Shakespeare Survey Volume 41: Shakespearian Stages and Staging*, edited by Stanley Wells, 119–32. Cambridge, UK: Cambridge University Press, 1989.
Holmes, Jonathan. "Adrian Lester." In *The Routledge Companion to Actors' Shakespeare*, edited by John Russell Brown and Kevin Ewert, 132–42. New York: Routledge, 2012.
Honigmann, E. A. J. *Shakespeare: Seven Tragedies Revisited: The Dramatist's Manipulation of Response*, second edition. Houndmills, UK: Palgrave Macmillan, 2002.
Hoole, Charles. *A New Discovery of the Old Art of Teaching School*. Edited by Thiselton Mark. Syracuse, NY: C. W. Bardeen, 1912.
Hopkins, D. J. "Performance and Urban Space in Shakespeare's Rome, or 'S.P.Q.L.'" In *Rematerializing Shakespeare: Authority and Representation on the Early Modern Stage*, ed. Bryan Reynolds and William N. West, 35–52. New York: Palgrave Macmillan, 2005.
Houston, John Porter. *Shakespearean Sentences: A Study in Style and Syntax*. Baton Rouge: Louisiana State University Press, 1988.
Howard, Jean. "The New Historicism in Renaissance Studies." *ELR* 16 (1986): 13–43.
Howard, Jean E. "Renaissance Antitheatricality and the Politics of Gender and Rank in *Much Ado About Nothing*." In *Shakespeare Reproduced: The Text in History and Ideology*, edited by Jean E. Howard and Marion F. O'Connor, 163–87. New York: Methuen, 1987.
Hunter, Lynette and Peter Lichtenfels, eds. *Shakespeare, Language and the Stage, The Fifth Wall: Approaches to Shakespeare from Criticism, Performance and Theatre Studies*. London: Thomson Learning, 2005.
Hutcheon, Elizabeth. "From Shrew to Subject: Petruchio's Humanist Education of Katherine in *The Taming of the Shrew*." *Comparative Drama* 45, no. 4 (2011): 95–119.
Hutson, Lorna. *The Invention of Suspicion: Law and Mimesis in Shakespeare and Renaissance Drama*. Oxford: Oxford University Press, 2011.

Hyman, Stanley Edgar. *Iago: Some Approaches to the Illusion of His Motivation: A Study in Pluralist Criticism.* New York: Atheneum, 1970.
Jackson, MacDonald P. *Defining Shakespeare: Pericles as Test Case.* Oxford: Oxford University Press, 2003.
James, Heather. "Shakespeare's Learned Heroines in Ovid's Schoolroom." In *Shakespeare and the Classics,* edited by Charles Martindale and A. B. Taylor, 66–85. Cambridge, UK: Cambridge University Press, 2004.
Jones, Emrys. *The Origins of Shakespeare.* Oxford: Oxford University Press, 1977.
———. "Stuart *Cymbeline.*" *Essays in Criticism* 11 (1961): 84–99.
Jonson, Ben. "Cynthia's Revels." In *Ben Jonson, Vol. IV,* edited by C. H. Herford and Percy Simpson, 1–184. Oxford: Clarendon Press, 1932.
———. "Volpone." In *English Renaissance Drama: A Norton Anthology.* Edited by Dave Bevington, Lars Engle, Katharine Eisaman Maus, and Eric Rasmussen. New York: W.W. Norton, 2002.
Jordan, Constance. *Shakespeare's Monarchies: Ruler and Subject in the Romances.* Ithaca, NY: Cornell University Press, 1997.
Jorgensen, Paul A. "Honesty in *Othello.*" *Studies in Philology* 47 (1950): 557–68.
Joseph, Bertram. *Acting Shakespeare,* second edition. New York: Theatre Arts Books, 1969.
Joseph, B. L. *Elizabethan Acting.* London: Oxford University Press, 1952.
Joseph, Miriam. *Shakespeare's Use of the Arts of Language.* New York: Hafner Publishing Company, 1966.
Kamaralli, Anna. *Shakespeare and the Shrew: Performing the Defiant Female Voice.* New York: Palgrave Macmillan, 2012.
Kathman, David. "How Old Were Shakespeare's Boy Actors?" In *Shakespeare Survey: Writing About Shakespeare, Vol. 58,* edited by Peter Holland, 220–46. Cambridge, UK: Cambridge University Press, 2005.
Keenan, Siobhan. *Acting Companies and Their Plays in Shakespeare's London.* London: Bloomsbury Arden Shakespeare, 2014.
Kennedy, George A., trans and ed. *Progymnasmata: Greek Textbooks of Prose Composition and Rhetoric.* Atlanta, GA: Society of Biblical Literature, 2003.
Khan, Victoria. "Machiavelli's Reputation to the Eighteenth Century." In *The Cambridge Companion to Machiavelli,* edited by John M. Najemy, 239–55. Cambridge, UK: Cambridge University Press, 2010.
Kiernan, Pauline. *Shakespeare's Theory of Drama.* Cambridge, UK: Cambridge University Press, 1996.
———. *Staging Shakespeare at the New Globe.* New York: Palgrave, 1999.
Kietzman, Mary Jo. "Will Personified: Viola as Actor-Author in *Twelfth Night.*" *Criticism* 54, no. 2 (2012): 257–89.
King, T. J. *Casting Shakespeare's Plays.* Cambridge, UK: Cambridge University Press, 1992.
Knight, G. Wilson. *The Crown of Life: Essays in Interpretation of Shakespeare's Final Plays.* London: Methuen, 1947.
Knight, G. Wilson. "The Writing of Pericles." In *Pericles: Critical Essays,* edited by David Skeele, 78–113. New York: Routledge, 2000.
Ko, Yu Jin. *Mutability and Division on Shakespeare's Stage.* Newark: University of Delaware Press, 2004.
Ko, Yu Jin and Michael W. Shurgot, eds. *Shakespeare's Sense of Character: On the Page and From the Stage.* Burlington, VT: Ashgate, 2012.
Kustow, Michael. *Peter Brook: A Biography.* New York: St. Martin's Press, 2005.
Kyd, Thomas. "The Spanish Tragedy." In *English Renaissance Drama: A Norton Anthology,* edited by David Bevington, 3–74. New York: W. W. Norton & Company, 2002.
Lamb, Edel. *Performing Childhood in the Early Modern Theatre: The Children's Playing Companies (1599–1613).* London: Palgrave Macmillan, 2009.
Lanham, Richard A. *A Handlist of Rhetorical Terms,* second edition. Berkeley: University of California Press, 1991.

Leavis, F. R. "Diabolic Intellect and the Noble Hero: Or the Sentimentalist's *Othello*." In *The Common Pursuit*. London: Chatto & Windus, 1953.

Lee, John. *Shakespeare's Hamlet and the Controversies of the Self*. Oxford: Oxford University Press, 2000.

Levin, Richard. *Looking for an Argument: Critical Encounters with the New Approaches of Shakespeare and His Contemporaries*. Madison, NJ: Fairleigh Dickinson University Press, 2003.

Levinson, Marjorie. "What Is New Formalism." *PMLA* 122, no. 2 (2007): 558–69.

Lewis, Cynthia. "'You Were an Actor with Your Handkerchief': Women, Windows, and Moral Agency." *Comparative Drama* 43, no. 4 (2009): 473–96.

Lichtenfels, Peter. "Shakespeare's Language in the Theatre." In *Reading Shakespeare's Dramatic Language: A Guide*, edited by Sylvia Adamson, Lynette Hunter, Lynne Magnusson, Ann Thompson, and Katie Wales, 158–72. London: Thomson Learning, 2001.

Lodge, Thomas. "A Reply to Stephen Gosson's School of Abuse, InDefence of Poetry, Music, and Stage Plays." In *Shakespeare's Theater: A Sourcebook*, edited by Tanya Pollard, 37–61. Oxford: Blackwell Publishing, 2004.

Longinus. "On Literary Excellence." In *Literary Criticism: Plato to Dryden*, edited by A. H. Gilbert, 146–98. Detroit: Wayne State University Press, 1967.

Lopez, Jeremy. "John Harrell." In *The Routledge Companion to Actors' Shakespeare*, edited by John Russell Brown and Kevin Ewert, 77–90. New York: Routledge, 2012.

Lopez, Jeremy. *Theatrical Convention and Audience Response in Early Modern England*. Cambridge, UK: Cambridge University Press, 2003.

Lucian. "How to Write History." In *Lucian*, vol. 6. Translated by K. Kilburn. Cambridge, MA: Harvard University Press, 1999.

Lupton, J. H. *A Life of John Colet: Dean of St. Paul's and Founder of St. Paul's School*. Eugene, OR: Wipf & Stock Publishers, 2004.

Mack, Peter. *Elizabethan Rhetoric: Theory and Practice*. Cambridge, UK: Cambridge University Press, 2002.

Maguire, Laurie and Emma Smith. *30 Great Myths about Shakespeare*. New York: Wiley-Blackwell, 2013.

Maher, Mary Z. *Modern Hamlets and Their Soliloquies: An Expanded Edition*. Iowa City: University of Iowa Press, 2003.

Mann, David. *Shakespeare's Women: Performance and Conception*. Cambridge, UK: Cambridge University Press, 2009.

Marcus, Leah S. *Puzzling Shakespeare: Local Reading and Its Discontents*. Berkeley: University of California Press, 1988.

Maus, Katharine Eisaman. *Inwardness and Theater in the English Renaissance*. Chicago: University of Chicago Press, 1995.

Mazer, Cary M. "Historicizing Spontaneity: The Illusion of the First Time of 'The Illusion of the First Time.'" In *Shakespeare's Sense of Character: On the Page and From the Stage*, edited by Yu Jin Ko and Michael Shurgot, 85–98. Burlington, VT: Ashgate 2012.

McDonald, Charles. *Rhetoric of Tragedy*. Amherst: University of Massachusetts Press, 1966.

McDonald, Russ. *Shakespeare's Late Style*. Cambridge, UK: Cambridge University Press, 2006.

McManus, Donald. "Kevin Kline." In *The Routledge Companion to Actors' Shakespeare*, edited by John Russell Brown and Kevin Ewert, 120–31. New York: Routledge, 2012.

McMullan, Gordon A. *Shakespeare and the Idea of Late Writing: Authorship in the Proximity of Death*. Cambridge, UK: Cambridge University Press, 2008.

Menzer, Paul. "That Old Saw: Early Modern Acting and the Infinite Regress." *Shakespeare Bulletin* 22 (2004): 27–44.

Miola, Robert. "The Influence of New Comedy on *The Comedy of Errors* and *The Taming of the Shrew*." In *Shakespeare's Sweet Thunder: Essays on the Early Comedies*, edited by Michael J. Collins, 27–33. Newark: Associated University Presses, 1997.

———. *Shakespeare and Classical Comedy: The Influence of Plautus and Terence*. Oxford: Oxford University Press, 1994.

Moore, Jeanie Grant. "Riddled Romance: Kingship and Kinship in *Pericles*." *Rocky Mountain Review of Language and Literature* 57, no. 1 (2003): 33–48.

More, Thomas. *The Correspondence of Sir Thomas More*. Edited by Elizabeth Frances Rogers. Princeton, NJ: Princeton University Press, 1947.

———. *The History of Richard the Third: A Reading Edition*. Edited by George M. Logan. Indianapolis: Indiana University Press, 2005.

———. *The Yale Edition of the Complete Works of St. Thomas More, Volume 2: The History of King Richard III*. Edited by Richard S. Sylvester. New Haven, CT: Yale University Press, 1963.

———. *The Yale Edition of the Complete Works of St. Thomas More, Volume 3, Part 1: Translations of Lucian*. Edited by Craig R. Thompson. New Haven, CT: Yale University Press, 1974.

———. *The Yale Edition of the Complete Works of St. Thomas More, Volume 4: Utopia*. Edited by Edward Surtz and J. H. Hexter. New Haven, CT: Yale University Press, 1979.

———. *The Yale Edition of the Complete Works of St. Thomas More, Volume 6, Part 1: A Dialogue Concerning Heresies*. Edited by Thomas M. C. Lawler et al. New Haven, CT: Yale University Press, 1981.

———. *The Yale Edition of the Complete Works of St. Thomas More, Volume 12: A Dialogue of Comfort Against Tribulation*. Edited by Louis L. Martz and Frank Manley. New Haven, CT: Yale University Press, 1976.

———. *The Yale Edition of the Complete Works of St. Thomas More, Volume 15: In Defense of Humanism*. Edited and translated by Daniel Kinney. New Haven, CT: Yale University Press, 1986.

Munday, Anthony. "A Second and Third Blast of Retreat from Plays and Theaters (1580)." In *Shakespeare's Theater: A Sourcebook*, edited by Tanya Pollard, 62–83. Oxford: Blackwell Publishing, 2004.

Myhill, Nova. "Spectatorship in/of *Much Ado about Nothing*." *Studies in English Literature 1500–1900* 39, no. 2 (1999): 291–311.

Nashe, Thomas. "Pierce Penniless his Supplication to the Devil (1592)." In *Thomas Nashe: Selected Writings*, edited by Stanley Wells, 23–88. London: Edward Arnold, 1964.

Navarro, Juan Huarte. *The Examination of Mens' Wits*. New York: Da Capo Press, 1969.

Nelson, William. *A Fifteenth Century School Book*. Oxford: Clarendon Press, 1956.

Northbrooke, John. "A Treatise Against Dicing, Dancing, Plays, and Interludes, with Other Idle Pastimes (1577)." In *Shakespeare's Theater: A Sourcebook*, edited by Tanya Pollard, 1–18. Oxford: Blackwell Publishing, 2004.

Novy, Marianne. "Multiple Parenting in *Pericles*." In *Pericles: Critical Essays*, edited by David Skeele, 238–48. New York: Routledge, 2000.

Nussbaum, Martha. "Aristotle on Emotions and Rational Persuasion." In *Essays on Aristotle's Rhetoric*. Berkeley: University of California Press, 1996.

O'Brien, Ellen J. "Mapping the Role: Criticism and Construction of Shakespearean Character." In *Shakespearean Illuminations: Essays in Honor of Marvin Rosenburg*. Newark: University of Delaware Press, 1998.

O'Dell, Leslie. *Shakespearean Characterization: A Guide for Actors and Students*. London: Greenwood Press, 2002.

Orgel, Stephen. *The Authentic Shakespeare: And Other Problems of the Early Modern Stage*. New York: Routledge, 2002.

———. "Nobody's Perfect: Or Why Did the English Stage Take Boys for Women?" *South Atlantic Quarterly* 88 (1989): 7–29.

Palfrey, Simon. *Doing Shakespeare*. London: Arden, 2011.

———. *Late Shakespeare: A New World of Words*. Oxford: Oxford University Press, 1997.
Palfrey, Simon and Tiffany Stern. *Shakespeare in Parts*. Oxford: Oxford University Press, 2007.
Parker, Patricia. "Construing Gender: Mastering Bianca in *The Taming of the Shrew*." In *The Impact of Feminism in English Renaissance Studies*, edited by Dympna Callaghan, 193–209. New York: Palgrave Macmillan, 2007.
———. "Shakespeare and Rhetoric: 'Dilation' and 'Delation' in Othello." In *Shakespeare and the Question of Theory*, edited by Patricia Parker and Geoffrey Hartman, 54–74. London: Routledge, 1985.
Parvini, Neema. *Shakespeare and Contemporary Theory: New Historicism and Cultural Materialism*. London: Bloomsbury Academic, 2012.
Peacham, Henry. *The Garden of Eloquence* (1593). London: Historical Collection from the British Library, 1593.
Pearson, Velvet D. "In Search of a Liberated Kate in *The Taming of the Shrew*." *Rocky Mountain Review of Language and Literature* 44, no. 4 (January 1, 1990): 229–242.
Pigman, G. W. III. "Versions of Imitation in the Renaissance." *Renaissance Quarterly* 33 (1980): 1–32.
Plett, Heinrich F. *Enargeia in Classical Antiquity and the Early Modern Age*. Boston: Brill, 2012.
———. *Rhetoric and Renaissance Culture*. Berlin: DeGruyter, 2004.
Plutarch. *Plutarch's Moralia: Twenty Essays Translated by Philemon Holland*. Edited by E. H. Blakeney. London: Dent, 1911.
Pollard, Tanya, ed. *Shakespeare's Theater: A Sourcebook*. Oxford: Blackwell Publishing, 2004.
Poole, William. "'Unpointed Words': Shakespearean Syntax in Action." *Cambridge Quarterly* 32 (2003): 27–42.
Potter, Lois. *The Life of Shakespeare: A Critical Biography*. Malden, MA: Wiley-Blackwell, 2012.
Potter, Ursula. "Performing Arts in the Tudor Classroom." In *Tudor Drama before Shakespeare 1485–1590*, edited by Lloyd Kermode, Jason Scott-Warren, and Martine Van Elk, 143–65. New York: Palgrave Macmillan, 2004.
Puttenham, George. *The Art of English Poesy: A Critical Edition*. Edited by Frank Whigham and Wayne A. Rebhorn. Ithaca, NY: Cornell University Press, 2007.
———. *The Arte of English Poesy: A Facsimile Reproduction*. Kent, OH: Kent State University Press, 1970.
Quintillian. *Institutio Oratoria*. Translated by H. E. Butler. Cambridge, MA: Harvard University Press, 1922.
———. *Quintillian's Insitutes of Oratory*. Translated by John Selby Watson. London: George Bell and Sons, 1907.
———. *Quintillian: The Orator's Education, Book 12*. Translated by Donald A. Russell. Cambridge, MA: Harvard University Press, 2001.
Rackin, Phyllis. *Shakespeare and Women*. Oxford: Oxford University Press, 2005.
Rainolds, John. "The Overthrow of Stage-Plays (1599)." In *Shakespeare's Theater: A Sourcebook*, edited by Tanya llard, 170–78. Oxford: Blackwell Publishing, 2004.
Rasmussen, Mark David, ed. *Renaissance Literature and Its Formal Engagements*. New York: Palgrave, 2002.
Reiman, Donald H. and Neil Fraistat, eds. "Prometheus Unbound." In *Shelley's Poetry and Prose*, second edition. New York: W.W. Norton & Co., 2002.
Reynolds, Bryan. and William N. West, eds. *Rematerializing Shakespeare: Authority and Representation on the Early Modern Stage*. New York: Palgrave Macmillan, 2005.
Rhodes, Neil. *The Power of Eloquence and English Renaissance Literature*. New York: St. Martin's Press, 1992.
Richmond, Hugh Macrae. *Shakespeare's Theatre: A Dictionary of his Stage Context*. London and New York: Continuum, 2004.
Roach, Joseph R. *The Player's Passion: Studies in the Science of Acting*. Ann Arbor: University of Michigan Press, 1993.

Roper, William. "Life of More." In *A Thomas More Source Book*, edited by Gerard B. Wegemer and Stephen Smith, 16–65. Washington, DC: Catholic University of America Press, 2004.

Rosenberg, Marvin. "Elizabethan Actors: Men or Marionettes?" *PMLA* 69, no. 4 (September 1954): 915–27.

Royce, Jacalyn. "Early Modern Naturalistic Acting: The Role of the Globe in the Development of Personation." In *The Oxford Handbook of Early Modern Theatre*, edited by Richard Dutton, 477–95. Oxford: Oxford University Press, 2009.

Russell, D. A. "De Imitatione." In *Creative Imitation and Latin Literature*, edited by D. West and A. Woodman, 1–16. Cambridge, UK: Cambridge University Press, 1979.

Rutter, Carol. *Clamorous Voices: Shakespeare's Women Today*. Edited by Faith Evans. London: The Women's Press, 1988.

Ryan, Kiernan, ed. *Shakespeare: The Last Plays*. London: Longman, 1999.

———. *Shakespeare's Universality: Here's Fine Revolution*. London: Bloomsbury, 2015.

Rylance, Mark. "Research, Materials, Craft: Principles of Performance at Shakespeare's Globe." In *Shakespeare's Globe: A Theatrical Experiment*, edited by Christie Carson and Farah Karim Cooper, 103–14. Cambridge: Cambridge University Press, 2008.

Sanders, Norman. "An Overview of Critical Approaches to the Romances." In *Shakespeare's Romances Reconsidered*, edited by Carol McGinnis Kay and Henry E. Jacobs, 1–10. Lincoln: University of Nebraska Press, 1978.

Sargeaunt, John. *Annals of Westminster School*. London: Methuen & Co., 1898.

Scolnicov, Hanna. "The Woman in the Window: A Theatrical Icon." In *Spectacle and Image in Renaissance Europe: Selected Papers of the XXXIInd Conference at the Centre D'Etudes Supérieures de la Renaissance de Tours, 29 June–8 July 1989*, edited by André Lascombes, 281–305. Leiden: Brill, 1993.

Seneca. *Seneca's Tragedies*. Translated by Frank Justus Miller. Cambridge, MA: Harvard University Press, 1960.

Shakespeare, William. *The Complete Pelican Shakespeare*, second edition. Edited by Stephen Orgel and A.R. Humphreys. New York: Penguin Classics, 2002.

———. *The Complete Works*, second edition. Edited by Stanley Wells and Gary Taylor. Oxford: Oxford University Press, 2005.

———. *The Complete Works*, fifth edition. Edited by David Bevington. New York: Longman, 2004.

———. *The Complete Works*, seventh edition. Edited by David Bevington. New York: Pearson Longman, 2014.

———. *Hamlet: Third Series (Arden Shakespeare)*. Edited by Ann Thompson and Neil Taylor. London: Thomson Learning, 2007.

———. *King Richard III: Second Series (Arden Shakespeare)*. Edited by Anthony Hammond. London and New York: Methuen Drama, 2000.

———. *King Richard III: Third Series (Arden Shakespeare)*. Edited by James R. Siemon. London: Thompson Learning, 2009.

———. *Love's Labour's Lost: Third Series (Arden Shakespeare)*. Edited by H. R. Woudhuysen. Walton-on-Thames: Thomas Nelson and Sons, 1998.

———. *Much Ado About Nothing: Second Series (Arden Shakespeare)*. Edited by Claire McEachern. London: Thomas Learning, 1981.

———. *A New Variorum Edition of Shakespeare: Much Ado About Nothing*. Edited by Horace Howard Furness. New York: Dover Publications, Inc., 1964.

———. *A New Variorum Edition of Shakespeare: Othello*. Edited by Horace Howard Furness. New York: Dover Publications, Inc., 1963.

———. *The Norton Shakespeare: Based on the Oxford Edition*, first edition. Edited by Stephen Greenblatt. New York: W. W. Norton & Co., 1997.

———. *The Norton Shakespeare*, second edition. Edited by Stephen Greenblatt. New York: W.W. Norton & Co., 2008.

———. *Othello (Arden Shakespeare)*. Edited by E. A. J. Honigmann. London: Thomas Learning, 2001.

———. *Pericles*. Edited by Jonathan Bate and Eric Rasmussen. New York: The Modern Library, 2012.
———. *Pericles: Third Series (Arden Shakespeare)*. Edited by Suzanne Gossett. London: Methuen, 2004.
———. *The Riverside Shakespeare*, second edition. Edited by G. Blakemore Evans. Boston: Houghton Mifflin, 1997.
———. *Taming of the Shrew: Third Series (Arden Shakespeare)*. Edited by Barbara Hodgdon. London: Methuen Drama, 2010.
———. *Twelfth Night, or What You Will: Third Series (Arden Shakespeare)*. Edited by Keir Elam. London: Cengage Learning, 2008.
Shapiro, James. *Rival Playwrights: Marlowe, Johnson, Shakespeare*. New York: Columbia University Press, 1991.
———. *A Year in the Life of William Shakespeare: 1599*. New York: HarperCollins, 2005.
———. *The Year of Lear: Shakespeare in 1606*. New York: Simon & Schuster, 2015.
Shapiro, Michael. "Framing the Taming: Metatheatrical Awareness of Female Impersonation in *The Taming of the Shrew*." In *The Taming of the Shrew: Critical Essays*, edited by Dana Aspinall, 210–35. New York: Routledge, 2002.
Shevtsova, Maria. "Peter Brook." In *The Routledge Companion to Director's Shakespeare*, edited by John Russell Brown, 16–36. London and New York: Routledge, 2008.
Sinfield, Alan. "From Bradley to Cultural Materialism." In *Shakespeare Studies, Volume XXXIV*, edited by Susan Zimmerman, 25–34. Cranbury, NJ: Associated University Presses, 2006.
———. "When Is a Character Not a Character? Desdemona, Olivia, Lady Macbeth, and Subjectivity." In *Faultlines: Cultural Materialism and the Politics of Dissident Reading*. Berkeley: University of California Press, 1992.
Skeele, David, ed. *Pericles: Critical Essays*. New York: Routledge, 2000.
———. *Thwarting the Wayward Seas: A Critical and Theatrical History of Pericles in the Nineteenth and Twentieth Centuries*. Newark: University of Delaware Press, 1988.
Skinner, Quentin. *Forensic Shakespeare*. Oxford: Oxford University Press, 2014.
———. *Reason and Rhetoric in the Philosophy of Hobbes*. Cambridge, UK: Cambridge University Press, 1996.
Skura, Meredith Anne. *Shakespeare the Actor and the Purposes of Playing*. Chicago: University of Chicago Press, 1993.
Spivack, Bernard. *Shakespeare and the Allegory for Evil*. New York: Columbia University Press, 1958.
Stanislavski, Constantin. *An Actor Prepares*. Translated by Elizabeth Reynolds Hapgood. New York: Theatre Arts Books, 1989.
———. *An Actor's Work: A Student's Diary*. Translated by Jean Benedetti. New York: Routledge, 2008.
———. *Building a Character*. Translated by Elizabeth Reynolds Hapgood. New York: Theatre Arts Books, 1985.
Stern, Tiffany. *Documents of Performance in Early Modern England*. Cambridge, UK: Cambridge University Press, 2009.
———. *Rehearsal from Shakespeare to Sheridan*. Oxford: Clarendon Press, 2000.
———. "(Re:)Historicizing Spontaneity: Original Practices, Stanislavski, and Characterization." In *Shakespeare's Sense of Character: On the Page and From the Stage*, edited by Yu Jin Ko and Michael W. Shurgot, 85–110. Burlington, VT: Ashgate, 2012.
Stoll, Elmer Edgar. "*The Tempest*." *PMLA* 47 (1932): 688–726.
Stubbes, Philip. "Anatomy of Abuses (1583)." In *Shakespeare's Theater: A Sourcebook*, edited by Tanya Pollard, 115–23. Oxford: Blackwell Publishing, 2004.
Styan, J.L. *Shakespeare's Stagecraft*. Cambridge, UK: Cambridge University Press, 1967.
Suetonius. *Lives of the Caesars*. Translated by J. C. Rolfe. Cambridge, MA: Harvard University Press, 1998.
Sutherland, James. "The Language of the Last Plays." In *More Talking of Shakespeare*, edited by John Garrett, 144–58. London: Longmans, 1959.
Swineburne, Algernon. *Pericles and Other Studies*. London: Private Circulation, 1914.

Tacitus, Cornelius. *The Annals*. Translated by A. J. Woodman. Indianapolis: Hackett Publishing, 2004.
———. *The Annals*. Translated by John Jackson. Cambridge, MA: Harvard University Press, 1998.
Taylor, Michael, "'Here Is a Thing Too Young for Such a Place': Innocence in *Pericles*." *Ariel* 13 (1982): 3–19.
———. *Shakespeare Criticism in the Twentieth Century*. Oxford: Oxford University Press, 2001.
Tennenhouse, Leonard. *Power on Display: The Politics of Shakespeare's Genres*. New York: Methuen, 1986.
Terence. *Terence, Volume 1*. Edited and translated by John Barsby. Cambridge, MA: Harvard University Press, 2001.
Theophrastus. *Characters*. Translated by Jeffrey Rusten. Cambridge, MA: Harvard University Press, 1993.
Thompson, Ann and Neil Taylor, eds. *The Arden Shakespeare: Hamlet*. Third series. London: Thomson Learning, 2007.
Thucydides. *History of the Peloponnesian War*. Translated by Rex Warner. New York: Penguin Books, 1954.
Traupman, John C. *The New College Latin and English Dictionary*, second edition. New York: Bantam Books, 1995.
Traversi, Derek. *Shakespeare: The Last Phase*. London: Hollis and Carter, 1954.
Tribble, Evelyn. *Cognition in the Globe: Attention and Memory in Shakespeare's Theatre*. New York: Palgrave Macmillan, 2011.
Tucker, Patrick. *Secrets of Acting Shakespeare: The Original Approach*. New York and London: Routledge, 2002.
Uphaus, Robert. *Beyond Tragedy: Structure and Experience in Shakespeare's Romances*. Lexington: University Press of Kentucky, 1981.
Van Es, Bart. "Reviving the Legacy of Indoor Performance." In *Moving Shakespeare Indoors: Performance and Repertoire in the Jacobean Playhouse*, edited by Andrew Gurr and Farah Karim-Cooper, 237–51. Cambridge, UK: Cambridge University Press, 2014.
———. *Shakespeare in Company*. Oxford: Oxford University Press, 2013.
Vergerio, Pier Paolo. "The Character and Studies Befitting a Free-Born Youth." In *Humanist Educational Treatises*, edited and Translated by Craig W. Kallendorf, 36–39. Cambridge, MA: Harvard University Press, 2002.
Vergil, Polydore. *Three Books of Polydore Vergil's English History*. Edited by Henry Ellis. New York and London: AMS Press, 1968.
Vickers, Brian. *Appropriating Shakespeare: Contemporary Critical Quarrels*. New Haven, CT: Yale University Press, 1993.
———. *Classical Rhetoric in English Poetry*. Carbondale: Southern Illinois University Press, 1989.
———. *In Defense of Rhetoric*. Oxford: Oxford University Press, 2002.
———. *Returning to Shakespeare*. London: Routledge, 1989.
———. "Rhetoric and Poetics." In *The Cambridge History of Renaissance Philosophy*, edited by Charles B. Schmitt, 715–45. Cambridge, UK: Cambridge University Press, 1988.
———. *Shakespeare, Co-Author: A Historical Study of Five Collaborative Plays*. Oxford: Oxford University Press, 2008.
———, ed. *William Shakespeare: The Critical Heritage, Vol 1, 1623–1692*. New York: Routledge, 2000.
Walker, Andrew D. "Enargeia and the Spectator in Greek History." *Transactions of the American Philological Association (1974–)* 123 (1993): 353–77.
Walker, B. *Annals of Tacitus: A Study in the Writing of History*. Manchester, UK: Manchester University Press, 1952.
Watson, Foster. *The English Grammar Schools to 1600: Their Curriculum and Practice*. Cambridge, UK: Cambridge University Press, 1908.

Wegemer, Gerard and Stephen Smith, eds. *A Thomas More Source Book*. Washington, DC: Catholic University of America Press, 2004.

Weimann, Robert. *Author's Pen and Actor's Voice: Playing and Writing in Shakespeare's Theatre*. Edited by Helen Higbee and William West. Cambridge, UK: Cambridge University Press, 2000.

———. *Shakespeare and the Popular Tradition in the Theater: Studies in the Social Dimension of Dramatic Form and Function*. Edited by Robert Schwartz. Baltimore: Johns Hopkins University Press, 1979.

Weimann, Robert and Douglas Bruster. *Shakespeare and the Power of Performance*. Cambridge, UK: Cambridge University Press, 2010.

Wells, Robin Headlam. *Shakespeare's Humanism*. Cambridge, UK: Cambridge University Press, 2005.

Wells, Stanley, ed. "Pierce Penniless his Supplication to the Devil (1592.)" In *Thomas Nashe: Selected Writings*. London: Edward Arnold, 1964.

Whitelocke, Sir James. *Liber Famelicus of Sir James Whitelock*. Edited by John Bruce. Westminster: J. B. Nichols and Sons, 1858.

Wickham, Glynne. "Riddle and Emblem: A Study in the Dramatic Structure of *Cymbeline*." In *English Renaissance Studies Presented to Dame Helen Gardner*, edited by John Carey, 94–113. Oxford: Clarendon Press, 1980.

Wiggins, Martin. *Shakespeare and the Drama of His Time*. Oxford: Oxford University Press, 2000.

Wills, Garry. *Rome and Rhetoric: Julius Caesar*. New Haven, CT: Yale University Press, 2011.

Wilson, Thomas. *The Art of Rhetoric*. Edited by Peter E. Medine. University Park: Pennsylvania State University Press, 1994.

Wimsatt, William K. and Monroe C. Beardsley. "The Intentional Fallacy." In *The Norton Anthology of Theory and Criticism*, edited by Vincent B. Leitch, 1371–87. New York: W.W. Norton, 2001.

Worthen, W. B. "The Rhetoric of Performance Criticism." *Shakespeare Quarterly* 40, no. 4 (Winter 1989): 441–55.

Wright, Thomas. *The Passions of the Mind in General: A Reprint Based on the 1604 Edition*. Chicago: University of Illinois Press, 1971.

Yachnin, Paul. "Personations: *The Taming of the Shrew* and the Limits of Theoretical Criticism." *Early Modern Literary Studies* 2, no. 1 (1996): 21–31.

Yachnin, Paul and Jessica Slights, eds. *Shakespeare and Character: Theory, History, Performance, and Theatrical Persons*. New York: Palgrave Macmillan, 2009.

Yates, Frances A. *Shakespeare's Last Plays: A New Approach*. London: Routledge & Kegan Paul, 1975.

Zenon, Luis Martinez. "Macbeth and the Passions' 'Proper Stuff.'" *SEDERI* 20 (2010): 71–101.

Index

Aaron (fictional character), 14
acting: delivery referred to by, 77; as good, 69n10; lively, 93n22, 93n23, 94n27; oratory as synonymous with, 48–49; playing and, 92n6; Richard III's expertise in, 30–36, 137. *See also* early modern acting styles; Elizabethan acting; formalism; naturalism; rhetoric
Acting Shakespeare (Joseph), 3, 9n10
actio. See delivery; gesture
actioning, 150–151, 154–155
actions, 9n6, 9n10, 22–23, 78–79, 122
actors (*discipuli*), 141n49, 156n6; characters as, 13–36; collaboration of, 146–155, 157n20, 157n21; dissemblers as, 29–30; More on, 40n45; as orators, 1–8, 31; as oscillating, 13–14; parts studied by, 126; pneumatism empowering, 9n12; *Richard III* and, 13–36; tyrants as, 19–27, 32–33; voice of, 13–14. *See also* boy actors; Burbage, Richard; direct address; modern actors; personation; players
Ad Herennium (Cicero), 49, 78–79, 119, 120, 122, 123, 124, 129, 131, 132; on debate, 142n70; forensic debate in, 139n19; *interrogatio* in, 73n84, 152; on narrative, 133–134; Wilson following, 132
Alleyn, Edward, 9n9, 78–79
ambassadors of love, boy actors as, 52–59
American Shakespeare Center (ASC), 145, 146, 155n2, 156n6, 156n9
anacoenosis. *See* audience dialogue rhetorical question
anaphora. *See* repetition

Annals (Tacitus), 6, 16–17, 19–20, 24–27, 40n59; Sylvester on, 37n17; vice in, 41n66
Anne (queen), 23–24, 33–36, 42n102, 42n104
Apelles, 16, 18, 37n15, 38n30
Aphthonius. *See Progymnasmata*
Apology for Actors (Heywood, T.), 49, 52–53, 77–81
aporia. See doubtful
aposiopesis. See breaking off, of speech; half telling
appeal to emotions (*pathos*), 35, 100, 122, 130. *See also* figure of speech
appeal to ethics (*ethos*), 100; characterization reflected by, 137; forensic rhetoric revealing, 122; importance of, 119; Marina voicing, 119–125, 129, 134–137; *martyria* establishing, 132; Quintilian on, 135; *See also Pericles, Prince of Tyre*
argumentum. See spoken subject
Aristides, 17, 18
Aristotle, 99–100, 113n19, 119, 124, 125; *See also Rhetoric*
The Arte of English Poesie: A Facsimile Reproduction (Puttenham), 73n84, 141n63
ASC. *See* American Shakespeare Center
assassin. *See* Leonine
Astington, John, 32, 102, 106, 114n44
As You Like It (Shakespeare), 30, 69n10. *See also* Rosalind
audacity, 47–52, 54, 58, 66–67, 69n10, 73n85
audience dialogue rhetorical question (*anacoenosis*), 153–155
audiences: collaboration of, 146–155, 157n20, 157n21; humoral bodies

173

174   Index

influencing, 9n14; involvement, 147; *Much Ado About Nothing* gulling, 81–92; as onstage, 90–92; paradox of, 91; participatory mode for, 110; scopic management directing, 95n47; theater went to by, 115n59; women in, 74n87. *See also* direct address
auricular defect, 101–104
author's pen, 13–14

Baldwin, T., 48, 61, 63
Bale, John, 48, 71n24
Barabas (fictional character), 15, 40n44
Barton, Anne, 118, 131, 137
Baumlin, Tita, 64, 73n82
Beatrice (fictional character), 81–92, 95n58
beholders, 18, 75, 77, 84, 88–90, 91
Belsey, Catherine, 69n10, 112n4
Benedick (fictional character), 81–92, 95n58
Bennett, Susan, 151
Bentley, Gerald, 69n10
Berger, Harry, 10n23
Berowne (fictional character), 52–54, 54, 55, 55–56
Bevington, David, 73n75
Bianca (fictional character), 64–65, 66, 68, 74n93, 106–108
bishops, 23–24, 26
Blackfriars theater, 145, 146, 156n5
Blake, Anne, 70n17
Bloom, Harold, 15, 110
bodies, 91–92. *See also* female bodies; humoral bodies
bodily abuse (*probra corporis*), 24–25, 27
bodily form figure (*effictio*), 21
Booth, Edwin, 98, 104–105, 109, 114n40
Borachio (fictional character), 7, 62–63, 75, 83–86, 88, 89, 90
Bottom (fictional character), 77, 90
boy actors, 6–7, 45–47, 52–59, 70n17, 72n43, 72n61. *See also* grammar schools; Minola, Katherina; Moth; speech of submission; Viola/Cesario
Boyet (fictional character), 52
Bradbrook, M., 1–2, 4, 9n4
Bradley, A., 4, 9n4, 99

bravery. *See* audacity
breaking off, of speech (*aposiopesis*), 35
Brinsley, John, 46, 48, 50, 58, 62, 65, 66, 73n67; *See also Ludus Literarius*
Brooke, Nicholas, 14–15
Brown, John, 3, 10n15, 10n16
Browne, Thomas, 16
Bruster, Douglas, 13, 43n108, 78–79
Buckingham (fictional character), 25–27, 30, 31–32, 43n108
Burbage, Richard, 1, 3, 4, 8, 9n9, 36n2, 78–79, 152, 154, 155. *See also* "An Excellent Actor"
Burns, Edward, 97–98, 105
Burrow, Colin, 29, 59

Caldarone, Marina, 150–151
Cambyses (king) (fictional character), 30–31
Caplan, H. *See Rhetorica Ad Herennium*
Carson, Christie, 156n13, 157n20, 157n22
Cassio (fictional character), 99, 105–107, 109
causa. See question to adjudicate
causa honesta. See honorable cause
causa turpis. See discreditable cause
Cesario/Viola. *See* Viola/Cesario
Chamberlain's Men, 1, 147
Chambers, E., 13–14, 19
character creation (*ethopoeia*), 50, 114n40
character delineation (*notatio*), 133–137
character-effects, 4–5, 10n23, 91–92; of coherent self, 136; forensic rhetoric revealing, 125; of innocence, 130; language creating, 121; Minola and, 46; patience as, 133–134; in *Pericles, Prince of Tyre*, 8; in *Richard III*, 21–22, 22–23
characterization, 6, 15, 26–27, 76–81, 78–79, 137. *See also* Marina
characters: as actors, 13–36; collaboration, 146–148; criticism, 5–6, 140n46; definition, 19, 151; *enargeia* bringing to life, 22; flat, 97; in grammar schools, 50–51; individual, 2; lifelike, 4–6; Marina as, 117–137; *Much Ado About*

Nothing offstage, 90–92; as narrative device, 131; as offstage, 90–92; performance infiltrating, 13–14; as persons, 76; persuasion's relationship to, 139n17; portrayal, 41n78; *Richard III* and, 13–36; as role, 115n50; sketch, 97–98; studies, 43n107; as unified self, 10n21. *See also* direct address; embodied characters; formalism; Hamlet; naturalism; performance; personation; types
charorator, Marina as, 117–137
The Child Actors: A Chapter in Elizabethan Stage History (Hillebrand), 49, 71n24, 71n25
Cicero, 50, 61, 62, 63, 100, 120, 121, 128–129, 139n22; on friendship, 107–108; good will recommended by, 119, 123, 127; on language, 140n43. *See also Ad Herennium*; *De Inventione*
Clarence (fictional character), 20, 30, 31
Clark, Donald, 50, 72n61
Claudio (fictional character), 63, 73n75, 81–92
Cohen, Ralph, 146, 147
Coleridge, Samuel, 2, 4
Colet, John, 50, 60, 72n61
collaboration, 146–155, 157n20, 157n21
commoners, 25–27
conduplicatio. *See* repetition of words
conquestio. *See* lament, or complaint
Conrade (fictional character), 62–63, 89
controversiae. *See* debate
copia. *See* copy
copy (*copia*), 64, 66–68
coronation, 23–24
The Correspondence of Sir Thomas More (More, T.), 41n82
counterfeiting, 15–45, 17, 42n97, 43n108, 82–90; Rainolds on, 94n39; Shakespeare and, 30–33; *See also Much Ado About Nothing*
covert drama, *The Taming of the Shrew* influenced by, 45–46
Crane, Mary, 83, 94n31
criticism, 5–6, 131–132, 137n1, 140n46
critics, 10n18, 15, 138n8, 140n41

crown, 25–27, 28–29
cues, 126–130
cue scripts. *See* parts
Cynthia's Revels (Jonson), 51, 72n43

Davus (fictional character), 27–29, 29, 30, 33, 36, 41n82
Dawson, Anthony, 5, 91, 95n47
day by day descriptions (*descripta per dies*), 24–25
De Amicitia (Cicero), 108
debate (*controversiae*), 127–128, 132, 142n70
declamation, 46–47, 48–49, 50–52. *See also* audacity; Moth; Viola/Cesario
deep characterization, 78–79
Defense of Poetry (Sidney), 88–89
deformity, 21, 40n49
De Inventione (Cicero), 139n22, 140n37
delivery (*actio*), 3, 9n6, 22, 46, 77. *See also* action
"Democratising the Audience?" (Carson), 157n20
demonstrative oratory. *See* epideictic oratory
descripta per dies. *See* day by day descriptions
description of events (*narratio*), 132–137
Desdemona (fictional character), 34–35, 69n10, 99, 103, 105–107, 114n44
Desmet, Christy, 98, 103
dicendi primordia. *See* rudiments of speaking
Dionyza (fictional character), 121–122, 125
direct address, 8, 73n85, 145–155
Direct Opening (*principium*), 123–125, 128
discipuli. *See* actors
discreditable cause (*causa turpis*), 120–122, 127–132
display candor, 99–100, 100
dissemblers, 19–23, 26–27, 28–30, 32–33, 33. *See also* Davus; Richard III
dissimulation, 30–33, 40n59, 115n60. *See also* dynamic dissimulation
dissimulator, 19–23
division (*divisio*), 61–65, 73n75, 73n78

Dogberry (fictional character), 62–63
Donawerth, Jane, 78–79
Don John (fictional character), 75–76, 92
Donohue, Dan, 109
Don Pedro (fictional character). *See* Pedro
double vision, 25–27, 29
doubtful (*aporia*), 102–103, 103, 153, 154–155
dramatic persons, 22–23, 91–92
dual awareness, 110–111
Dumaine (fictional character), 52–54
Dusinberre, Juliet, 6–7, 45, 59, 68
dynamic dissimulation, 22–23, 34

early modern acting styles, 10n18, 112n1
Edward IV (king) (fictional character), 20, 28–29
effictio. *See* bodily form figure
Elizabethan acting, 1, 2–5, 45, 69n10
Elizabethan Acting (Joseph), 3, 9n6
"Elizabethan Acting" (Harbage), 9n5, 10n16
"Elizabethan Action" (Gurr), 93n12, 93n23
Elizabethanists, 145–155, 156n5
eloquence, 134–136
embodied characters, 5
embodied performance, 31, 47
emotions, 113n17, 113n19
enargeia. *See* vivid description
Enterline, Lynn, 46, 48, 65
epanorthosis. *See* figures of interruption
epideictic oratory, 55, 119–120
episodes, 27–29
Erasmus, 17, 50, 55, 60, 62–63
erotema. *See* figure of speech
Escolme, Bridget, 73n86, 150, 151
ethopoeia. *See* character creation
ethos. *See* appeal to ethics
Evans, Robert, 98, 100, 112n9, 113n10, 114n23
evidentia. *See* vivid description
Ewbank, Inga-Stina, 135
examination (*interrogatio*), 73n84, 152–153

"An Excellent Actor" (Webster), 1, 8n1, 10n16
executions, 23–24, 24–25
exordium, 122–125, 126–127, 128, 132, 140n37

Falstaff (fictional character), 30–31, 42n94, 42n97, 111
female bodies, 65, 66–68
Ferdinand (king) (fictional character), 52–54
Feste (fictional character), 32
figure of speech (*erotema*), 65, 73n84, 152–153, 153, 154–155
figures of interruption (*hyperbaton* or *epanorthosis*), 127–128, 141n54
flatterers, 7, 37n15, 98–100, 100–111, 113n12
flattery, rhetorical figures and, 101–104
"Flattery in Shakespeare's *Othello*: The Relevance of Plutarch and Sir Thomas Elyot" (Evans), 112n9, 113n10, 114n23
Folly (lady) (fictional character), 62–63
forensic rhetoric, 139n19, 140n41, 142n70; character-effects revealed by, 125; *ethos* revealing of, 122; late style or, 125–132; opening, 123–125; in *Pericles, Prince of Tyre*, 7–8, 117–137. *See also* Marina
formalism, 1–6, 102–103, 149; Harbage on, 9n5; natural distinction *versus*, 110–111, 112n1; new, 138n8
fourth wall, 146–147, 147
friends, flatterers and, 98–100, 111, 113n12
friendship, Cicero on, 108

Galenic theories, 3, 9n14
gazes, 106–107, 114n44
gesture (*actio*), 1, 105–107, 114n44
Globe theater, 2, 36, 103, 138n5, 146, 147, 148. *See also* London Bankside Globe; New Globe theater
God, 28–29
good men, 100, 119
good will, 100, 113n17, 119, 122–125, 127, 130–131
Gosson, Stephen, 74n87, 84, 85, 86

Index

grammar schools, 47, 48–68. *See also* Brinsley, John; Minola, Katherina; *The Taming of the Shrew*
Greenblatt, Stephen, 37n6, 87
gulling scenes, 81–92, 95n47
Gurr, Andrew, 77, 77–78, 92n6. *See also* "Elizabethan Action"

Hal (fictional character), 30–31
half telling (*aposiopesis*), 101–104
Hamlet (fictional character), 58, 87, 120, 146–155, 148–155, 158n45
Hamlet (Shakespeare), 8, 11n26
Harbage, Alfred, 1, 2, 4, 9n5, 10n16. *See also* "Elizabethan Acting"
Hastings, William (fictional character), 24–25, 27–28, 41n70, 42n96
Hecuba (fictional character), 50–51, 55
Henry VI (Shakespeare), 37n8, 40n51, 40n52
Hercules Furens (Seneca), 42n102, 42n106
Hero (fictional character), 75, 83–86, 88, 89
heroines, 6–7. *See also* Marina
Heywood, Thomas, 49–50, 51, 52–53, 88; *See also Apology for Actors*
Hillebrand, Harold, 49, 71n24, 71n25, 71n30
historians, 17–19
Historia Richardi Tertii (More, T.), 20, 27–29, 39n42, 40n43
history, 17–19, 23–24, 132–137
History of Richard III (More, T.), 6, 13–36, 37n17, 38n31
Holland, Peter, 110, 110–111
Holland, Philemon, 98–101, 105, 113n10
Holofernes (fictional character), 63, 90
Homer, 16, 110. *See also* Ulysses
honesty, 100, 112n9
Honigmann, E., 99, 112n4, 112n8
honorable cause (*causa honesta*), 120–122, 127–132, 129, 140n41, 154
Hoole, Charles, 47, 51
Hortensio (fictional character), 64, 73n82
house style, 15
Howard, Jean, 7, 85

humoral bodies, 3, 9n14
Hutson, Lorna, 14, 37n6, 118
hyperbaton. *See* figures of interruption

Iago (fictional character), 7, 112n4, 112n8, 114n23, 114n44, 153; acting style of, 97–111; display candor used by, 99; Donohue on, 109; dual awareness, 110–111; Othello persuaded by, 100–111; as soldier, 99; soliloquies of, 110–111
identification, 60–61
illusions of depth, 5
imaginary circumstances, 7
imitation (*imitatio*), 14–19
impressions of mind, 86–90
individual characterization, 76–81
individuality, body corresponding to, 91–92
innocence, 130, 142n79
insinuatio. *See* Subtle Approach
Institutio (Quintilian), 3, 31
intentionality, Richard III possessing, 23, 33–34
interiority, 33, 37n8, 58, 149, 150–151, 151
interiorized personhood, 5, 6
interrogatio. *See* examination
inventio. *See* reimagining
The Invention of Suspicion: Law and Mimesis in Shakespeare and Renaissance Drama (Hutson), 37n6, 118

Johnson, Samuel, 2, 63
Jones, Emrys, 40n44, 41n76
Jonson, Ben, 36, 51, 72n43, 77, 92n6
Jorgensen, Paul, 98, 112n9
Joseph, Bertram, 3, 10n15, 46, 60–61, 94n27; *See also Acting Shakespeare*; *Elizabethan Acting*
judicial oratory. *See* forensic rhetoric
junior scholars, 49–50

Kamaralli, Anna, 66, 141n58
Kate (fictional character). *See* Minola, Katherina
Kiernan, Pauline, 69n10, 76, 146
Kietzman, Mary, 56–57, 58

kindly counterfeiting, 15–45, 17
King Richard III (Shakespeare). See *Richard III*
kings' games, 26–27, 36, 41n76
King's Men, 1, 138n5, 147
Kline, Kevin, 149, 149–150, 151, 153
knave, 107, 112n9
Ko, Yu, 5–6
Kyd, Thomas, 15, 40n44, 42n97

lament, or complaint (*conquestio*), 129, 141n57
language, 24, 121, 131, 140n43
late style, 118–119, 125–132, 137n1, 141n60
Latin New Comedy, 117
Leonato (fictional character), 81–83
Leonine (fictional character), 119–125, 126–127, 128–129, 130–131, 139n26, 140n41
Leontes (fictional character), 131, 135
Lester, Adrian, 149, 150, 151, 154
lifelike characters, 4–6
lifelike performance, 78–81
lifelike types, 104–109
lively acting, 93n22, 93n23, 94n27
lively performance, 78–81; See also *Much Ado About Nothing*
Lives of the Caesars (Suetonius), 23–24, 40n61
Lloyd-Williams, Maggie, 150–151
Logan, M., 40n49, 40n61, 41n70
London Bankside Globe, 145, 146
Longaville (fictional character), 52–54
Lopez, Jeremy, 90–91, 155n2
Lorenzo (fictional character), 15, 40n44
love, 52–59, 54–55, 100–111
Love's Labor's Lost (Shakespeare), 46, 61, 90. See also Moth
Lucentio (fictional character), 64–65, 68, 73n82
Lucian of Samosata, 17–18, 38n30
Ludus Literarius (Brinsley), 46, 59–61, 72n56, 73n78
Lycus (fictional character), 42n102, 42n106
Lysimachus (fictional character), 127–128, 129–131, 139n26, 141n53, 141n58

Machiavelli, Niccolò, 20, 39n40
Malvolio (fictional character), 32, 76–77
Margaret (fictional character), 75, 83–86, 89
Maria (fictional character), 32, 76–77, 79
Marina (fictional character), 7–8, 138n6, 139n26, 140n41, 141n53, 141n58, 141n59, 152–153, 155; as charorator, 117–137; eloquence of, 134–136; *ethos* voiced by, 119–125, 129, 134–137; exordium of, 122–125, 126–127, 128, 132; good will secured by, 122–125, 130–131; innocence exemplified by, 142n79; Leonine persuaded by, 119–125, 126–127, 128–129; *narratio* of, 132–137; Novy on, 142n88; overview, 117–137; patience of, 142n79; peroration of, 129, 130, 132; recognition scene and, 132–137; self-defense of, 119–125; superhuman power of, 142n81
Marlowe, Christopher, 14–15, 37n8, 78–79. See also Barabas
marriage, 27–29
martyria. See testimony
Maus, Katherine, 33–34
McDonald, Russ, 118, 125–126, 126, 127, 131, 140n46, 141n60
McMullan, Gordon, 118, 137n1
Measure for Measure (Shakespeare), 88, 117
Megara (fictional character), 42n102, 42n106
men, 64–65. See also good men; *The Taming of the Shrew*
Menzer, Paul, 10n18
A Midsummer Night's Dream (Shakespeare), 59, 63, 77, 90
mimesis, 6, 36n4, 37n6, 46–47, 51, 53
mimicry, 22–23
mind, impressions of, 86–90
Minola, Katherina (fictional character), 6–7, 70n13, 70n14, 70n18; as audacious, 47, 66–67, 69n10; Bianca as under, 74n93; character-effects and, 46; declamation of, 46–47; division of, 61–65; partition of, 61–68; Petruchio's direction

required by, 61–62; resistance of, 47; singular parts of, 46–47. *See also* speech of submission
Miola, Robert, 117
miracle, 28–29
modern actors, 7, 106, 108–111. *See also* early modern acting styles
More, Thomas, 37n15, 40n59; on actor, 40n45; comparisons to, 41n70; on Davus, 41n82; dissemblers considered by, 29–30; dramatic *enargeia* of, 23–27; goal of, 18; Jones on, 40n44; liberal arts version of, 38n19; merchant of, 42n96; Shakespeare influenced by, 6, 11n26, 32–33; Suetonius influencing, 40n61; *See also Historia Richardi Tertii; History of Richard III*; Richard III
Moth (fictional character), 52–59, 61–62, 65
Much Ado About Nothing (Shakespeare), 7, 62–63, 95n45, 95n58; audiences gulled by, 81–92; impressions, 86–90; mind, 86–90; offstage characters, 90–92; overview, 75–92; title of, 87–88. *See also* Beatrice; Benedick; Claudio; Leonato; Pedro
Munday, Anthony, 85–86, 86, 87–88
murder, of Clarence, 30, 31
murderer, Richard III as, 34–35
Myhill, Nova, 75–76, 87
Mysis (fictional character), 29

narratio. See description of events
narrative, *Ad Herennium* on, 133–134
Nashe, Thomas, 4
naturalism, 1–6, 149; Bradbrook disputing, 9n4; formal distinction *versus*, 110–111, 112n1; Harbage on, 9n5; personation and, 10n16; rhetorical acting styles overlapping with, 7; Richard III indicating, 29–30
new Globe theater, 69n10, 147, 151–152, 157n20. *See also* Rylance, Mark
Niobe (fictional character), 50–51, 55
Nobilitas Literata (Sturm), 16

"Nobody's Perfect: Or Why Did the English Stage Take Boys for Women?" (Orgel), 74n87
non-naturalistic practices, 5–6
notatio. See character delineation
noting practices, 88, 90

obedience, 60–61, 64–65
OED. *See* Oxford English Dictionary
Olivia (lady) (fictional character), 55–59, 61–62
OP. *See* original practices
orators, 1–8, 10n16, 22–23, 31, 117–137, 139n35. *See also* boy actors; delivery; mimesis
oratory, 10n15, 10n16, 48–49, 77, 119–120. *See also* rudiments of speaking
Oregon Shakespeare Festival (2008), 109
Orgel, Stephen, 74n87, 108, 151
original practices (OP), 8, 145–155, 155n2
Orlando (fictional character), 30, 111
Orsino (duke) (fictional character), 55–59, 56–58
Othello (fictional character), 34, 83, 100–111, 114n23, 114n44
"The Overthrow of Stage-Plays (1599)" (Rainolds), 94n39. *See also* Th'Overthrow of Stage-Playes
Oxford English Dictionary (OED), 73n71, 84

painting, 16, 18, 37n15, 77. *See also* Apelles
Palfrey, Simon, 91, 94n24, 102, 103, 115n59, 126, 126–127, 129
Pamphilus (fictional character), 27–29
parody, 14–19, 15
partition (*partitio*), 61–68, 73n75
parts, 10n15, 73n67, 126, 148, 149
passions, 3, 81–83, 89–90, 95n47, 102. *See also* late style
The Passions of the Minde in Generall: A Reprint Based on the 1604 Edition (Wright), 9n6, 94n27
pathos. See appeal to emotions
patience, 133–134, 138n12, 142n79

Peacham, Henry, 6, 46–47, 51, 53, 66, 152–154
Pedro (fictional character), 7, 63, 75–76, 81–92, 95n58
performance, 43n108; audacity and, 48–52; Booth's divide with, 114n40; character infiltrated by, 13–14; of childbirth, 28; as false, 28; lifelike, 78–81; lively, 78–81; persuasion's distinction with, 103–104; playgoers influenced by, 90–92; protagonist assimilation, 13; rhetoric directing, 4; of Richard III, 25–27, 30–36. *See also* embodied performance; formalism; *Much Ado About Nothing*; naturalism; practices
Pericles (fictional character), 119, 132–137, 138n12, 142n79, 142n88
Pericles, Prince of Tyre (Shakespeare and Wilkins), 7–8, 117–137, 137n1, 138n5, 138n6. *See also* Marina
peroration (*peroratio*), 128–129, 130, 132
personages, 16–19. *See also* Richard III
personation, 1–2, 4–8; *Apology for Actors* on, 77–81; characterization and, 76–81; critics discussing, 10n18; declamation signifying, 46–47; naturalism and, 10n16. *See also* character-effects; *Much Ado About Nothing*; *Richard III*
person-effects. *See* character-effects
personhood, interiorized, 5, 6
persons, 10n20, 18–19, 76
persuasion, 100, 103–104, 139n17
Petruchio (fictional character), 45, 46, 59, 64–65, 68; Baumlin on, 73n82; Minola requiring direction of, 61–62
"Petruchio the Sophist and Language as Creation in *The Taming of the Shrew*" (Baumlin), 73n82
Phidias, 17–18
Philoponus (fictional character), 59–60, 61
platea. *See* presentational space
players, 58, 77
The Player's Passion (Roach), 3–4, 10n15
playgoers, 9n14, 18, 90, 90–92
playing, 84, 92n6
playwright, 18, 141n49

ploche. *See* speedy word iteration
Plutarch, 7, 18, 98, 103, 105; essay of, 98–101; Evans on, 114n23. *See also* flatterers; Holland, Philemon
poetry, 17–19
poets, 16–19
Potter, Ursula, 47, 70n19
practice of playing, 84
practices, 83–92; *See also Much Ado About Nothing*
praecisio. *See* stop
presentational space (*platea*), 73n85, 95n58
principium. *See* Direct Opening
probra corporis. *See* bodily abuse
Progymnasmata (Aphthonius), 50–51, 59, 61
pronunciation, 102–103
pronuntio. *See* figures
proscenium stage, 146, 147, 152, 157n21
Puritans, 79–80, 84–85
Puttenham, George, 15–45, 17, 101, 102, 104, 105; on *ploche*, 142n64; on repetition, 130, 141n63; *See also The Arte of English Poesie: A Facsimile Reproduction*
Pyramus (fictional character), 90

quaestioiudicii. *See* question to adjudicate
question to adjudicate (*quaestioiudicii* or *causa*), 120, 139n25
Quintilian, 3, 17, 18, 31, 50, 121, 123, 130; on *ethos*, 135; on rhetoric, 139n26; Skinner on, 139n35

Rainolds, John, 79–80, 88–89, 94n39
rape, 23–24, 127–128
real inner feeling, 3, 9n10
recognition scene, 132–137
reimagining (*inventio*), 16–19
repetition (*anaphora*), 130, 141n60, 141n63
repetition of words (*conduplicatio*), 129–131
report, 132, 141n63
representation, 43n108, 110
rhetoric: art of, 48; definition, 139n26; genres of, 119–120; history's

Index

relationship with, 17–19; overview, 1–8; performance directed by, 4; poetry's relationship with, 17–19; Quintilian on, 139n26. *See also* boy actors; forensic rhetoric; grammar schools
Rhetoric (Aristotle), 100, 139n21
Rhetorica Ad Herennium (Cicero). *See Ad Herennium*
rhetorical acting styles, 1–8, 7, 22–23, 35
rhetorical delivery. *See* delivery
rhetorical figures, flattery and, 101–104
Richard III (fictional character), 6; acting expertise of, 30–36, 137; Anne courted by, 33–36, 42n102, 42n104; Buckingham's exchange with, 30, 31–32; Chambers's account of, 19; continuity of, 40n52; crown rejected by, 25–27, 28–29; deformity of, 21, 40n49; delivery and, 22; dissimulation of, 40n59; Hastings executed by, 24–25; histrionics of, 13–14, 29–30, 36n2, 41n76; intentionality possessed by, 23, 33–34; Jones on, 40n44; as lover, 34–35; mimesis of, 36n4; monologue of, 37n8; as murderer, 34–35; natural acting style indicated by, 29–30; overview, 13–14; *pathos* used by, 35; performance of, 25–27, 30–36; rhetorical acting style illustrated by, 35; role adopted by, 21–22; soliloquy of, 21–23, 33–34, 36, 40n51; spacing influencing, 27–29; typological genealogy of, 14–23; Vergil on, 41n74; *See also Historia Richardi Tertii*; *History of Richard III*; kings' games
Richard III (Shakespeare), 11n26, 75; actors and, 13–36; character-effects in, 21–22, 22–23; characters and, 13–36; as historical example stage, 19; *See also Historia Richardi Tertii*; *History of Richard III*
A Rich Storehouse or Treasure for Nobility and Gentlemen (Browne), 16
Roach, Joseph, 3–4, 9n12; *See also The Player's Passion*
roles, 21–22, 46, 115n50

Roman history, 23–24
Roper, William, 23–24
Rosalind (fictional character), 30, 65, 69n10, 111
Rosenberg, Marvin, 3, 9n9, 10n15, 102–103
Royce, Jacalyn, 147, 148
rudiments of speaking (*dicendi primordia*), 50–52. *See also* Moth; Viola/Cesario
Rylance, Mark, 147, 148–155, 154, 155, 156n13

St. Paul's School, 50, 60
schoolmasters, 27, 48–49, 71n25
self, 5, 10n21
self-defense, 119–125
selfhood, 91
Seneca, 42n102, 42n106
Shaa, John, 28–29
Shakespeare, William, 37n8, 86; counterfeiting and, 30–33; *History of Richard III* influencing, 35–36; More influencing, 6, 11n26, 32–33; sonnet of, 54–55. *See also* Hamlet; Richard III; *specific plays*
The Shakespearean Stage (Gurr), 92n6, 93n12
Shakespeare in Parts (Palfrey and Stern), 94n24, 115n59
Shakespeare: Seven Tragedies Revisited: The Dramatist's Manipulation of Response (Honigmann), 112n4, 112n8
Shakespeare's Late Style (McDonald), 118, 140n46, 141n60
Shakespeare's Sense of Character: On the Page and From the Stage (Ko and Shurgot), 5–6
Shakespeare's Stagecraft (Styan), 147, 157n21
Shapiro, James, 14–15, 27, 32
Shore, Jane (fictional character), 20, 25, 41n70
Shrewsbury School, 60, 71n25
Shurgot, Michael, 5–6
sides. *See* parts
Sidney, Philip, 88–89
Siemon, James, 33, 40n52

Simo (fictional character), 27–29
singular parts, 46–47
Sir John (fictional character). *See* Falstaff
Skinner, Quentin, 118, 120, 139n35
Snout (fictional character), 63
soliloquies: of Hamlet, 148–155; of Iago, 110–111; of Richard III, 21–23, 33–34, 36, 40n51
sonnet, 54–55
"Sonnet 23", 54–55
spacing, 27–29
speaker, language's division with, 131, 140n43
spectators, 9n14, 87–92, 95n49, 115n59
speech composition knowledge (*technê*), 53–55
speeches, 6–7, 7–8, 35, 38n29, 45–68. *See also* forensic rhetoric; Marina; Moth; rudiments of speaking; Viola/Cesario
speech of submission, 6–7, 45–68
speedy word iteration (*ploche*), 130, 142n64
spoken subject (*argumentum*), 50, 59
Spoudeus (fictional character), 59–60
staged body, 91–92
stairs of Mourning, 23–24
statesman (*vircivilis*), 48–51. *See also* audacity
statuesque performance, 2, 3
Stern, Tiffany, 94n24, 102, 103, 105, 115n59, 126, 126–127, 129
stop (*praecisio*), 101–104, 108, 114n23
story, 148
storyteller, 149
Stubbes, Philip, 91
study, 102–103
Sturm, Johannes, 16, 22
Styan, J., 146–147, 148, 157n21
submission. *See* speech of submission
Subtle Approach (*insinuatio*), 123–125
Suetonius, 23–24, 40n61
Sylvester, Richard, 20, 25, 26, 37n17, 39n42, 40n59

Tacitus, Cornelius, 18, 33–34, 39n40, 41n78; *See also Annals*; double vision; Tiberius

The Taming of the Shrew (Shakespeare), 6–7, 45–46, 45–68, 70n12, 74n93, 75
tears, 31
technê. *See* speech composition knowledge
Terence, 6, 27–30, 33–34. *See also* Davus
testimony (*martyria*), 133–137
"That Old Saw: Early Modern Acting and the Infinite Regress" (Menzer), 10n18
theater, 25, 94n31, 115n59
theatricality, 6, 7, 25–27
themes, 50–52, 59–61, 73n67. *See also* Moth; Viola/Cesario
Theophrastus, 19–20, 33, 103
Th'Overthrow of Stage-Playes (Rainolds), 79–80. *See also* "The Overthrow of Stage Plays (1599)"
Thucydides, 18, 38n29
Tiberius (emperor) (fictional character), 17, 19, 20, 20–21, 33; dissimulation of, 40n59; stairs of Mourning of, 23–24; theater employing license against, 25
Timon of Athens (Shakespeare), 118, 136
Titus Andronicus, 14–15
"To Discern a Flatterer from a Friend" (Plutarch), 98–101
Tribble, Evelyn, 52, 55, 56, 58
Tudor schoolroom, 6–7, 46, 64, 70n12. *See also* grammar schools
Twelfth Night, Or What You Will (Shakespeare), 32, 61. *See also* Malvolio; Maria; Viola/Cesario
types, 2, 6, 7, 103, 104–109. *See also* flatterers; Iago; Richard III
tyrants, 19–27, 23, 32–33, 35–36. *See also* Richard III

Ulysses (fictional character), 16

van Es, Bart, 15
Variorum Othello (Furness), 104–105
Vergil, Polydore, 21, 24, 25, 41n70, 41n74
vice, 41n66, 110, 112n5
Viola/Cesario (fictional character), 52, 55–59, 59, 61–62, 65, 67
vircivilis. *See* statesman

virgins, 23–24
vita. See life
vivid description (*enargeia* or *evidentia*), 14–19, 22, 22–27, 37n6. *See also* bodily form figure; dynamic dissimulation

Warner, David, 154
Webster, John. *See* "An Excellent Actor"
wedding, 27–29
Weimann, Robert, 13–14, 43n108, 78–79, 95n58
Widow (fictional character), 64–65, 66, 68

Wilkins, George. *See Pericles, Prince of Tyre*
Wilson, Thomas, 30, 101, 104, 105, 129–130, 132
The Winter's Tale (Shakespeare), 103, 135
wives. *See The Taming of the Shrew*
The Woman of Andros (Terence), 6, 27–30
Wright, Thomas, 9n6, 94n27
writing style, 118–119

Yachnin, Paul, 43n107, 47

About the Author

Travis Curtright is associate professor of humanities and literature at Ave Maria University, where he directs the minor of studies in Shakespeare in Performance. He is the author of *The One Thomas More* and coeditor of *Shakespeare's Last Plays: Essays in Literature and Politics*.